6/29/89

Pocket Flora
of the
Redwood
Forest

Pocket Flora
of the
Redwood
Forest

Dr. Rudolf W. Becking

Island Press   Covelo, California

Printed in the United States of America.

Library of Congress Cataloging in Publication Data

Becking, Rudolf Willem, 1922–
  Pocket flora of the redwood forest.

  Includes index.
  1. Forest flora—California—Identification.
2. Redwood. 3. Redwood—Ecology. I. Title. II. Title: Redwood forest.
QK149.B38   582.0979   82-201
ISBN 0-933280-02-5   AACR2

The map on page 3 is adapted from the map appearing on page 26 of *The Redwoods,* a report issued in 1964 by the U.S. Department of the Interior, National Park Service, San Francisco Regional Office.

For a free catalogue of other Island Press titles, write to: Island Press, Star Route 1, Box 38, Covelo, California 95428.

To all those who had the foresight and dedication to fight for the preservation of this precious creation: the indomitable coastal redwood.

Contents

Preface

The California coastal redwoods are known all over the world for their majestic size and beauty. The dense groves, with their impressive dominance, height, and deep shade, resemble large forest cathedrals in which all sounds of life are hushed. The sense of solitude and silence is overwhelming; one can lose all sense of time.

These trees of incredible size and age crowded together so closely have no equals on earth. They are the last sentinels of a remote past, a living testimony of prehistoric forests, seemingly unaltered by the forces of time and impervious to the many changes and pace of modern civilization. Visitors who enter these redwood groves are enveloped. Foggy mists pierced by shafts of shifting sunlight preserve the serenity of the forest. Hardly a sound is heard; nor are there visible signs of life. Yet one feels deeply the impact of the vibrant life forces that have created the tallest trees in the world.

It is with profound awe for these sublime trees that this pocket flora has been created. I hope it will inspire users with an understanding of and admiration for the numerous forms of plant life that can be discovered within the redwood forest. It is a unique environment; in the narrow coastal belt of northern and central California the redwoods have found their last existence. They are one of the very few survivors of a long bygone era, some 80 to 100 million years before the beginning of human life on this planet.

I wish to develop this pocket flora into an accurate tool for the efficient identification of the most common and frequent plants within the redwood forests. Any omissions, errors, or weaknesses either in keys or descriptions can only be found through intensive use by interested visitors there. I would be much indebted if they would report any deficiencies to me. Comments on the general format and organization of the flora and on the clarity of the illustrations are equally welcome.

Acknowledgments

Encouragement for the production of *Pocket Flora of the Redwood Forest* and the commitment to publish came from Barbara Dean, Executive Director of Island Press, Covelo, California, during the summer of 1978. I wish to thank Barbara for her continuous support and encouragement during all the phases of this tedious process. My thanks go to all those who participated in the preparations. For their help with creating and revising the descriptions, thanks go to: Lynette Dobler, Frank Enright, Michele Forrest, Jack

Lewis, and Thomas Overturf. For rechecking the descriptions and keys: Paula Carson, Lisa Ganio, Dwain L. Goforth, Lee Hollis, Kelly Logan, Esther Nelsen, Richard Rushforth, Michelle Seidl, Jane E. Smith, David Waller, and Peggy Woo. For clerical assistance: Suzette Davis, Lisa Holding, and David Horowitz.

Thanks too to Judy Chaffin, production supervisor and copy editor, and to Marilyn Langfeld, designer, and her assistant, Phil Lieb. I also want to express my appreciation to the staff and consultants of Island Press for their continued efforts.

I am much indebted to Dr. F. Raymond Fosberg, who painstakingly reviewed the manuscript and made many valuable comments and corrections enhancing immeasurably the quality and practical usefulness of the pocket flora.

Finally, I feel a deep sense of gratitude toward my wife and my family for letting me finish this flora project, with its endless hours of drawing and writing and checking and rechecking every page. Without their understanding and support, it would have been impossible for me to complete this arduous task.

January 5, 1982
Arcata, California

Note to the Reader

Pocket Flora of the Redwood Forest is a comprehensive guide to a unique plant community. Nowhere else on earth do the forces of terrain, climate, soil, and living matter combine to form a habitat for the world's tallest trees and the plants that surround them. Until now, no guide has offered a complete and accurate source of identification for the plants of this region.

During two decades of studying and drawing the plants of the redwood forest, Dr. Rudolf W. Becking has developed a system of identification that serves both informed laypeople and scientists. He has applied simplified terminology in descriptions and keys for field identification of living plants or parts of specimens, so that everyone who uses this book can systematically follow the family and genus/species keys to determine precisely which plant is being examined. Dr. Becking is one of the first authors to use this system of keys in an American pocket flora. Although the use of these keys and the scientific names of plants may seem challenging, mastery of this highly effective system requires only a bit of curiosity and persistence, for which you will be rewarded with a true working knowledge of some essentials in botanical study.

Equally important, *Pocket Flora of the Redwood Forest* presents clear, accurate drawings of 212 of the most frequently seen plants in this region. Dr. Becking has made these drawings from living plants rather than from the dried or pressed specimens often used for illustrations. In combination with the selection of color photographs, they make this guide as close to the natural forest environment as pages can come.

For all of these reasons, Island Press is confident that you will find *Pocket Flora of the Redwood Forest* a complete guide to a very special natural community and an enriching tool for self-education.

Introduction

Some 100 million years ago, during the Cretaceous era, redwoods were among the dominant forest trees in the Northern Hemisphere. They coexisted with the now-extinct giant horsetail trees and dinosaurs. Coastal redwoods (*Sequoia sempervirens*) first appear in the fossil record in Cretaceous coal deposits. Since that time they have remained virtually unchanged in their botanical features. Miraculously, they survived not only the ordinary, day-to-day battering of the physical elements but all the more dramatic upheavals of the past as well: ice ages and other drastic climatic changes, volcanic eruptions, geological uplift of massive mountain ranges, and the forces associated with continental drift. Once widely distributed, their range has gradually shrunk until it has become totally restricted to the Coastal Redwood Belt along the Pacific Ocean in California.

This narrow and irregular coastal strip is some 500 km (310 mi) long and 5–10 km (3–6 mi) wide, stretching from Brookings, Oregon, south to the Monterey–San Luis Obispo county line in central California; but it is by no means continuous (see map on p. 3). In the mild maritime climate that characterizes the redwood belt, summers are cool, with dense, damp morning and night fogs but no precipitation. Winters are very mild, with an abundance of precipitation and frequent storms, and frost and snow are quite uncommon. Redwoods are a typical lowland species, commonly reaching an elevation of 500 m (1640 ft) and occasionally 1000 m (3280 ft). Their optimal habitat is always directly in line with the moist air currents coming by westerly or northwesterly winds from the Pacific Ocean. Sites most congenial to them are wide river valleys and the lower slopes of foothills and mountains. In such river valleys with a northwest-southeasterly orientation, redwoods can occur for more than 50 km (30 mi) upstream inland as long as the ocean fogs can penetrate that deeply. Summer fog seems to be one of the critical factors encouraging their patchy inland distribution. Their massive, tall crowns absorb huge quantities of this aerial moisture, which significantly supplements soil moisture as it declines with the advent of summer droughts. Large quantities of moisture, fog drip, fall from their crowns. In fact, the dense redwood groves create their own localized climate, with the favorable moisture, shade, and shelter on which all plant and animal life associated with the redwood forests depends. The size of the trees and the extent of the groves create a balance vital for the health and maintenance of the entire redwood forest community. When these delicate balances are upset by human forces, communities are destroyed.

Of all species, redwoods are one of the most naturally resilient. Throughout their long evolutionary history, these trees have developed adaptations that have allowed them to survive the devastating effects of natural forces. Extensive, shallow, surface root systems frequently interlock, allowing individual trees of great height and massive crown, to become extremely wind firm. In severe wind storms redwood trees usually break off in the trunk rather than becoming uprooted. Trees are only uprooted when they are very old and decayed or when their root systems fail.

Significant concentrations of tannic acids in wood, bark, and foliage render redwoods very resistant to attacks by insects or fungi. The heartwood, tannin rich and dark colored, is virtually immune to rot for a period of several hundred years; fallen tree trunks remain intact for a very long time in the damp forest environment. Fewer than a dozen insect species attack redwoods in their native habitat, and practically all attack only sick and dying trees. This is extraordinary for a tree species with such a long evolutionary history.

Redwoods can withstand the forces of the severe flooding that occurs in river valleys. In fact, where severe floods are common, redwoods rapidly become the dominant tree species. They are sensitive, however, to lack of aeration in the soil. Their root systems are readily suffocated and killed by sedimentary deposits that do not crack and permit soil aeration. Recurring forest fires tend to favor redwoods, creating beds favorable for seed germination and stimulating abundant seed production in the periods immediately following these fires. Redwood is extremely fire-resistant; its tough, dense, fibrous bark does not burn (giving it its renowned insulating properties). Even when fire destroys the crown, a redwood resprouts from its trunk and develops a new crown. This remarkable tenacity in the face of catastrophe is appropriately reflected in the redwood's scientific name, *Sequoia sempervirens,* the ever-living redwood.

One of the redwood's most unusual adaptations is that it can resprout continuously from the burl growth at the base of its trunk. This kind of burl tissue, inherent to every redwood tree, is extremely rare in conifer species. When the burl is damaged or irritated, dormant buds embedded in it easily develop into leafy shoots toward sunlight and roots toward darkness. After the tiny redwood seedling unfolds its 2 or 3 primary leaves, or cotyledons, above the ground, burl formation begins, in the axils of these cotyledons, some 15–35 mm (6–14 in) above the ground. The position of the burl is fixed at the time of germination and remains constant for the life of the tree. In the second or third year the axillary buds become more visible, and in each subsequent year these buds expand, gradually encircling the entire stem. In the fourth or fifth year under natural conditions, the seedling collapses from the weight of the burl mass, and the swollen stem bends to the ground. The burl tissue is immediately incorporated into the

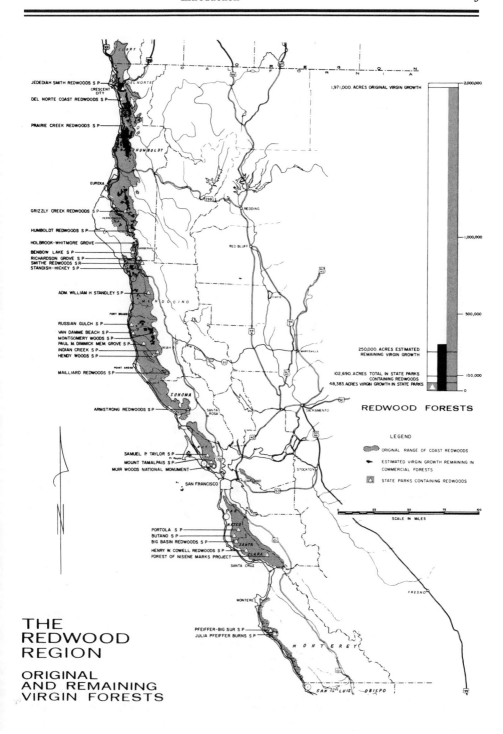

JEDEDIAH SMITH REDWOODS S P
CRESCENT CITY
DEL NORTE COAST REDWOODS S P
PRAIRIE CREEK REDWOODS S P
EUREKA
GRIZZLY CREEK REDWOODS S P
HUMBOLDT REDWOODS S P
HOLBROOK-WHITMORE GROVE
BENBOW LAKE S P
RICHARDSON GROVE S P
SMITHE REDWOODS S R
STANDISH-HICKEY S P
ADM WILLIAM H STANDLEY S P
RUSSIAN GULCH S P
VAN DAMME BEACH S P
MONTGOMERY WOODS S P
PAUL M DIMMICK MEM GROVE S P
INDIAN CREEK S P
HENDY WOODS S P
MAILLIARD REDWOODS S P
ARMSTRONG REDWOODS S P
SAMUEL P TAYLOR S P
MOUNT TAMALPAIS S P
MUIR WOODS NATIONAL MONUMENT
SAN FRANCISCO
PORTOLA S P
BUTANO S P
BIG BASIN REDWOODS S P
HENRY W COWELL REDWOODS S P
FOREST OF NISENE MARKS PROJECT
SANTA CRUZ
MONTEREY
PFEIFFER-BIG SUR S P
JULIA PFEIFFER BURNS S P

1,971,000 ACRES ORIGINAL VIRGIN GROWTH

250,000 ACRES ESTIMATED
REMAINING VIRGIN GROWTH

102,690 ACRES TOTAL IN STATE PARKS
CONTAINING REDWOODS
48,383 ACRES VIRGIN GROWTH IN STATE PARKS

REDWOOD FORESTS

LEGEND

ORIGINAL RANGE OF COAST REDWOODS

ESTIMATED VIRGIN GROWTH REMAINING IN
COMMERCIAL FORESTS

STATE PARKS CONTAINING REDWOODS

SCALE IN MILES

THE
REDWOOD
REGION

ORIGINAL
AND REMAINING
VIRGIN FORESTS

soil, where it forms a new, more vigorous root system. Eventually the bent seedling erects its main bole and continues to grow in height. At the same time that the main bole expands, the burl tissue expands outwardly, developing actually into a massive root collar from which massive intertwining roots emerge. All major roots will continue to originate from this burl throughout the life of the tree. Since a burl cannot shift its position upward along the tree bole when it is buried by sedimentary deposits in floods, it must immediately send out new roots to the soil surface if it is to avoid being suffocated. Sometimes cancerous growths caused by disease or injury are observed on redwood trunks. They outwardly resemble the root collar burls, but they appear to lack the capacity to resprout or regenerate. The burl wood with its many dormant buds is much sought by craftworkers for use in making novelty products that draw part of their appeal from its swollen, gnarled appearance. Burl wood is also used industrially in producing valuable veneers.

Redwood trees flower in the midst of the rainy winter, from December to January. They are prolific cone producers, and in virgin redwood forests, trees bear thousands of cones each year. Cones mature the following fall, shedding their seeds in October and November. Each cone contains 90–150 seeds. The seeds seem to germinate instantly, as soon as they get wet, although the ability to germinate is lost within a few months. Normal germination rates for redwood seeds are very low, averaging 3–10 percent, because many seeds are empty; and few seedlings survive the first 3 years. Thus, although large quantities of seeds are produced annually, natural regeneration of redwoods remains a slow process. Some form of environmental disturbance (such as flood or fire) that reduces root competition for the germinating redwood seedling is required for its successful survival. Redwoods partially compensate for their sporadic regeneration with exceptional longevity: Mature redwoods can reach 2200 years of age, and numerous trees are known to be over 1500 years old. This longevity allows them eventually to gain dominance within a forest, triumphing over all competitors.

Redwoods do not easily withstand the impact of timber harvesting. Formerly, a conservative system of selective tree harvesting was practiced. This system allowed for abundant resprouting from cut redwood stumps and maintained to some extent the essential elements of the protective forest environment. However, only rarely did these conditions contribute to establishing natural regeneration, and future timber crops depended entirely on residual trees and sprout regrowth.

Nowadays, clear-cutting, or total removal of all trees, is commonly advocated as the standard forest management practice in the redwood region. This practice is especially detrimental to redwood survival. The sudden exposure causes rapid deterioration of the special forest environment on which redwoods depend. Without it, even undamaged, healthy, mature, residual redwoods die within 10–15 years. Isolated trees gradually lose branches, foliage, and crowns, and their root systems begin to decay. Eventually they are weakened to the point where they can be blown down, no longer able to withstand winds, desiccation, and harsh exposure to the elements. In addition, the mechanized logging equipment associated with clear-cutting deleteriously affects the soil, compacting it as well as disturbing it in other ways and accelerating erosion. Artificial redwood plantings in such barren clear-cuts have yielded only mediocre results. Sadly, these magnificent and ancient trees—uniquely adapted against almost any natural catastrophe—do not seem to be able to weather the onslaught of people and their machines. Ironically, the protection and preservation of this precious heritage rests in the same hands that shape its destruction.

Plant Identification and Use of the Keys

The first step in using this pocket flora is understanding how the plant identification process works. Plants are classified according to their most typical and significant features in groups called families. Families are further subdivided by common features into more restricted or specific groups called genera (the singular form of *genera* is *genus*). Likewise, genera are divided into species (the singular and plural forms of *species* are the same).

Plants are named according to the binomial system of Latin names first proposed in 1753 by a Swedish botanist, Carl von Linné (commonly referred to as Carolus Linnaeus). For example, redwoods are given the scientific name *Sequoia sempervirens*. The first part of this name, *Sequoia*, is that of the genus; the second part, *sempervirens*, is termed the specific epithet. Together they constitute the species name. Both parts of species names have variable endings. Family names all end in *-aceae*, pronounced *a see ee* (for example, Taxodi-aceae). Officially, the Latin, scientific name is followed by an abbreviation identifying according to a standard key the original author and the publication in which the plant species is described for the first time in scientific literature. For example, "*Sequoia sempervirens* (Lamb.) Endl. Syn. Conif. 198. 1847" indicates that the species was first described by Lambert, Aylmer Bourke, 1761–1842 (= Lamb.), redescribed by Endlicher, Stephen Friedrich Ladislaus, 1804–1849 (= Endl.), and the description first published in *Synonyma Coniferae* in 1847 on page 198. Usually except in reference books publication sources are omitted from the scientific names.

Identifying families, genera, and species by choosing between opposing statements is called keying, and the particular arrangement of statements is called a key. The botanical keys in this flora are framed in the standard binary format. Each numbered key entry offers a clear choice between two contrasting statements. One of the alternatives will apply to the unknown specimen at hand. Following each alternative is either a number or a scientific name; in the genus/species keys sometimes there are both. In all cases whenever a number is present the next step is to proceed to the key entry bearing that number, there repeating the identical process of choosing between two alternatives. Each step leads to another key entry and its alternatives, until a family, genus, or species identity is reached.

It is important to note that most family, genus, and species distinctions are based on flower and fruit structure. Thus, for identification purposes, flowering and fruiting material is usually required; underground plant parts may be needed as well. Sometimes a hand lens or pocket magnifier can reveal identifying details that would otherwise be obscure.

To identify a particular unknown plant species one must first place it in a family by using the Family Key. Reading the appropriate family description next will allow users to determine if they have keyed a plant correctly. The family characteristics listed should agree with the specimen under consideration. When the family is established, the plant can be taken through the genus/species key, first to the genus, then to the species. Finally, to check for keying accuracy, the individual species descriptions and drawings should be consulted.

In the middle of this pocket flora 29 plant species are reproduced in color. These plates provide an independent visual means of identification, based strictly on color and shape of the flower. Users are encouraged to study the color plates carefully, comparing them when possible to actual specimens, to facilitate this kind of visual identification.

This pocket flora is intended to be a handy and ready reference to 212 of the species most frequently encountered in the redwood forest. Included are native species and common exotic species (species introduced from abroad), species of the dense redwood forest, of the roadsides, of the forest edge, and of disturbed or logged forest. The flora is not exhaustive: Although it treats the most common plants from the entire redwood region stretching from about Santa Cruz, California, along the coast to Brookings, Oregon, it does not cover plant species common to habitats outside the redwood forests.

Certain large plant families although very familiar in the redwood forests have nonetheless been omitted either because they are not very conspicuous or because identifying them requires a sophisticated understanding of technical nomenclature. The sedge family (Cyperaceae) is one of these, as is the grass family (Poaceae), which is also absent except for one exotic species, pampas grass *(Cortaderia selloana)*. I have not developed separate keys for such major divisions of the plant kingdom as the ferns (Pteridophyta), the club mosses (Lycopodophyta), the horsetails (Equisitophyta), or the conifers (Gymnospermae). These divisions have been incorporated into the single Family Key.

Users of this pocket flora will find it helpful to familiarize themselves with the organization of the material. A glossary appears at the end of the flora. It has been carefully compiled to define unavoidable technical terms in nontechnical language, and many of the more important terms are illustrated. It should be consulted before the keys are used. One should also look at the various drawings (particularly, before beginning, see the drawings, pp. 8–11) and color plates to learn to recognize flower parts and details and to gain an appreciation of plant and flower variability. The first and major key in the flora is the Family Key. In this key, only the most typical and significant features of plants are introduced for family identification. This key is followed by descriptions of individual families, with each family description followed, when applicable, by its respective genus/species key. For easy reference, running heads indicate the families under consideration. In addition, a strictly alphabetical order of the family names is maintained. Individual family sections each include a detailed and complete general description of the primary family features relevant to species treated in the flora.

Not all the general family descriptions are followed by separate keys leading to individual genus and species names. When only a single species of a family is considered, there is no separate genus/species key. Whether or not there is a key, each species is described in a brief, comprehensive paragraph giving its major features, its general geographical range, its specific distribution within the redwood region, and its ecology. Line drawings illustrating the characteristic features of each species accompany the text. Genera and species are arranged in alphabetical order within each family. In case the plant specimen does not match the descriptions in exact detail there is a likelihood that the species is not included in this pocket flora, and users must then consult a more comprehensive and less portable standard flora.

FLOWERS

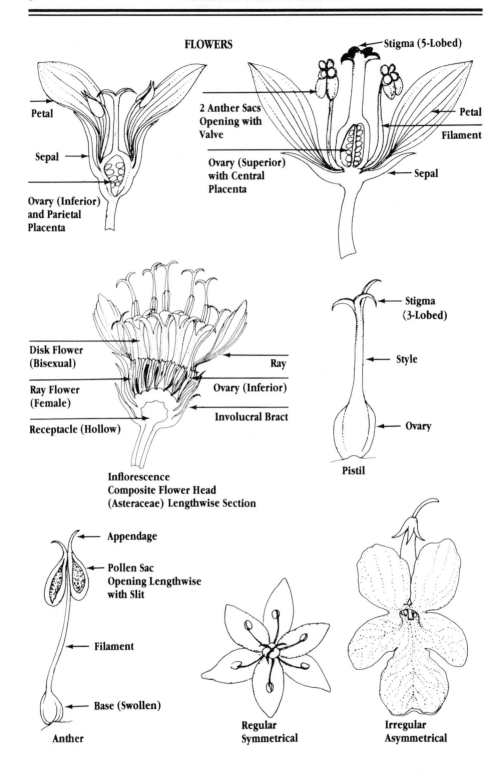

Petal

Sepal

Ovary (Inferior) and Parietal Placenta

Stigma (5-Lobed)

2 Anther Sacs Opening with Valve

Ovary (Superior) with Central Placenta

Petal

Filament

Sepal

Disk Flower (Bisexual)

Ray Flower (Female)

Receptacle (Hollow)

Ray

Ovary (Inferior)

Involucral Bract

Inflorescence Composite Flower Head (Asteraceae) Lengthwise Section

Stigma (3-Lobed)

Style

Ovary

Pistil

Appendage

Pollen Sac Opening Lengthwise with Slit

Filament

Base (Swollen)

Anther

Regular Symmetrical

Irregular Asymmetrical

FRUITS

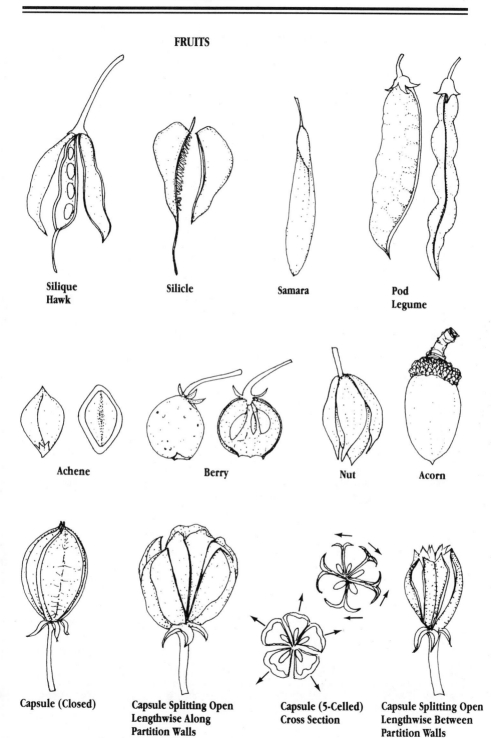

Silique
Hawk

Silicle

Samara

Pod
Legume

Achene

Berry

Nut

Acorn

Capsule (Closed)

Capsule Splitting Open
Lengthwise Along
Partition Walls

Capsule (5-Celled)
Cross Section

Capsule Splitting Open
Lengthwise Between
Partition Walls

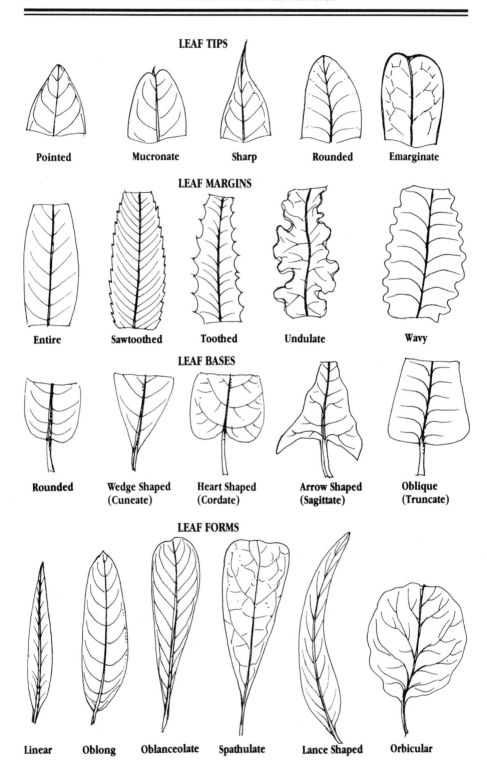

LEAF TIPS

Pointed   Mucronate   Sharp   Rounded   Emarginate

LEAF MARGINS

Entire   Sawtoothed   Toothed   Undulate   Wavy

LEAF BASES

Rounded   Wedge Shaped   Heart Shaped   Arrow Shaped   Oblique
            (Cuneate)   (Cordate)   (Sagittate)   (Truncate)

LEAF FORMS

Linear   Oblong   Oblanceolate   Spathulate   Lance Shaped   Orbicular

LEAF ARRANGEMENTS

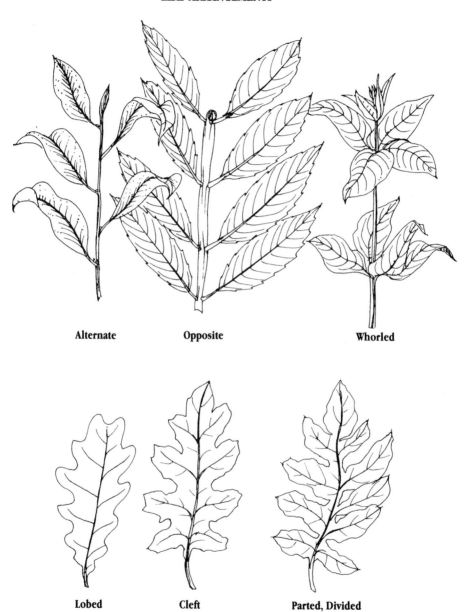

Alternate   Opposite   Whorled

Lobed   Cleft   Parted, Divided

Family Key

This key is intended to be used only for those members of a family growing in the redwood region of California. These members are described in this pocket flora.

1   Plants without flowers (without perianth) and without fruits. Reproductive structures borne on the upper surface, lower surface or base of leaves, or in axillary or terminal cones. Ovules without carpels. (Ferns, horsetails, and gymnosperms and allied families.)   **2**

1   Plants with flowers (with a perianth) and with fruits containing 1–many seeds. Ovules borne in carpels. (Flowering plants, or angiosperms.)   **13**

2   Plants without a woody stem, not treelike in stature. No seeds present, only spores. (Lower vascular plants.)   **3**

2   Plants with a woody stem, treelike in stature. Seed present, no spores. (Gymnosperms.)   **10**

3   Stems usually with hollow internodes, simple or with whorled branches at the solid nodes. Stems segmented into internodes, can be readily pulled apart into segments, without leaves or needlelike scales. Stems hollow, fluted, or grooved but roundish in cross section. Leaves reduced to a whorl of minute, fused scales at each node.   *Horsetail Family*—EQUISETACEAE

3   Stems not so segmented or fluted. Leaves various but not reduced to a whorl of fused scales at each node.   **4**

4   Stems aerial, spreading, often forked, and branching into 2. Leaves bractlike, with a single, straight midvein, seldom over 8 mm long, densely arranged along the branches. Spore-producing organs often aggregated into a terminal cone.   **5**

4   Stems underground or at ground surface, either elongate and horizontal or compact and vertical. Leaves well-developed, with a branching vein system, more than 5 mm long. Plants not producing cones.   **6**

5   Leaves without appendages, entire, up to 8 mm long. Plants of coastal bogs and cool, damp sites of the redwood forest.   *Club Moss Family*—LYCOPODIACEAE

5   Leaves with a small appendage a little above the base, toothed or fringed with hairs, less than 5 mm long. Plants typically of exposed rocks and cliffs of inland areas or growing from tree branches. *Spike Moss Family*—SELAGINELLACEAE

6   Sori usually not in distinct clusters; either at or near the margins of the pinnae (or pinnules) or covering all but the midrib and margins of pinnately lobed pinnae (or pinnules).   **7**

6 Sori either in distinct clusters away from the leaf margins or in continuous rows on each side of the midrib of the narrow and entire pinnae (or pinnules).   **8**

7 Large, coarse ferns, fronds arching, spreading, on light-colored stalks, mostly up to 150 cm high. Stem cross section reveals numerous scattered vascular bundles.   *Bracken Fern Family—* **DENNSTAEDTIACEAE**

7 Small to medium-sized ferns, on dark, usually shining stalks, less than 100 cm high. Stem cross section reveals a single central cavity. *Maidenhair Fern Family—***ADIANTACEAE**

8 Sorus cover (indusium) present and well-developed.   **9**

8 Sorus cover absent or lacking.   *Polypody Fern Family—* **POLYPODIACEAE**

9 Sorus cover rounded to kidney shaped, usually attached in the center of its underside and opening around the margin. Sori are on the veins or at the end of the veins.   *Wood Fern Family—* **ASPIDIACEAE**

9 Sorus cover elongate, opening at one side only, facing the midrib of the leaf-frond segment, never centrally attached and never opening all around the margin. Sori in rows or bands on each side of and parallel to the midrib of the leaf-frond segment.   *Deer Fern Family—***BLECHNACEAE**

10 "Fruit" a red drupe, berrylike, fleshy, 1-seeded. Leaves needlelike, flat, sharp pointed, spreading in 2 horizontal rows.   *Yew Family—***TAXACEAE**

10 "Fruit" a dry cone, consisting of several to many woody scales, each scale bearing 1 to several seeds. Leaves needlelike to scalelike, sometimes spreading in 2 horizontal rows.   **11**

11 Leaves needlelike to linear, not all scalelike. If scalelike, also needlelike leaves present.   **12**

11 Leaves all scalelike, adpressed to and thickly covering the branches. *Cedar (Cypress) Family—***CUPRESSACEAE**

12 Cone scales overlapping, each bearing 2 seeds usually with a long, papery wing at one end.   *Pine Family—***PINACEAE**

12 Cone scales not overlapping, each bearing 5–7 seeds, usually with a narrow, papery wing surrounding the seed.   *Bald Cypress (Redwood) Family—***TAXODIACEAE**

13 Perianth (sepals or petals) much reduced, undeveloped, or absent.   **14**

13 Perianth (sepals or petals) well-developed.   **24**

14 Plants with distinctly woody stems, like trees or shrubs.   **15**

14 Plants with no distinctly woody stems, herblike.   **20**

15 Leaves palmately lobed and palmately veined, the margins never toothed. Inflorescence globose, hanging on long stalks. *Sycamore Family*—PLATANACEAE

15 Leaves not palmately lobed or palmately veined, the margins often toothed. Inflorescence not globose, not hanging on long stalks.   **16**

16 Plants unisexual, male and female flowers on separate plants. All flowers in elongated, similar catkins. *Willow Family*— SALICACEAE

16 Plants bisexual, male and female flowers on the same plant. Female flowers not in elongated catkins, female catkins very dissimilar from male catkins.   **17**

17 Leaves nearly entire or remotely toothed, aromatic, gland dotted. Male catkins short, erect. Fruit a drupelike nut, covered with whitish wax. Ovary 1-celled. Stipules absent. *Sweet Gale (Wax Myrtle) Family*—MYRICACEAE

17 Leaves toothed or lobed, not aromatic or gland dotted. Male catkins elongate, usually hanging. Fruit an acorn, a winged nutlet, or a nut enclosed in a leafy involucre. Ovary 1–7-celled. Stipules deciduous.   **18**

18 Female inflorescence cylindrical, conelike. Female flowers lacking a calyx, ovary free. Fruit a small, winged nutlet, often crowned with persistent styles. *Birch Family*—BETULACEAE

18 Female inflorescence not conelike. Female flowers with calyx joined to and enclosing the ovary. Fruit not a winged nutlet but an acorn or a nut enclosed in a leafy involucre.   **19**

19 Fruit an acorn. Ovary 3-celled with 2 ovules per cell. Male flowers with a 4–6-lobed calyx. Stamen filament split to its base, each half bearing a 1-celled anther. *Beech Family*—FAGACEAE

19 Fruit a nut enclosed in the enlarged, tubular, leaflike involucre. Ovary 1–2-celled with 1 ovule per cell. Male flowers without a calyx. Anthers 2-celled. *Hazelnut (Filbert) Family*— CORYLACEAE

20 Leaves compound, long stalked, with 3 leaflets. *May Apple Family*—PODOPHYLLACEAE (Achlys)

20 Leaves simple, entire to lobed or incised.   **21**

21 Leaves not bladelike, net veined, either foul smelling, bluish glossy, or with stinging hairs.   **22**

21 Leaves bladelike, parallel veined, not foul smelling or stinging. **23**

22 Flowers aggregated into a cylindrical spadix subtended by a conspicuous yellow or white spathe. Fruit a berry. Plants foul smelling, not with stinging hairs. Leaves very large, basal. *Arum Family*—ARACEAE

22   Flowers in various clusters but not in a spadix and spathe arrangement. Fruit an achene. Plants with stinging hairs, not foul smelling. Leaves opposite.   *Nettle Family*—URTICACEAE

23   Flowers without a perianth, consisting of pairs of reduced, opposite, overlapping bracts concealing the stamens and the ovary. Inflorescence an open or condensed spike, raceme, or panicle. Flowers bisexual or unisexual. Not aquatic plants.   *Grass Family*—POACEAE

23   Flowers with a perianth reduced to hairs, lacking overlapping bracts. Inflorescence always a dense spike or spikes. Flowers all unisexual, limited to separate spikes or separate parts of the same spike. Aquatic plants.   *Cattail Family*—TYPHACEAE

24   Flower or perianth parts basically in 1 or more whorls of 3 or 6.   **25**

24   Flower or perianth parts basically in 1 or more whorls of 2, 4, or 5, or, rarely, 7–9.   **31**

25   Flowers irregular, perianth parts not symmetrically arranged, the lower petal sometimes pouchlike or spurred.   *Orchid Family*—ORCHIDACEAE

25   Flower regular. Perianth parts symmetrically arranged.   **26**

26   Perianth of 12 or more segments. Leaves compound.   **27**

26   Perianth of 6 or fewer segments. Leaves simple.   **28**

27   Plants woody. Perianth of 12 segments. Leaves with spiny margins. *Barberry Family*—BERBERIDACEAE

27   Plants herbaceous. Perianth of 18–21 segments. Leaves not spiny margined.   *May Apple Family*—PODOPHYLLA-CEAE (Vancouveria)

28   Stamens 12. Sepals 3. Petals absent. Flowers solitary in the leaf axils, not terminal. Leaves net veined, the bases not sheathlike or covering the stems.   *Birthwort Family*—ARISTOLO-CHIACEAE

28   Stamens 3 or 6. Perianth usually consisting of 6 segments. Flowers mostly showy, single or clustered in terminal heads or racemes. Venation running parallel, not intersecting or forking, leaf bases typically ensheathing the stems.   **29**

29   Ovary inferior, stamens 3.   *Iris Family*—IRIDACEAE

29   Ovary superior to half inferior. Stamens 6.   **30**

30   Leaves alternate, never all whorled at the top of the stem.   *Lily Family*—LILIACEAE

30   Leaves opposite or whorled at the top of the stem.   *Trillium Family*—TRILLIACEAE

31 Stamens numerous, more than twice the number of perianth segments. **32**

31 Stamens no more than twice as many as perianth segments. **34**

32 Shrubs, small trees, or herbs. Sepals, petals, and stamens inserted on the rim of an open cup (hypanthium) becoming fleshy in fruit. Stipules usually present. *Rose Family*—**ROSACEAE**

32 Plants always herbaceous. Sepals, petals, and stamens inserted directly on the flat or elevated receptacle, which is not cup shaped (no hypanthium). Stipules absent. **33**

33 Ovules several to many per carpel. Fruit a follicle or berry. Flowers regular or irregular. *Hellebore (Baneberry) Family*—**HELLEBORACEAE**

33 Ovule 1 per carpel. Fruit a cluster of dry achenes, sometimes with long, feathery tails. Flowers always regular. *Buttercup Family*—**RANUNCULACEAE**

34 Only 1 perianth whorl present, the perianth segments all quite similar to one another. When there are 2 perianth whorls, the outer perianth whorl inconspicuous, reduced to a row of hairs, bristles, or pappus (Asteraceae). **35**

34 2 or more perianth whorls present, the 2 perianth whorls distinguished by differences in shape, color, or placement on the receptacle, but the second perianth whorl not reduced to hairs, bristles, or pappus. **41**

35 Trees or shrubs. Stems distinctly woody. **36**

35 Plants herbaceous or vinelike. Stems not woody. **37**

36 Leaves opposite. Fruits 2 nutlets free but paired, each with a large, hard, terminal wing. *Maple Family*—**ACERACEAE**

36 Leaves alternate. Fruit a berry or drupe. *Laurel Family*—**LAURACEAE**

37 Stems 4-angled. Leaves in apparent whorls because of large leaflike stipules. *Madder Family*—**RUBIACEAE**

37 Stems not 4-angled. Leaves not whorled. **38**

38 Plants bearing tendrils opposite the leaves. Fruit a pepo or cucumber. *Gourd Family*—**CUCURBITACEAE**

38 Plants without tendrils. Fruit not a pepo or cucumber. **39**

39 Ovary superior. Stamens 4. Fruit a berry. *Lily Family*—**LILIACEAE (Maianthemum)**

39 Ovary inferior. Stamens 5 when present. Fruit an achene or a dry fruit with 2 carpels splitting into 2 halves. **40**

40 Inflorescence a compound umbel. Leaves compound or deeply dissected. Flowers bisexual. Fruit a dry fruit with 2 carpels splitting

          into 2 halves.   *Carrot (Parsley) Family*—API-ACEAE

40   Inflorescence a compact head. Leaves various but never compound. Flowers often unisexual. Fruit an achene, usually with persistent hairs, bristles, or pappus.   *Aster (Sunflower) Family*—ASTERACEAE

41   Petals or inner whorl of perianth segments more or less separate and free to their bases.   **42**

41   2 or more petals united for at least one-fourth their length.   **62**

42   Trees, shrubs, or woody vines.   **43**

42   Plants always herbaceous, without woody stems.   **49**

43   Leaves simple, lobed or entire, not compound.   **44**

43   Leaves compound.   **48**

44   Trailing vinelike herb, often shrubby. Fruit a 4- or 5-celled capsule. *Hydrangea (Syringa) Family*—PHILADELPHIACEAE (Whipplea)

44   Erect shrubs or trees. Fruit not a 4- or 5-celled capsule.   **45**

45   Ovary inferior.   **46**

45   Ovary superior.   **47**

46   Receptacle enlarged into a cuplike structure (hypanthium). Leaves variously lobed. Fruit a spiny or spineless berry.   *Gooseberry (Currant) Family*—GROSSULARIACEAE

46   No cuplike structure present. Leaves entire. Fruit a drupe.   *Dogwood Family*—CORNACEAE

47   Leaves opposite, palmately lobed.   *Maple Family*—ACERACEAE

47   Leaves alternate, not palmately lobed.   *Buckthorn Family*—RHAMNACEAE (Ceanothus)

48   Leaves opposite. Leaflets 5–7.   *Buckeye Family*—HIPPOCASTANACEAE

48   Leaves alternate. Leaflets 3.   *Sumac Family*—ANACARDIACEAE

49   Plants whitish yellowish, lacking chlorophyll.   *Indian Pipe Family*—MONOTROPACEAE

49   Plants green, with chlorophyll.   **50**

50   Flowers irregular.   **51**

50   Flowers regular.   **53**

51   Fruit a pod or legume. Leaves compound, often tendril bearing. Petals 5, an upper "banner," 2 lateral "wings," and 2 lower petals joined to form a "keel."   *Pea Family*—FABACEAE

51 Fruit a capsule. Leaves simple, entire to dissected. Flower not as described above. **52**

52 Stamens 5. Sepals 5. Petals 5, the lower one usually larger than the others and spurred or pouchlike. *Violet Family*—VIO-LACEAE

52 Stamens in 2 groups of 3. Sepals 2. Petals 4, forming an inner and outer pair. *Fumitory (Fumewort) Family*—FUMARIACEAE

53 Flowers in compound umbels or racemes of umbels. **54**

53 Flowers not in umbels. **55**

54 Inflorescence a compound umbel. Fruit a dry fruit with 2 carpels splitting into 2 halves. *Carrot (Parsley) Family*—APIACEAE

54 Inflorescence a raceme of umbels. Fruit a berry. *Ginseng Family*—ARALIACEAE

55 Styles 4 or 5. **56**

55 Styles 1 or 2. **57**

56 Leaves compound. Leaflets 3, not succulent. *Wood Sorrel (Oxalis) Family*—OXALIDACEAE

56 Leaves simple, succulent. *Stonecrop (Orpine) Family*—CRASSULACEAE

57 Styles 2, forming divergent beaks. Leaves palmately veined and palmately lobed. *Saxifrage Family*—SAXIFRAGA-CEAE

57 Style 1, entire or branched. Leaves not palmately veined nor palmately lobed. **58**

58 Ovary inferior. *Evening Primrose Family*—ONA-GRACEAE

58 Ovary superior. **59**

59 Sepals 2. Style with 3 branches. *Purslane Family*—PORTULACACEAE

59 Sepals 4–7. Style entire or merely lobed. **60**

60 Petals 5. Stamens 10. *Wintergreen Family*—PYRO-LACEAE

60 Petals 4. Stamens 5 or 6. **61**

61 Sepals 4, not united. Petals not united. Stamens 6, 2 of them shorter than the others. *Mustard Family*—BRASSICACEAE

61 Sepals 5–7, united. Petals united. Stamens 5. *Primrose Family*—PRIMULACEAE

62 Leaves palmately veined and palmately lobed. **63**

62   Leaves not palmately veined and palmately lobed.   **66**

63   Plants bearing tendrils opposite the leaves. Flowers unisexual. Fruit a pepo or cucumber.   ***Gourd Family***—CUCURBITA-CEAE

63   Plants without tendrils. Flowers bisexual. Fruit a capsule or berry.   **64**

64   Stamens 2. Sepals 4.   ***Figwort (Snapdragon) Family***—SCROPHULARIACEAE (Synthyris)

64   Stamens 5 or 10, or if stamens 2, then sepals 5.   **65**

65   Plants herbaceous. Leaves mostly basal.   ***Saxifrage Family***—SAXIFRAGACEAE

65   Plants shrubby. Leaves well distributed along stem.   ***Gooseberry (Currant) Family***—GROSSULARIACEAE

66   Plants woody (or at least woody toward base).   **67**

66   Plants herbaceous.   **71**

67   Leaves opposite or whorled.   **68**

67   Leaves alternate.   **69**

68   Ovary superior. Fruit a capsule.   ***Figwort (Snapdragon) Family***—SCROPHULARIACEAE (Mimulus aurantiacus)

68   Ovary inferior. Fruit a drupe or berry.   ***Honeysuckle Family***—CAPRIFOLIACEAE

69   Flowers bisexual, in racemes or panicles. Fruit a capsule, berry, or drupe.   **70**

69   Flowers unisexual, in compact heads. Male and female flowers on separate plants. Fruit an achene.   ***Aster (Sunflower) Family***—ASTERACEAE (Baccharis)

70   Ovary inferior. Stamens inserted on the outer edge of a disk on top of the ovary. Anther cells elongated into more or less long, tubelike horns.   ***Huckleberry (Blueberry, Cranberry, Bilberry) Family***—VACCINIACEAE

70   Ovary superior. Stamens inserted on the outer edge of a disk at the base of the ovary. Anther cells not elongated at the apex into tubelike horns.   ***Heath Family***—ERICACEAE

71   Plants without chlorophyll. Leaves much reduced, scalelike bracts.   **72**

71   Plants with chlorophyll. Leaves well-developed.   **73**

72   Stamen 4, in 2 pairs. Corolla irregular, 2-lipped.   ***Broomrape Family***—OROBANCHACEAE

72   Stamens 6–12. Corolla regular.   ***Indian Pipe Family***—MONOTROPACEAE

73   Flowers irregular.   74
73   Flowers regular.   79

74   Flowers borne in a head on a common receptacle surrounded by involucral bracts.   *Aster (Sunflower) Family—*ASTERACEAE

74   Flowers not borne in heads with involucral bracts.   75

75   Stamens 2 or 4.   76
75   Stamens 5 or more.   77

76   Ovary 4-lobed. Fruit of 4 separate-seeded nutlets. Plants usually aromatic. Stem usually square in cross section. Plants mostly less than 1 m tall. Lower lip of corolla generally enlarged.   *Mint Family*—LAMIACEAE

76   Ovary not 4-lobed. Fruit a 2-celled capsule. If stem 4-angled (*Scrophularia*), then plant at least 1 m tall. Upper lip of corolla generally enlarged.   *Figwort (Snapdragon) Family*—SCRO-PHULARIACEAE

77   Leaves simple. Sepals not united, 3. Petals 5 or 4, 2 separate, the other 2 or 3 united.   *Milkwort Family*—POLYGALA-CEAE

77   Leaves compound. Sepals united, 2 or 5 toothed or cleft. Corolla of 4 or 5 united petals.   78

78   Leaflets of compound leaf entire. Fruit a pod. Stamens 10, 9 of these united, or in 2 groups of 5.   *Pea Family*—FABACEAE

78   Leaflets of compound leaf dissected. Fruit a capsule. Stamens 6, in 2 sets of 3.   *Fumitory (Fumewort) Family*—FUMARIACEAE

79   Ovary inferior.   80
79   Ovary superior.   81

80   Flowers in a head on a common receptacle surrounded by involucral bracts.   *Aster (Sunflower) Family*—ASTERA-CEAE

80   Flowers in scattered clusters, not in involucrate heads.   *Bellflower (Bluebell, Harebell) Family*—CAMPAN-ULACEAE

81   Stamens 4. Stems square in cross section.   *Mint Family*—LAMIACEAE (Mentha)

81   Stamens 5. Stems not square in cross section.   *Waterleaf Family*—HYDROPHYLLACEAE

Genus/Species
Keys/
Descriptions

ACERACEAE
Maple Family

Habit	Deciduous trees or shrubs with generally rounded tops and watery, often sweet, syrupy sap.
Life Form	Phanerophyte.
Roots	Surface roots, often heavy.
Stems	Multibranched, stems ascending or often declining and forming dense thickets. Bark on old trees often furrowed.
Leaves	Opposite, entire, simple or pinnately lobed or more infrequently palmately or pinnately compound, changing color in the fall of the year, often to brilliant yellow or red before leaf fall.
Inflorescence	Flattopped panicles or racemes, terminal or in leaf axils, often elongated and drooping.
Flowers	Bisexual, but often bearing unisexual and bisexual flowers on the same plant, regular. Calyx generally 5-parted (4–9), greenish, overlapping in bud. Petals as many as calyx lobes or none, yellowish. Stamens 3–12, often 8 with threadlike filaments inserted on margin of disk. Ovary superior, 2-celled, 2-lobed. Styles 2, inserted between the lobes.
Fruit	Achenes 2, long winged, joined at the base but usually separating before falling.
Seeds	Generally 1, occasionally 2 per achene with compressed, ascending embryo. Endosperm none. Cotyledons 1-folded, thin.
Distribution	Family of 2 genera and about 125 species native to the Northern Hemisphere.
Uses	Often used as ornamental trees or shrubs or shade trees.
Varieties	Several varieties having dark red or variegated leaves or brilliantly colored red or yellow fall foliage. Widely used as ornamentals in parks and gardens or as shade trees in urban areas.

Key to ACERACEAE

Only 1 genus, *Acer,* is represented.

1   Flowers in large, 10–50-flowered, dense, drooping, 7–15 cm long, elongated racemes. Body of long-winged achene densely grayish yellow, stiff-hairy, achene wings spreading 30–45 degrees. Leaves long stalked, 10–25 cm broad, deeply 3–5 parted with irregular, coarse, few-toothed leaf margins. Tall trees with multibranched arching and ascending stems.   **ACER MACROPHYLLUM**

1   Flowers in small 3–10(20), spreading to drooping, 2–4 cm long, open flattopped panicles or convex racemes. Body of achene not hairy, achene wings often changing in color to brilliant red, spreading about 180 degrees. Leaves short stalked, 5–12 cm broad, round-heart shaped in outline, shallowly 5–11 lobed. Lobes pointed and sharply sawtoothed. Small trees to tall erect shrubs, heavily branched, declining stems forming dense thickets.   **ACER CIR-CINATUM**

001 ACER CIRCINATUM Pursh.
Vine Maple

Shrub to small tree, to 15 m tall. Multistemmed, ascending, or often reclining and rooting, forming dense thickets. Bark smooth, brownish gray, often dark red on full exposure to the sun. Leaves heart shaped, palmately (5)7–9(11) lobed. Leaves green, changing in the fall season to bright red or red with yellow mottling. Raceme short, drooping, spreading, 3–10(20)-flowered, 2–4 cm long. Fruit 2–3 cm long. Wings spreading at 180 degrees. *Flowering:* March–June, on appearance of young foliage. *Fruiting:* October–December.

Found along shaded stream banks and on moist, wooded, seepage slopes from southern Alaska along the Pacific coast to Mendocino County, California; from the east side of the Cascades to Yuba and Butte counties, California. Below 1700 m elevation.

002 ACER MACROPHYLLUM Pursh.
Big-Leaf Maple

Tree up to 40 m tall with massive, rounded crown, multistemmed, with heavy surface roots. Bark smooth, textured, grayish. On older trees bark is thick, furrowed, and brownish gray. Leaves roundish, dark green, paler beneath, 10–25 cm. Lobes deeply 3–5 parted, irregularly few toothed. Foliage changing to bright yellow in the fall season. Stalks 5–12 cm long. Terminal raceme, dense, cylindrical, drooping, 10–60-flowered, 7–15 cm long. Fruit a long-winged achene, wings spreading at 30–45 degree angle, hairy along main vein, 20–40 mm long. *Flowering:* April–May. *Fruiting:* October–December. (See Plate I.)

Common in alluvial flood plains along stream banks, in canyons, and on moist lower slopes. From coastal southern Alaska along the Pacific coast to southern California, west of the Cascades and the Sierra Nevada. Below 1700 m elevation.

ADIANTACEAE
Maidenhair Fern Family

Habit	Terrestrial ferns growing in moist to dry areas.
Rootstock	Rootstocks short, creeping or ascending.
Fronds	Pinnate in plan, simple to compound, not jointed to the rootstock. Stalks erect, blackish, and hollow.
Sori	Typically marginal and protected by a reflexed margin, or elongate along the veins and without an indusium, or covering the whole fertile surface.
Indusium	None or the reflexed pinna margin functioning as a false indusium.
Sporangia	Encircled by a ring (annulus), which is usually lengthwise and interrupted, the sporangia opening by a definite slit.
Spores	Almost always tetrahedral.
Distribution	About 62 genera of temperate and tropical regions.

Key to ADIANTACEAE

1   Sporangia following the veins throughout, not covered by the reflexed pinna margins. Fronds evergreen, powdery-waxy beneath. Sporangia encircled by a ring of 20–24 cells. Spores irregularly ribbed.   **PITYROGRAMMA**

Portion of frond with pinnae triangular to pentagonal in outline, 4–18 cm long, almost as wide. Pinnae few, opposite. The lowest pair of pinnae by far the largest with pinnately divided segments, the lower basal segments by far the longest. The other pinnae pinnately lobed, or the upper ones entire.   **PITYROGRAMMA TRIANGULARIS**

1   Sporangia borne at or near the tips of the veins, hence close to and covered by the reflexed margin of the frond when young. Fronds deciduous, not powdery-waxy beneath. Sporangia encircled by a ring of about 18 cells. Spores smooth.   **ADIANTUM**

Portion of frond with pinnae forked at the base, the branches bearing 2 to several pinnae on the outer side. Pinnae 10–40 cm long, pinnately divided, with 15–35 segments on the larger ones. The segments short stalked, asymmetrical, the lower margin entire and straight or concave, the upper margin lobed or cleft and more convex.   **ADIANTUM PEDATUM**

003   ADIANTUM PEDATUM   L.
Maidenhair Fern, Five-Finger Fern

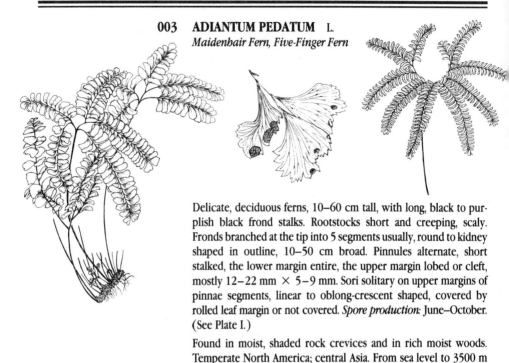

Delicate, deciduous ferns, 10–60 cm tall, with long, black to purplish black frond stalks. Rootstocks short and creeping, scaly. Fronds branched at the tip into 5 segments usually, round to kidney shaped in outline, 10–50 cm broad. Pinnules alternate, short stalked, the lower margin entire, the upper margin lobed or cleft, mostly 12–22 mm × 5–9 mm. Sori solitary on upper margins of pinnae segments, linear to oblong-crescent shaped, covered by rolled leaf margin or not covered. *Spore production:* June–October. (See Plate I.)

Found in moist, shaded rock crevices and in rich moist woods. Temperate North America; central Asia. From sea level to 3500 m elevation.

004   PITYROGRAMMA TRIANGULARIS   (Kaulf.) Maxon
Goldenback Fern

Small, evergreen fern, 6–40 cm tall. Fronds long stalked, triangle shaped, 4–18 cm long. Rootstock short, ascending, densely covered with blackish scales. Fronds yellow powdery beneath due to dense cover of sporangia. During drought periods fronds shrivel up and curl. Pinnae few, opposite, the lower pair largest and longest with pinnately divided segments. Frond stalk red brown when young, blackish in age, 6–22 cm long. Sori indistinct with no cover. *Spore production:* June–August.

Common in rocky, shaded places, in drier sites. From southern British Columbia to northern Baja California, east to Arizona, southern Nevada, and extreme southwestern Utah. Below 1700 m elevation.

ANACARDIACEAE
Sumac Family

Habit Shrubs or trees with sharp, stinging, resinous or milky sap and alternate (rarely, opposite) leaves. Plants with bisexual flowers or male and female flowers on separate plants, or sometimes unisexual flowers, both sexes on the same plant.

Leaves Simple or pinnately compound with 3 leaflets, lacking stipules, persistent or deciduous.

Inflorescence Axillary or terminal racemes or panicles.

Flowers Mostly rather small, regular. Sepals fused, 5(3–7)-parted, a glandular ring or cuplike disk lining its base. Petals fused to calyx, equal in number to the sepals, or lacking. Stamens usually equal in number to the sepals, or twice as many. Ovary superior, 1-celled, with 1 ovule, free from calyx and disk, styles 3, or single with 3 stigma lobes.

Fruit Drupe, dry, berrylike.

Seeds Small, with a bony or crustaceous seed coat without endosperm.

Distribution About 70 genera and 600 species, mostly from warm regions.

---

005 RHUS DIVERSILOBA Torr. & Gray
Poison Oak

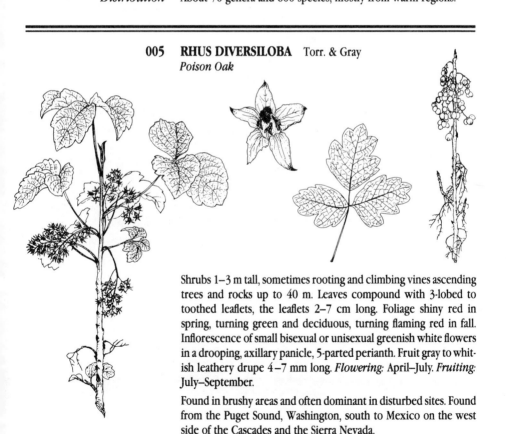

Shrubs 1–3 m tall, sometimes rooting and climbing vines ascending trees and rocks up to 40 m. Leaves compound with 3-lobed to toothed leaflets, the leaflets 2–7 cm long. Foliage shiny red in spring, turning green and deciduous, turning flaming red in fall. Inflorescence of small bisexual or unisexual greenish white flowers in a drooping, axillary panicle, 5-parted perianth. Fruit gray to whitish leathery drupe 4–7 mm long. *Flowering:* April–July. *Fruiting:* July–September.

Found in brushy areas and often dominant in disturbed sites. Found from the Puget Sound, Washington, south to Mexico on the west side of the Cascades and the Sierra Nevada.

APIACEAE
Carrot (Parsley) Family

Habit Annual or perennial herbs, often hollow stemmed with aromatic foliage or seed, and flowers in umbels.

Leaves Alternate or rarely opposite, or even all basal, usually compound to variously cleft or dissected, the stalks commonly widened at the base and sheathing the stem. Stipules, when present, minute.

Inflorescence Typically a compound umbel subtended by a few bracts, the individual, small umbels subtended by small bracts.

Flowers Mostly regular and bisexual, small. Sepals usually 5, or lacking. Petals 5, the tips often recurved inward, typically yellow or white. Stamens 5, alternate with the petals, inserted on a disk above the ovary. Filaments threadlike. Ovary inferior of 2 carpels, 2-celled. Ovules 1 in each cell, hanging. Styles 2, distinct, slender, greatly swollen at the base (forming a stylopodium).

Fruit A dry splitting fruit, consisting of 2 halves united along their common faces, each half ribbed or winged, usually with 1 or more vertical oil tubes in the fruit wall. Fruit splitting or separating at maturity into 2 halves, revealing the slender central thread to which they are originally attached by the tip, each half not opening or splitting.

Seeds Embryo small. Endosperm copious, firm.

Distribution About 300 genera and 3000 species, most abundant in the drier parts of temperate zones.

Key to APIACEAE

1 Fruit linear to club shaped, beaked at the tip, tapering to a tail at the base. Oil tubes in fruit wall absent or obscure. **OSMORHIZA**

Fruit 12–22 mm long, tapering to a slender beak at the tip. Flowers usually greenish white. Enlarged basal portion of style as high as or higher than wide. **OSMORHIZA CHILENSIS**

1 Fruit oblong or ovoid to spherical. Oil tubes evident in fruit wall. **2**

2 Ovary and fruit with prickles or bristles. Primary involucre usually present. **3**

2 Ovary and fruit without prickles or bristles. Primary involucre usually absent. **4**

3 Leaves palmately or pinnately divided, the divisions not small and narrow. Plants hairless or nearly so. Enlarged basal portions of style flattened and disklike or lacking. Fruit not ribbed. Some flowers male, others bisexual, the male flowers stalked, the others sessile. **SANICULA**

Apiaceae = Umbelliferae.

Flowers yellow. Leaves deeply palmately 3–5-lobed, 4–14 cm long and about as broad. Umbels irregularly compound, each with 3 or 4, small, about 20-flowered secondary umbels.   **SANICULA CRASSICAULIS**

3   Leaves 2 or 3 times pinnately compound, the ultimate divisions small and narrow. Plants more or less hairy or bristly. Enlarged basal portion of style conical. Fruit ribbed. Flowers bisexual. Umbels irregularly compound. Ovary and fruit with hooked prickles. Fruit somewhat compressed laterally. Sepals present.   **CAU-CALIS**

Leaf blades 2–6 cm long, 2–5 cm wide. Individual flower stalks very unequal in length. Involucres well-developed.   **CAUCALIS MICROCARPA**

4   Leaves once compound. Leaflets 3, very large, mostly 10–40 cm long and wide.   **HERACLEUM**

Flowers white. At least inflorescence and lower side of leaves hairy. Primary involucre present, deciduous. Plants sturdy, 1–3 m tall.   **HERACLEUM LANATUM**

4   Leaves 1–3 times compound, the leaflets seldom as much as 10 cm wide.   **5**

5   Fruit with prominent, corky, thickened ribs wider than the intervals. Enlarged base of style none or lowered. Sepals evident, persistent. Plants of marshes, streams, and wetlands.   **OENANTHE**

Herb generally reclining, rootstock slender, solid. Stem trailing, rooting at nodes, 50–150 cm long. Leaves twice pinnately compound. Leafstalks not sheathing.   **OENANTHE SARMENTOSA**

5   Ribs of the fruit not corky and thickened. Leafstalks sheathing. Sepals present or absent. Plants stout. Seed face flat to concave. Fruit strongly flattened in the plane of the partition between the seeds. Flowers white, seldom pinkish.   **ANGELICA**

Plants growing on bluffs and sand dunes along the coast. Leaves twice compound, with short, densely matted, soft, white, woolly hairs beneath. Primary involucre absent.   **ANGELICA HENDER-SONII**

006   ANGELICA HENDERSONII   Coult. & Rose
Coastal Angelica, Henderson's Angelica

Perennial, 30–150 cm tall with large leaves and a stout taproot. Leaves compound with 3 stalked leaflets, woolly beneath. Leaflets oval to lance-ovate, 4–8 cm long, sawtoothed. Woolly compound umbels, each with 30–45 secondary umbels on stalks up to 7 cm. Primary involucre lacking; secondary involucre of narrow woolly haired bracts. Sepals minute or lacking, petals white, seldom pink or purplish. Fruit oval 7–10 mm long, the ribs on the back slightly elevated, lateral ribs winged and as wide as the body of the fruit. *Flowering:* June–September. *Fruiting:* September–November.

Found along bluffs and sand dunes from southern Washington to Monterey County, California.

007   CAUCALIS MICROCARPA   Hook. & Arn.
California Hedge Parsley

Slender annual, 8–40 cm tall, hairy throughout. Leaves mostly on the stem, the blade 2–6 cm × 2–5 cm, pinnately dissected into small, narrow segments. Secondary umbels 1–9 per primary umbel on unequal, 1–8 cm long stalks. Primary involucre of almost unmodified leaves; secondary involucre of several small, entire or pinnately divided bracts. Sepals present; petals white; styles short. Fruit oblong, 3–7 mm long, densely covered with rows of hooked bristles. *Flowering:* April–July. *Fruiting:* June–September.

Found along streams, on slopes, or on sandy or rocky soils from southern British Columbia to Baja California, Idaho, Utah, Arizona, and Sonora, Mexico. Below 1600 m elevation.

008 HERACLEUM LANATUM Michx.
Cow Parsnip

Large, single-stemmed perennial, 1–3 m tall, lower surface of leaves woolly. Leaves 20–50 cm long, compound, with 3 leaflets. The leaflets palmately lobed, 10–30(40) cm long and wide, coarsely toothed. Leafstalks distinctly enlarged, the upper ones inflated and sheathing. Large terminal umbel compound, often 10–20 cm wide with several smaller, axillary umbels. Involucres of 5–10 narrow, deciduous bracts. Sepals absent, petals white. Fruit obovate, 7–12 mm × 5–9 mm, slightly hairy or hairless. *Flowering:* February–August. *Fruiting:* July–October.

Found along stream banks and low swampy sites, often forming dominant patches. From Alaska south to Monterey County, California, Arizona, Atlantic coast, Siberia. Below 3000 m elevation.

009 OENANTHE SARMENTOSA Presl.
Pacific Oenanthe, American Oenanthe

Loose-ascending perennial herb, .5–1.5 m, with fibrous roots and also rooting at the nodes. Leaves 10–30 cm long, twice pinnately compound, leaf divisions ovate, 10–60 mm × 7–50 mm. Leafstalks 10–30 cm. Umbels appearing axillary to the leaves on 5–13 cm stalks. Involucre of a few stipules or lacking. Secondary umbels 10–20 on 15–30 mm stalks. Secondary involucre of evident, narrow bractlets. Sepals lance shaped. Petals white with recurved tip. Fruit oblong, cut off squarely, often purplish and with prominent ribs. *Flowering:* June–October. *Fruiting:* July–November.

In low, wet areas, in thickets and along streams, often dominant in open ditches with stagnant water. From southeastern Alaska south to central and southern California, extending inland to Idaho, below 1200 m elevation.

010   OSMORHIZA CHILENSIS H. & A.
Mountain Sweet-Cicely

Slender perennial, 30–100 cm tall, stems 1–3 from a well-developed taproot. Leaves 5–15 cm, compound with 3 leaflets, each leaflet of 3 segments, coarsely toothed. Basal leaves several, on 5–15 cm stalks. Stem leaves 1–3 with shorter stalks. Umbels several, small, short stalked in flower, becoming open and long stalked at maturity of the seeds, the stalks 5–25 cm long. Secondary umbels 3–8. Involucres lacking. Sepals lacking. Petals greenish white. Stamens white. Base of style enlarged and conical. Fruit linear to oblong, 12–22 mm, tapering at ends, stiff-hairy at base. *Flowering:* April–July. *Fruiting:* June–September.

Found in woods and along woodland trails. Southern Alaska to San Diego County, California, Sierra Nevada and Coast Ranges; Alberta south to Arizona, Great Lakes region; and from northern New Hampshire to Newfoundland; also Chile, Argentina.

011   SANICULA CRASSICAULIS Poepp.
Pacific Sanicle

Perennial herb, 25–80(125) cm tall branching above, with a well-developed taproot. Leaves triangular in outline but deeply 3–5 palmately lobed, the lobes toothed and cleft; 4–14 cm long on stalks of equal length. Leaves of upper stem becoming smaller and sessile. Primary umbels 3 or 4, irregular. Secondary umbels 1 cm wide or less. Primary involucre of 2 or 3 leaflike bracts. Flowers bisexual and male. Bisexual flowers sessile; male flowers short stalked. Sepals lance shaped, light green. Petals yellow. Fruit 2–5 mm long, dark brown, covered with stout, hooked prickles. *Flowering:* March–July. *Fruiting:* June–October.

Found in moist or dry woods. From southern British Columbia to northern Baja California; Columbia River Gorge to Klickitat County, Washington; Chile. Below 1500 m elevation. Pacific sanicle is a weedy species commonly growing along roads and deer trails; its seed is dispersed by hooking into clothing and fur.

ARACEAE
Arum Family

Habit	Herbs, deciduous.
Stems	Erect, climbing or horizontally spreading, sometimes hard and woody, with sharp, bitter, biting sap or milky juice.
Leaves	Large, mostly basal, simple or compound.
Inflorescence	Flowers reduced, often without perianth, crowded on a fleshy, elongated spadix, usually surrounded by a large, often colored bract or spathe.
Flowers	Usually unisexual with the male flowers above and the female flowers below on the spadix, or bisexual, or separate male and female plants. Perianth of 4–6 scalelike segments or lacking. Stamens 2–10, filaments short, anthers 2-celled. Ovary 2–several-celled, ovules 1–several per cell. Style short or none. Stigma terminal, usually minute and sessile.
Fruit	Berrylike, 1–many-seeded, inflated, bladderlike.
Seeds	Seed coat hard, with or without endosperm.
Distribution	About 105 genera and 1500 species, mostly tropical, a few in temperate zones.
Uses	Several species used as decorative house plants because of their multicolored foliage.

012   LYSICHITUM AMERICANUM   Hult. & St. John
Skunk Cabbage

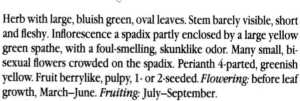

Herb with large, bluish green, oval leaves. Stem barely visible, short and fleshy. Inflorescence a spadix partly enclosed by a large yellow green spathe, with a foul-smelling, skunklike odor. Many small, bisexual flowers crowded on the spadix. Perianth 4-parted, greenish yellow. Fruit berrylike, pulpy, 1- or 2-seeded. *Flowering:* before leaf growth, March–June. *Fruiting:* July–September.

Often dominant in open swamps and wet woods, prefers boggy sites. Thick, horizontal rootstocks form dominant understory patches. Easily transplanted or propagated by division of rootstock. The range is from the Santa Cruz Mountains, California, north along the Pacific coast to Alaska, east to Montana and Idaho.

ARALIACEAE
Ginseng Family

Habit	Herbs, shrubs, and trees, sometimes climbing.
Rootstock	Well-developed rootstock.
Stems	Woody, often armed with thorns and prickles.
Leaves	Alternate to whorled, entire to compound with major veins radiating from 1 point.
Inflorescence	Umbels or umbellate heads or panicle of umbels of small greenish or whitish flowers.
Flowers	Bisexual or unisexual. Floral tube attached to the ovary. Calyx small, often absent. Petals usually 5, folded in bud or overlapping. Stamens 5. Ovary inferior, 1–5, mostly 3-celled with 1 ovule in each cell, surrounded or embedded in a fleshy disk. Styles 1–5, almost entirely free.
Fruit	Berry or drupe.
Seeds	Flattened or 3-angled, thin seed coat. Embryo small in mealy endosperm.
Distribution	About 60 genera and 800 species, widely distributed in temperate and tropical regions all over the world.

013   ARALIA CALIFORNICA   Wats.
California Spikenard

Perennial herb, 1–3 m tall. Stem erect but straggling and branched, with many prominent leaf scars. Leaves hairless, twice compound, with 3–5 leaflets per division. Leaf blade 35–75 cm long. Leaflets oblong-oval with a toothed margin. Inflorescence an erect or drooping panicle, 30–50 cm long. Sepals 5, white, minute, .5–1 mm long. Petals 5, white, 2–3 mm long. Stamens 5, white, with long filaments. Style and stigma 5, white. Fruit a dark purple black berry, 3–5 mm in diameter. *Flowering:* June–August. *Fruiting:* August–October. (See Plate I.)

Located in open to shaded canyons, roots always reaching flowing water. From southwestern Oregon to Orange County, California, in low elevations of the Coast Ranges.

ARISTOLOCHIACEAE
Birthwort Family

Habit	Low, perennial herbs or twining shrubs.
Life Form	Hemicryptophyte.
Rootstock	Often creeping rootstocks.
Stems	Herbaceous or woody, trailing or climbing.
Leaves	Basal or alternate, stalked, mainly entire, heart shaped or kidney shaped.
Inflorescence	Flowers in leaf axils or terminal, solitary or clustered.
Flowers	Bisexual, regular or irregular. Sepals petallike, purplish or pale, 3- or 6-lobed, usually partially fused, and mostly attached to the ovary. Petals lacking, reduced to 3 tiny, linear bracts at the base of the stamens. Stamens 5–12, somewhat fused at the base, partially united to the style. Anthers 2-celled, facing outward from the style. Ovary wholly or partly inferior, 6-celled with placenta along the central axis or, sometimes, along the side walls.
Fruit	Many-seeded capsule.
Seeds	Angled or compressed, smooth or wrinkled, usually with well-developed fleshy attachment.
Distribution	About 200 species, widely distributed, mostly in the tropics and subtropics.

014   ASARUM CAUDATUM   Lindl.
Wild Ginger

Perennial herb with branching rootstock and runnerlike stem. Leaves evergreen, in pairs, heart shaped to kidney shaped, 2–12 cm long, on stalks 3–20(30) cm long. Flowers terminal and solitary in the leaf axils. Sepals 3-parted, petallike, brownish purple to greenish or yellowish or both; the lower portions fused, upper portions tapering into narrow segments, 25–85 mm long. Stamens 12, anthers pointed; stigma fleshy and ridged. Fruit a fleshy capsule, the seeds ovate, 3–4 mm long, dark olive green with a large, gelatinous, yellow arillus. *Flowering:* April–July. *Fruiting:* May–November. (See Plate II.)

In moist, shaded woods or alluvial flats, rich soils with abundant moisture; often dominant in large patches. From British Columbia south to the Santa Cruz Mountains, California, especially along the coast, northeastern Oregon, Idaho, western Montana. Below 1700 m elevation.

ASPIDIACEAE
Wood Fern Family

Habit	Mostly terrestrial ferns, with creeping or erect rootstocks.
Rootstock	With thin, dry scales, rarely forming a short trunk or climbing.
Fronds	Pinnate, simple to compoundly divided, mostly of 1 form only. Stalks rarely jointed.
Sori	Sporangia grouped into distinct sori on the veins or at the ends of the veins. Sori rarely marginal, typically round, sometimes elongate; or the sporangia extending indefinitely along the veins and even on the surface.
Indusium	Usually present, fixed at the middle of its underside, opening around the margin, round to kidney shaped, or elongate, sometimes lacking.
Sporangia	Encircled by a lengthwise ring (annulus) of 10–40 thick-walled cells, interrupted by the stalk.
Spores	Two-sided.
Distribution	About 66 genera, largely tropical.

Key to ASPIDIACEAE

1 Fronds once or twice pinnate, leathery in texture, evergreen. Indusium round, centrally attached to the frond.   **POLY-STICHUM**   **2**

1 Fronds at least twice pinnate, usually more, but not leathery, rarely evergreen. Indusium not centrally attached, or absent.   **5**

2 Fronds once pinnate.   **3**

2 Fronds twice pinnate.   **4**

3 Frond stalk persistently scaly, the scales dry, thin, greater than 1 mm wide. Indusium fringed with hairs on the margin. Pinnae wedge shaped at the base.   **POLYSTICHUM MUNITUM**

3 Frond stalk usually without scales. If scales are present, less than 1 mm wide. Indusium entire on the margin. Pinnae oblique at the base.   **POLYSTICHUM IMBRICANS**

4 Basal pinnae about one-half the length of the middle pinnae. **POLYSTICHUM DUDLEYI**

4 Basal pinnae about as long or longer than the middle pinnae.   **5**

5 Frond stalks very slender, less than 1.5 mm in diameter. Fronds delicate, the portion of the frond with pinnae mostly less than 25 cm long and 10 cm wide.   **CYSTOPTERIS**

Portion of the frond with pinnae longer than the stalk portion, at least twice as long as wide, with 8–18 pairs of pinnately cleft pinnae. Veinlets mostly projecting beyond the marginal teeth.   **CYS-TOPTERIS FRAGILIS**

5   Frond stalks coarse, 2–4 mm in diameter. Portions of frond with pinnae mostly more than 25 cm long and 10 cm wide.   6

6   Indusium kidney to horseshoe shaped, quite circular in outline, attached by the inner end of the notch. Fronds borne in a compact crown, triangular in outline. Stalks of the fronds at the base, in cross section, with 5 circular vascular bundles.   **DRYOPTERIS**   7

6   Indusium merely curved, elongate rather than round, attached along the inner side. Fronds tightly bunched in a vaselike cluster, deciduous, elliptical in outline. Stalk of the fronds at the base, in cross section, with 2 elongated vascular bundles.   **ATHYRIUM**

     Indusium straight or often curved, toothed or fringed on the free edge, deciduous. Sori mostly round or round-elliptic. Fronds 20–200 cm long, delicate, 2 or 3 times pinnate, with 20–35 pairs of pinnae.   **ATHYRIUM FILIX-FEMINA**

7   Fronds essentially 3 times pinnate, rather coarse and evergreen. Basal pinnae distinctly asymmetrical and longer toward the basal and outer side, the most basal and outer pinnae distinctly the longest and largest pinna of the entire frond. Indusium generally shrivels up.   **DRYOPTERIS EXPANSA**

7   Fronds only 1 or 2 times pinnate. Basal pinnae symmetrical. Indusium persistent.   **DRYOPTERIS ARGUTA**

015   **ATHYRIUM FILIX-FEMINA**   (L.) Roth.
      Lady Fern

Tall, deciduous fern, 20–200 cm, from a stout rootstock covered with persistent frond-stalk bases. Fronds pointed-elliptical in outline, 30–200 cm long, 2 or 3 times pinnate. Pinnae lance-oblong, pointed, ascending-spreading, the basal pinnae often reduced; pinnae near the top end progressively reduced and joined together. Frond stalk coarse, straw colored, flattened below, with many dried, brown or blackish, 1 cm long scales. Sori roundish, usually .1 mm long. Indusium straight, curved, or kidney shaped, toothed or fringed on the free edge, deciduous. Sporangium on stalk of about equal length. *Spore production:* June–August.

Found in moist woods, meadows, and along stream banks. From Alaska to southern California, in the Rocky Mountains to Nevada and New Mexico; also in Eurasia. From the lowlands to 3200 m elevation. Locally dominant in alluvial flats and in wet areas.

016   CYSTOPTERIS FRAGILIS   (L.) Bernh.
Brittle Fern

Delicate, small fern, 5–45 cm, from a short and erect or long and creeping rootstock, which is densely beset with dark brown, thin, lance-shaped scales. Fronds lance-oblong-ovate, 1–25 cm × .5–10 cm, (1)2 or 3 times pinnate. Pinnae in 8–18 pairs, triangular-oblong, the segments pinnately cleft or incised. Frond stalk slender, brittle, smooth, 5–20 cm long. Sori small, with round-ovate cover that is pointed and deeply convex. Light brown sporangia encircled by a dark brown, shiny ring (annulus). *Spore production:* May–August.

Found in moist, rocky places, common in sheltered or shaded sites. Present in Northern and Southern Hemispheres, up to 4000 m in elevation.

017   DRYOPTERIS ARGUTA   (Kaulf.) Watt
Coastal Wood Fern

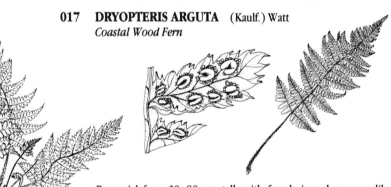

Perennial fern, 30–90 cm tall, with fronds in a dense, vaselike clump (30–90 cm), from stout, woody, short-creeping rootstocks. Scales on rootstocks brown, thin, and densely covered by persistent frond bases. Fronds 25–65 cm long, 10–30 cm broad, mostly twice pinnate. Pinnae close together, the lower ones broadest. Pinnae segments spreading, somewhat tough, sawtoothed or incised, the teeth often spiny. Sori in 2 rows, close together. Indusium round, firm, strongly convex, with a deep narrow notch. *Spore production:* May–October.

Found in mesic sites of shaded and open woods, more common inland, not coastal. From southern Washington to San Diego County, California, east to Arizona. Mostly below 1700 m elevation.

018 DRYOPTERIS EXPANSA (C. Presl.) Fraser-Jenkins & Jermy.
Spreading Wood Fern

Rather tall, perennial fern, 30–100 cm, with loose, open clump of erect and spreading fronds. Rootstocks stout, woody, creeping or ascending, with thin, dry, brownish scales. Fronds ovate-triangular or ovate-oblong, 15–90 cm long, 10–40 cm broad, thrice pinnate. Pinnae numerous, up to 20 cm long and 10 cm wide, upper pinnae progressively less dissected. Lower pinnae as large or larger than those above, asymmetrical. Segments of pinnae oblong-ovate, deeply pinnately cleft, softly spine toothed. Frond stalks coarse, dark, 15–45 cm long. Sori not usually reaching ends of pinnae segments. Indusium pale yellow, centrally implanted at the edge of the sorus nearer the midvein, persistent. *Spore production:* May–November.

In dense woods, on decaying logs and along stream banks. From San Mateo County, California, north to Alaska; Atlantic coast; Eurasia. Below 500 m elevation.

019 POLYSTICHUM DUDLEYI Maxon
Dudley's Sword Fern

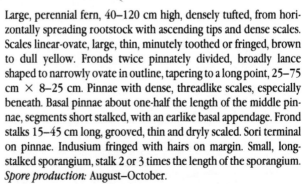

Large, perennial fern, 40–120 cm high, densely tufted, from horizontally spreading rootstock with ascending tips and dense scales. Scales linear-ovate, large, thin, minutely toothed or fringed, brown to dull yellow. Fronds twice pinnately divided, broadly lance shaped to narrowly ovate in outline, tapering to a long point, 25–75 cm × 8–25 cm. Pinnae with dense, threadlike scales, especially beneath. Basal pinnae about one-half the length of the middle pinnae, segments short stalked, with an earlike basal appendage. Frond stalks 15–45 cm long, grooved, thin and dryly scaled. Sori terminal on pinnae. Indusium fringed with hairs on margin. Small, long-stalked sporangium, stalk 2 or 3 times the length of the sporangium. *Spore production:* August–October.

Found in shaded woods of rocky canyons, always near streams. Rare, confined near the coast from northern San Luis Obispo County, California, to Marin and Napa counties, California.

020   **POLYSTICHUM IMBRICANS**   (D. C. Eat.) D. H. Wagner
      Imbricated Sword Fern

Perennial, medium-sized ferns, ascending 20–50(60) cm high, from horizontally spreading rootstocks with ascending tips. Fronds pinnately divided, linear and lance shaped, 25–50 cm long. Pinnae crowded, obliquely overlapping, up to 70 on each side of the midrib, shortly lance shaped, folded inward and horizontally oriented, 2–4(5.5) cm long. Sori near the midvein or slightly closer to the margin. Indusium entire. *Spore production:* May–November.

Found in rock crevices, rocky soil in dry woods or open places from southern British Columbia to southern California, mostly along the Sierra–Cascade axis, in the Klamath region of southwestern Oregon and northwestern California, and in the Olympic Mountains of northwestern Washington.

021   **POLYSTICHUM MUNITUM**   (Kaulf.) Presl.
      Sword Fern, Christmas Fern

Perennial fern with large, coarse fronds, 20–180 cm high, from an erect, much-branched rootstock covered with old frond stalks. Fronds pinnately divided, lance shaped, 15–60(100) cm long, 9–16(25) cm wide, dark green above, paler below. Pinnae offset, narrowly lance shaped, the lower side tapered, the upper side extending into a single, small, projecting lobe, which is wedge shaped to triangular in the upper portion of the blade. The pinnae toothed or incut, the teeth short, firm, bristle tipped. Frond stalks stout, 5–60 cm long, thinly dry scaled, the scales bright glossy green, often dark centered. Numerous sori borne mostly on the middle and upper pinnae, generally in a single row on each side of the midvein halfway between the midvein and the margin. Indusium round and fringed, tardily deciduous. *Spore production:* May–November.

Common in moist-dry shaded woods. From Alaska to northern Baja California, east to northern Idaho and northwestern Montana. Below 800 m elevation.

ASTERACEAE
Aster (Sunflower) Family

Habit Annual, biennial, or perennial herbs, or, less commonly, shrubs, or even trees in the tropics, sometimes with milky cell sap, diverse in habit, foliage, and inflorescence.

Leaves Opposite or alternate, sometimes basal only, entire or more or less dissected. Stipules lacking.

Inflorescence Flowers usually many, sessile, borne in a close head on a common receptacle surrounded by an involucre of variously modified bracts in 1 to several series and often overlapping. Heads solitary or in an inflorescence of several to many heads. Heads are often composed of 2 types of flowers, disk flowers and ray flowers, but may be composed of either.

Flowers Individual flowers sometimes subtended by a small bract, in which case the receptacle is said to be "chaffy"; otherwise the receptacle is "naked." Calyx sometimes absent or modified into scales, bristles, or hairs. Corolla tubular, usually 5-lobed. Stamens as many as the corolla lobes (usually 5) and alternate with them, the anthers elongated and usually united into a tube around the lengthening style, sometimes with appendages at the tip. Ovary inferior, 2 carpels, 1-celled. Style 1, usually with 2 branches, each bearing a stigmatic surface and often with elongated tips. Functionally male flowers often with an undivided style, which functions to eject the pollen from the tube of united anthers. The style branches of the ray (peripheral) flowers are mostly similar in all genera; those of the disk (central) flowers vary distinctly from genus to genus.

Disk Flowers Regular, bisexual, or functionally male, found at the center of the common receptacle, corolla tubular or trumpet shaped, with, typically, 5 short terminal lobes (petals).

Ray Flowers Borne at the periphery of the common receptacle, irregular, female, or lacking sexual parts (but bisexual in *Cichoreae,* a special case in which disk flowers are absent). Tubular only at the very base, above which the flower is flat, commonly bent to the outside of the head, and often exhibiting traces of 2 or 3 of the lobes as small, terminal teeth.

Fruit Achenes, without bristles or teeth or more commonly crowned with a pappus (modified calyx) of bristles, scales, awns, or teeth.

Distribution Worldwide distribution of 900 or more genera and over 15,000 species.

Uses Lettuce, safflower oil, sunflower seeds, artichokes, ornamentals.

Key to ASTERACEAE

1 Disk flowers absent. Heads composed of ray flowers only. Cell sap generally milky.   **17**

Asteraceae = Compositae.

1   Disk flowers present. Heads composed of disk flowers and periph-
     eral flowers that may or may not have rays. Cell sap usually watery,
     not milky white.   **2**

2   Plants spiny. Heads of bisexual disk flowers only. Style with a thick-
     ened, minutely hairy ring below the branches, which are joined
     nearly to the tip. Receptacle densely bristly-hairy.   **CIRSIUM 3**

2   Plants not spiny. Heads with peripheral female flowers that may or
     may not have a ray. Style and receptacle not as in *Cirsium.*   **4**

3   Heads unisexual, usually only 1 kind borne on any individual plant,
     15–25 mm long. Corolla tubes 12–15 mm long.   **CIRSIUM
     ARVENSE**

3   Male and female flowers borne together in heads on the same plant.
     Heads 30–50 mm long. Corolla tubes 25–35 mm long.   **CIRSIUM
     VULGARE**

4   Heads with an outer row of conspicuously rayed flowers.   **5**

4   Heads with an outer row of inconspicuously rayed flowers; or
     entirely rayless, disk flowers only.   **8**

5   Pappus of numerous bristles. Individual disk flowers without small
     subtending bracts.   **6**

5   Pappus absent. Individual disk flowers subtended by small
     bracts.   **7**

6   Disk flowers whitish, mostly functionally male, the styles undivided
     or nearly so. Achenes linear.   **PETASITES**

     Disk 3–5 mm wide. Involucre 5–9 mm high. Plants 10–50 cm tall
     with palmately lobed and toothed 10–40 cm broad leaves, white
     woolly beneath.   **PETASITES PALMATUS**

6   Disk flowers yellow, all bisexual. Style divided, the branches flat-
     tened and stigmatic along the inner margins. Achenes cylindrically
     flattened, 2-nerved.   **ERIGERON**

     Disk 6–15 mm wide, involucre 4–6 mm high. Plant 20–100 cm tall
     with sessile stem leaves and toothed or lobed basal leaves.
     ERIGERON PHILADELPHICUS

7   Disk flowers 6. Ray flowers 5, yellow. Receptacle with a central tuft
     of hairs. Floral bracts slightly united in a single row between ray
     and disk flowers, subtending each of the outer disk flowers. Annual,
     white woolly herb.   **LAGOPHYLLA**

     Heads in small clusters at ends of branchlets in a raceme. Ray flow-
     ers pale yellow turning purplish or reddish on the lower surface.
     LAGOPHYLLA RAMOSISSIMA

7   Disk flowers mostly 10–75. Ray flowers mostly 3–12, most often
     white. Floral bracts subtending all the disk flowers and nearly equal-
     ing them. Perennial herb.   **ACHILLEA**

Disk flowers 25–30, white. Ray flowers 5 or 6, white. Leaves 2 or 3 times pinnately cleft. **ACHILLEA BOREALIS var. CALIFORNICA**

8   Shrubs with woody stems. Plants with thickish evergreen leaves. Male and female flowers on separate plants. **BACCHARIS**

Heads whitish to yellowish, with disk flowers only. Leaves obovate to wedge shaped, .5–5(8) cm long × .5–2(3) cm wide. **BACCHARIS PILULARIS var. CONSANGUINEA**

8   Plants herbaceous or if woody, only at the base of otherwise herbaceous stems.   **9**

9   Plants woolly haired. Anther with a taillike basal appendage. Leaves entire. Involucral bracts dry and membranous, at least at the tips.   **10**

9   Plants variously hairy. Anthers not tailed. Involucral bracts usually green. Leaves usually lobed or toothed.   **13**

10   Male and female flower heads on separate plants, except the female heads usually with a few central male flowers. Pappus bristles not thickened at the tip. Involucral bracts overlapping in several series, almost wholly dry and membranous. Roots fibrous.   **ANAPHALIS**

Lance-shaped to linear leaves, dark green, hairless upperside and white woolly underside. Heads white. Involucre spherical with papery white, ovate bracts.   **ANAPHALIS MARGARITACEA**

10   Disk flowers bisexual. Peripheral flowers female, numerous, in several series. Pappus bristles sometimes thickened at the tip. Involucral bracts slightly to evidently overlapping, dry and membranous at least at the tip, thickened at the base. Usually taprooted. **GNAPHALIUM**   **11**

11   Pappus bristles falling separately. Flowers at least 180 per head. Upper leaves often broadened and clasping at the base, extending down the stem past the point of attachment.   **GNAPHALIUM CHILENSE**

11   Pappus bristles falling in a persistent or easily fragmented ring. Flowers less than 130 per head. Leaves narrowed to a sessile or stalklike base, not clasping or extending down the stem.   **12**

12   Heads in dense or spherical clusters, about 20-flowered. Involucral bracts not hairy. Pappus bristles cohering in an easily fragmented ring. Leaves lance shaped to linear, narrowed to a slender stalklike base.   **GNAPHALIUM JAPONICUM**

12   Heads in dense or interrupted spikes, about 90–130-flowered. Involucral bracts woolly toward the base. Pappus deciduous in a complete ring. Leaves obovate, gradually reduced up the stem. **GNAPHALIUM PURPUREUM**

13   Pappus none. Disk flowers functionally male, the styles undivided. Anthers strongly arrowhead shaped, with the basal lobes turned downward. Heads in a nearly naked panicle. Leaves large, mostly near the base.   **ADENOCAULON**

Leaves mostly near the base, triangular-ovate to heart shaped, 5–12 cm long, green, hairless upperside, white woolly underneath, achenes 5–8 mm long, blackish green, with coarse gland-tipped hairs.   **ADENOCAULON BICOLOR**

13   Pappus of hairlike bristles. Disk flowers generally bisexual, the styles branched. Anthers entire or slightly lobed at the base. Leaves well distributed over the entire stem.   **14**

14   Peripheral flowers with short inconspicuous rays. Style branches stiff-hairy above, with short ovate attachments. Involucral bracts more or less overlapping in 2 series, unequal, scarcely green. Achenes compressed, 0–2-nerved. Pappus bristles few.   **CONYZA**

Ray flowers numerous, female, threadlike and tubular, with an inconspicuous ray. Disk flowers few, with a slender 5-toothed tube.   **CONYZA CANADENSIS**

14   Peripheral flowers disklike, lacking rays. Style branches with a minute tuft of hairs near the tip, without appendages. Involucral bracts in a single series, equal, with a few minute bractlets at the base. Achenes 5-angled or 5–20-nerved. Pappus bristles many. **15**

15   Peripheral flowers bisexual. All disk flowers bisexual. Plants less than 50 cm tall.   **SENECIO**

Heads several or numerous, 5–10 mm wide, with disk flowers only. Involucre, 5–8 mm high, with about 21 black-tipped bracts.   **SENECIO VULGARIS**

15   Peripheral 2 or more rows of flowers female. Plant usually over 50 cm tall.   **ERECHTITES**   **16**

16   Leaves more or less deeply pinnately lobed or cleft. Plant thinly woolly haired, hairless when young.   **ERECHTITES ARGUTA**

16   Leaves finely and sharply toothed, not at all lobed or cleft. Plant obscurely hairy or almost hairless.   **ERECHTITES PRENAN-THOIDES**

17   Pappus hairs branched, featherlike, the branchlets covered with stiff hairs.   **18**

17   Pappus hairs unbranched, smooth, hairlike.   **19**

18   Involucral bracts scarcely overlapping, the outer bracts small and reduced, the inner bracts larger and almost equal in size. Receptacle without thin membranelike bracts subtending each flower. Flower stalk not swollen below the head.   **LEONTODON**

Leaves sharply toothed to pinnately compound in a basal rosette. Heads solitary on slender, usually unbranched, stalks. Yellow bisexual ray flowers only. Achene 3 – 6 mm long with thin, lengthwise furrows.   **LEONTODON LEYSSERI**

18   Involucral bracts overlapping. Receptacle with thin, membranous bracts subtending each flower. Flower stalk distinctly swollen below the head.   **HYPOCHOERIS**

Basal leaves flat spreading, toothed, stiff-hairy, no leaves along the stem. Ray flowers showy, yellow. Achenes brown, 4–7 mm long, with a slender beak.   **HYPOCHOERIS RADICATA**

19   Leaves entirely basal and large, or if along the stem, reduced, not deeply lobed but finely toothed. Achenes not flattened, pappus dull white or grayish yellow.   **21**

19   Basal leaves reduced, stem leaves larger, deeply lobed and finely toothed or prickly. Achenes slightly or strongly flattened, pappus white.   **SONCHUS**   **20**

20   Flowering heads deep yellow to orange, large, 3–5 cm wide in flower. Involucral bracts and the stalks of the heads with many conspicuous gland-tipped hairs. Leaves pinnately cleft and finely toothed, terminal lobes narrow and pointed.   **SONCHUS ARVEN-SIS**

20   Flowering heads light yellow, smaller, 1.5–2.5 cm wide in flower. Involucral bracts and the stalks of the heads with a few, sparse, gland-tipped hairs. Leaves pinnately cleft and finely toothed, the terminal lobe usually noticeably arrowhead shaped.   **SONCHUS OLERACEUS**

21   Leaves entirely basal. Heads solitary and terminal on unbranched flowering stalks, yellow flowered. Achenes roughened or spiny at least above, tapering to a slender beak.   **TARAXACUM**

Leaves oblong to spatula shaped, entire to pinnately divided with the terminal lobe being the largest. Heads 2–5 cm long, yellow or orange yellow, involucre green to grayish brown. Taproot thick and fleshy.   **TARAXACUM OFFICINALE**

21   Leaves along the stem and basal. Heads rarely solitary, usually in an open branching panicle, white flowers. Achene not beaked.   **HIERACIUM**

Leaves inversely lance shaped, entire, finely toothed with sparse, long, bristly hairs. Heads 2–7 mm long, white, involucre greenish to blackish. Taproot thick and woody.   **HIERACIUM ALBIFLO-RUM**

022   **ACHILLEA BOREALIS**   Bong.   **var. CALIFORNICA**
(Pollard) Keck
Yarrow

Perennial herb 50–100 cm tall with creeping rootstocks and aromatic foliage. Stems branched with long, soft hairs. Leaves alternate, linear, pinnately compound and deeply dissected, 10–15 cm long, 1.5–3 cm wide; lower leaves stalked, the upper leaves smaller, sessile, and clasping. Heads many, in a corymb. Involucral bracts in 4 series, blunt tipped with brown margins and long, soft hairs. Ray flowers 5 or 6, the rays white, 3–4 mm long. Disk flowers 25–30, corollas white, 3 mm long. Achenes 2 mm long, no pappus. *Flowering and fruiting:* all year. (See Plate II.)

Widespread weed. Open and grassy places below 800 m elevation from Washington to Baja California.

023   **ADENOCAULON BICOLOR**   Hook.
Trail Plant

Annual or perennial herbs, 50–100 cm tall, with slender stems, fibrous roots, and large, alternate leaves near the base. Leaves triangular-ovate to heart shaped, dark green above, white woolly beneath. Leaf stalks equal to or longer than the 5–12 cm long blades. Heads in a slender, branched, 40–60 cm long panicle. Involucre small, of less than 10 nearly equal, green bracts. Flowers whitish, some with arrowhead-shaped anthers. Achenes blackish green, 5–8 mm long, with gland-tipped hairs above. *Flowering:* May–September. *Fruiting:* June–October.

Found in moist, shaded woods frequently along roadsides and deer trails. From southern British Columbia to Santa Cruz and Tulare counties, California, east to northern Idaho, northwestern Montana, northern Michigan, and northern Minnesota. Below 2000 m elevation.

024 ANAPHALIS MARGARITACEA (L.) Benth. & Hook.
Pearly Everlasting

Erect, white woolly, perennial herb, 20–90 cm high, with slender, running rootstocks. Leaves alternate and entire, 2–8(15) cm long, 2–20 mm wide, woolly haired below. Male and female heads on separate plants (sometimes the same plant). Some heads with central bisexual flowers that are sterile. Female heads may have a few central male flowers. Heads small, numerous, crowded in a short, broad panicle. Involucral bracts pearly white, papery, sometimes with a small, basal, dark brown spot. Flowers tubular. Female flowers with a divided style. Male flowers with a sterile undivided style, anthers with a taillike basal appendage. Pappus of hairlike bristles. Achenes finely roughened with minute stiff hairs. *Flowering:* March–October. *Fruiting:* July–November.

Found in open areas, ravines, talus, pastures, and along roads; common in cutover areas. Coast Ranges of California, the Sierra Nevada, north to Alaska; Atlantic coast; and Eurasia. Below 2800 m elevation.

025 BACCHARIS PILULARIS DC.
var. CONSANGUINEA (DC.) Kuntze
Chaparral Broom, Coyote-Brush

Small shrubs, much branched, matted, and spreading or erect, 12–150 cm tall. Branchlets very leafy. Leaves thick, evergreen, wedge shaped or round, sessile or nearly so, .5–5 cm × .5–2 cm. Male and female heads on separate plants in terminal or axillary clusters. Female heads 8–10 mm high, the involucre 4–5 mm high, its bracts hardened, whitish. Pappus much longer than corolla and involucre in fruit. Male heads 4–5 mm high, the involucre 3–4 mm high. Pappus about as long as corolla and involucre. Fertile achenes 1–2 mm long, pappus sparse, 6–10 mm long, slightly reddish. *Flowering:* August–December. *Fruiting:* November–January.

Found in thickets and dunes along coast, common in the brush succession stage of cutover forest land, from Tillamook County, Oregon, to San Diego County, California.

026   CIRSIUM ARVENSE (L.) Scop.
Canada Thistle, Creeping Thistle

Perennial with creeping rootstocks. Stem mostly simple below and branched above, 3–15(20) cm tall. Stem leaves variously shaped, narrowed at the base or clasping, pinnately lobed-divided with spiny-bristly margins, 5–20 cm long, 3–7 cm wide. Uppermost leaves reduced, sometimes bractlike. Basal leaves wavy margined or pinnately lobed with spiny-bristly margins. All leaves hairless above and woolly haired below. Heads unisexual, sometimes bisexual, usually only 1 type on a plant, solitary or in a corymb. Involucral bracts numerous, in many series. Pappus of female heads exceeding the corollas. Corollas pinkish purple (white), 12–15 mm long, stamens white. Achene 3–4 mm long, tipped by a persistent style. *Flowering:* May–September. *Fruiting:* June–October.

Noxious weed of fields and waste places, often locally dominant. Widespread weed in northern United States and southern Canada, native of Eurasia.

027   CIRSIUM VULGARE (Savi) Ten.
Bull Thistle, Common Thistle

Biennial weed with erect, branched stem, .3–2 m tall, spiny winged by the leaf bases, which extend downward. Lower side of leaves woolly, upper side bristly-spiny. Stem leaves 30 cm long, 10 cm wide, shallowly to deeply pinnately lobed, the lobes ending in stiff, yellowish spines. Basal leaves wavy margined or shallowly lobed, coarsely toothed. Heads few, 30–50 mm long and nearly as broad, subtended by the uppermost reduced leaves. Involucral bracts in many series, the outer and middle spine tipped and woolly margined. Heads of bisexual disk flowers only, 25–35 mm long, rose purple (white). Achene 3–4 mm long, slightly widened upward, pappus 20–30 mm long. *Flowering:* June–October. *Fruiting:* June–October.

Found in waste places, pastures, and disturbed ground in cutover forest lands. Widespread in North America, native of Eurasia.

028 CONYZA CANADENSIS (L.) Cronq.
Horseweed

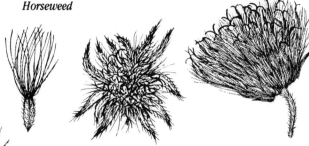

Annual weed 20–100 cm tall, many ascending branches above, stems hairy (var. *canadensis*) to hairless (var. *glabrata*). Lower leaves numerous, inversely lance shaped, 2–10 cm long, saw-toothed, short stalked. Upper leaves more linear, entire and sessile. Heads numerous, in a dense panicle. Involucre 3–4 mm high, bracts linear. Ray flowers 15–40, with white, inconspicuous rays barely exceeding the pappus. Disk flowers 7–12, light greenish yellow to light green. Achene hairy, light brown. Pappus dirty white. *Flowering:* May–September. *Fruiting:* June–October.

Common weed in waste ground at low elevations throughout the United States and southern Canada.

029 ERECHTITES ARGUTA DC.
Cut-Leaved Coast Fireweed

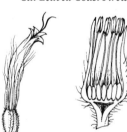

Annual or short-lived biennial weed, 60–200 cm tall. Stem somewhat sparse woolly-hairy to hairless, stout, erect, branched above, with light brown bark. Leaves many, well distributed, alternate, the lower stalked, the upper sessile and reduced, oblong-ovate to lance shaped, 5–15 cm × 4 cm, often irregularly toothed. Heads many in a loose or crowded cyme of dull yellow flowers. Involucre nearly cylindric, narrow, 5–7 mm high, often woolly. Achenes stiff haired, 2 mm long. Pappus white, sticky, 5 mm long. *Flowering:* February–August. *Fruiting:* June–October.

Found below 500 m elevation, in woods and waste places, abundant in burned-over and logged areas. San Mateo County, California, to Clatsop County, Oregon.

030   ERECHTITES PRENANTHOIDES   (A. Rich.) DC.
Toothed Coast Fireweed

Annual or short-lived perennial weed, 60–200 cm tall, almost hairless. Stem stout, erect, branched above, with blackish green bark. Leaves many, well distributed, alternate, lance-linear, 5–15 cm long, evenly and finely toothed, underside often purplish and tinged with cobwebby hairs. Heads many in a large, broad panicle, to 30 cm across. Involucre narrow, cylindric, 5–7 mm high. Corolla dull yellow, stamens yellow, ovary green. Achenes stiff haired, dark brown, 2 mm long. Pappus 6–7 mm long. *Flowering:* February–September. *Fruiting:* July–October.

Found below 500 m elevations in waste places along the coast, abundant in burned-over and logged areas. Marin County, California, to Lincoln County, Oregon.

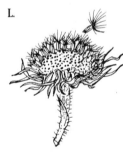

031   ERIGERON PHILADELPHICUS   L.
Philadelphia Daisy

Biennial, short-lived perennial or, rarely, annual, with fibrous roots. Stem 20–100 cm tall, unbranched below the middle. Leaves hairless to long-hairy, the upper ones smaller, sessile and clasping. Basal leaves inversely lance shaped to spatula shaped, toothed or lobed, sometimes entire, 8–15 cm × 1–3 cm. Heads 1–many in a corymb. Involucral bracts sometimes purplish, slightly unequal, usually with a hairy brownish and broad translucent margin. Ray flowers deep pink to white, female. Disk flowers yellow, bisexual. Achenes 2-nerved, pappus of 20–30 fragile bristles. *Flowering:* April–July. *Fruiting:* May–August.

Found in disturbed open, moist, grassy areas throughout the United States and most of Canada.

032   GNAPHALIUM CHILENSE   Spreng.
Cotton-Batting Plant

Annual or biennial herb 10–60 cm tall, several stemmed and leafy, loosely woolly haired, usually aromatic. Lower leaves obovate or oblong, 2–10 cm × 3–10 mm. When young often in a basal rosette, but mostly stem leaves when in flower. Stem leaves inversely lance shaped to linear, 1–6 cm × 1–8 mm, often with broadened, clasping base. Heads in terminal clusters, 180–230-flowered. Involucres 4–6 mm high. Bracts white, greenish, or yellowish, browning with age. Peripheral flowers 160–200, female. Disk flowers 20–30, bisexual. Corollas yellow to orange. Achene olive brown with white pappus. *Flowering and fruiting:* all year.

Found in moist waste places, common in cutover forest lands. From Washington south to northern Baja California, east to Montana, south to Arizona, New Mexico, western Texas. Below 2000 m elevation.

033   GNAPHALIUM JAPONICUM   Thunb.
Japanese Cudweed

Erect annual 10–40 cm high, simple or branched, more or less cottony white or woolly. Leaves thick, cottony haired beneath, margins rolled under, 3–5(7) cm long, narrowly spatula shaped to inversely lance shaped, narrowed to stalklike base. Stem leaves more linear, sessile. Heads 20-flowered in terminal clusters. Involucres, 4 mm high, the bracts brown, straw colored, or purplish tinged. Peripheral flowers female, with a white, tubular corolla. Disk flowers bisexual, corolla yellow. Achenes with minute conical processes. Pappus bristles cohering in an easily fragmented ring. *Flowering:* July–October. *Fruiting:* July–October.

An introduced weed of grassy open spots in wooded areas, common in cutover areas. From Curry County, Oregon, to Humboldt and Trinity counties, California, native of Japan.

034 GNAPHALIUM PURPUREUM L.
Purple Cudweed

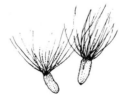

Annual or biennial herb 10–50 cm tall, erect or spreading, somewhat woolly. Leaves obovate, inversely lance shaped or spatula shaped, 10 cm × 2 cm, gradually smaller upward, thickish, usually narrowed to a stalklike base, white woolly beneath. Heads in a terminal, spikelike panicle 1–18 cm long, with leafy bracts. Heads bell shaped, 4–5 mm high, the involucral bracts light brown, often pink or purple tinged. Peripheral flowers female, with a translucent style. Disk flowers bisexual, corolla purple tipped, white below. Achenes olive brown. Pappus united at the base, separating as a complete ring. *Flowering:* April–October. *Fruiting:* May–October.

A native weed in disturbed places, common in cutover areas. From British Columbia south to Baja California, mostly west of the Cascades and the Sierra Nevada; eastern and central United States.

035 HIERACIUM ALBIFLORUM Hook.
White-Flowered Hawkweed

Perennial herb with woody taproot. Stem usually solitary, 30–120 cm high from a short, woody base; long, bristly hairs below, becoming hairless upward. Stem leaves few, mainly basal leaves, oblong to inversely lance shaped, 4–18 cm × 1–5 cm. Wavy margined and finely toothed with sparse, bristly hairs or entire. Heads on slender stalks in a panicle. Involucral bracts lance-linear, hairless, or bristly haired and glandular. Ray flowers only, bisexual, white, rays 3–4 mm. Achenes red brown, 2–3 mm, with dull white or tawny pappus longer than the achene. *Flowering:* June–August. *Fruiting:* June–September.

Common in dry, forested areas below 3200 m elevation from Alaska and northwestern Canada south to Colorado and San Diego County, California.

036 HYPOCHOERIS RADICATA L.
Hairy Cat's-Ear

Perennial herb with a woody root crown and with several, slender, branched, and leafless stems, 15–80 cm tall, often with stiff, spreading, basal hairs. Leaves basal, rosettelike and spreading, ovate to inversely lance shaped, toothed, or pinnately divided, stiff-hairy, 3–35 cm × 5–70 mm. Heads several, usually terminal, stalk distinctly swollen below head. Involucre oblong-cylindric, 1–2.5 cm, the bracts overlapping. Bisexual ray flowers only, yellow, well surpassing the involucre, rays 12–18 mm × 3–5 mm. Achene brown, 4–7 mm long, with a 4–7 mm long, slender beak. *Flowering:* April–November. *Fruiting:* April–December.

A weed of lawns and pastures common in cutover areas along compacted tractor trails. Widely established in the United States and southern Canada, also in many cooler, high-elevation, open areas in the tropics.

037 LAGOPHYLLA RAMOSISSIMA Nutt.
Common Hareleaf

Slender, annual herb 20–100(150) cm tall, more or less woolly. Lower basal and stem leaves spatula shaped 1–12 cm × 5–12 mm, deciduous before flowering. Upper stem leaves smaller, lance shaped to linear. Heads short stalked, along the branchlets or terminal. Involucre 4.5–8 mm, the bracts hairy on the ridges, hairs emitting sticky black droplets. Ray flowers pale yellow, the rays 2.5–5 mm long, turning red or purple on lower surface. Disk flowers pale yellow, male. Achene club shaped, black and shiny. *Flowering:* May–October. *Fruiting:* June–October.

Common in cutover areas along trails and in drier sites. Found on dry plains and foothills in eastern and central Washington and central Idaho south to San Diego County, California, northern and western Nevada, up to 1700 m elevation.

038   LEONTODON LEYSSERI   (Wallr.) G. Beck
Hairy Hawkbit

Perennial herb with fibrous roots and a short, reduced stem. Leaves in a basal rosette, inversely lance shaped, sharply toothed to pinnately compound, 4–15 cm long × 6–25 mm wide, with stiff, spreading hairs. Heads solitary, elevated above basal leaves on slender stalks 10–35 cm high. Involucre 6–11 mm high with 6–12 narrowly lance-shaped bracts, the outer ones small, inner ones larger and almost equal. Yellow, bisexual ray flowers only. Achenes 3–6 mm long, blackish brown, roughened with narrow, lengthwise furrows. Pappus of inner flowers of featherlike bristles, outer flowers with reduced pappus. *Flowering:* May–August. *Fruiting:* June–September.

A weed of lawns, roadsides, and open fields and hills. From Vancouver Island and British Columbia to Santa Clara County, California, west of the Cascade Mountains, especially along the coast. Introduced from Europe.

039   PETASITES PALMATUS   (Ait.) Gray
Western Coltsfoot

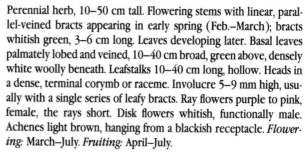

Perennial herb, 10–50 cm tall. Flowering stems with linear, parallel-veined bracts appearing in early spring (Feb.–March); bracts whitish green, 3–6 cm long. Leaves developing later. Basal leaves palmately lobed and veined, 10–40 cm broad, green above, densely white woolly beneath. Leafstalks 10–40 cm long, hollow. Heads in a dense, terminal corymb or raceme. Involucre 5–9 mm high, usually with a single series of leafy bracts. Ray flowers purple to pink, female, the rays short. Disk flowers whitish, functionally male. Achenes light brown, hanging from a blackish receptacle. *Flowering:* March–July. *Fruiting:* April–July.

Found in moist areas, often dominant in flood plains and along roadside ditches. From the Santa Lucia Mountains north to Siskiyou and Del Norte counties, California, to Alaska and Massachusetts. Below 330 m elevation.

040 SENECIO VULGARIS L.
Common Groundsel

Leafy, annual herb, 10–50 cm tall, simple or branched hairless to sparsely stiff-hairy. Taproot usually evident. Leaves alternate coarsely pinnately cleft and toothed, or toothed only, 2–10 cm × 5–45 mm. Lower leaves tapered to a stalk, the upper sessile and clasping. Several heads in a lax panicle. Involucral bracts distinctly black tipped, short bractlets well-developed. Heads of bisexual disk flowers only, tubular, yellow and white. Achenes minutely rough haired. *Flowering and fruiting:* all year.

A common weed in disturbed soils, gardens, and waste places. Common in cutover areas, especially after a slash burn. Widely distributed throughout the temperate zone. Native to Europe.

041 SONCHUS ARVENSIS L.
Perennial Sow Thistle

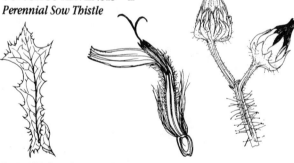

Biennial, 40–200 cm tall, with creeping rootstock. Stem usually hairless below, conspicuously glandular-hairy above. Leaves deeply and sharply divided to merely toothed, 3–40 cm long, 2–15 cm wide. The margins prickly toothed. Leafstalks short, the base winged. Upper leaves usually reduced, often not divided. Heads in an open, terminal corymb, composed of bisexual ray flowers only, the rays orange yellow. Heads large, 3–5 cm broad when flowering. Achenes oblong, flattened, 2.5–3.5 mm long. Pappus 8–10 mm long. *Flowering:* April–November. *Fruiting:* May–December.

A widespread weed of European origin. Common on roadsides, and in gardens and waste places.

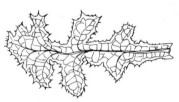

042   SONCHUS OLERACEUS L.
Common Sow Thistle

Annual herb, 10–100 cm tall with a short taproot, producing white milky sap when injured. Hairless, though sometimes sparsely glandular-hairy on the involucres and flower stalks. Leaves simple to pinnately divided, 6–30 cm × 1–15 cm, toothed but not prickly, clasping the stem, the earlike lobes pointed. Heads small, several in a lax corymb. Bisexual ray flowers only, yellow, peripheral rays purple on the back. Achenes 2–3 mm long, somewhat compressed, light brown, 3–5 lengthwise ribs on each face, roughly wrinkled across the ribs. Pappus of many soft, thin, white bristles, separating as a ring of hairs. *Flowering:* April–November. *Fruiting:* April–November.

Common weed on roadsides and in cutover areas, gardens, and waste places. Worldwide distribution; native to Europe.

043   TARAXACUM OFFICINALE Weber
Dandelion

Perennial herb with a thick, deep taproot and short, reduced stem. Flower stalks producing white, milky sap when injured. Leaves in a spreading basal rosette, oblong to spatula shaped, with spear-shaped lobes, the terminal lobe the largest one; 5–30(40) cm × 1–15 cm. Heads terminal on leafless, hollow flower stalks, 5–50 cm tall. Involucre 15–25 mm high, green to grayish brown. Bisexual ray flowers only, yellow, rays squarely cut off and 5-toothed. Achenes gray brown, 3–4 mm long, with a 6–16 mm long beak, ending in a long, white pappus parachute, 6–8 mm long. Mature achenes and pappus form a conspicuous ball easily disintegrated by the wind. *Flowering:* May–October. *Fruiting:* all year.

Common weed of lawns and compacted trails in cutover areas. Worldwide distribution.

BERBERIDACEAE
Barberry Family

Habit	Shrubs and woody perennial herbs, spreading, erect, or treelike.
Life Form	Phanerophyte.
Roots	Gray brown, creeping rootstock with deep yellow inner bark.
Stems	Woody, erect to horizontally spreading, much branched, bark grayish, inner bark and wood yellow.
Leaves	Alternate, simple or pinnately compound, without stipules, often spiny.
Inflorescence	Racemes, solitary in axils, or usually bunched near the top of the stems with numerous bracts.
Flowers	Bisexual, regular, perianth in 4 or 5 alternating whorls of 3 segments, similarly colored. Smaller outer whorl considered bracts; 2 whorls successively larger in size are sepals; the innermost 1 or 2 whorls smaller in size are petals. Petals distinctly 2-lobed and with 2 basal glands or with 2 nectar glands near the recurved tip. Stamens 4–18, mostly 6, in 2 whorls opposite the petals and connected to their bases. Filaments widened and toothed. Anthers opening with 2 uplifting valves. Ovary 1-celled, superior. Style short or lacking, stigma shieldlike, ovules many, implanted at base or along walls.
Fruit	Berry, 1–several-seeded, bluish with a bloom.
Seeds	Triangular with hard seed coat.
Distribution	About 9 genera and 590 species, largely Asian, widely distributed over South America, a few in North America, Europe, and Africa.
Uses	Many species because of attractive yellow inflorescence, bluish fruits, and dark, shiny evergreen foliage sought as ornamentals in gardens.

Key to BERBERIDACEAE

Only 1 genus, *Berberis,* is represented.

Woody, perennial shrubs, erect or spreading. Leaves pinnately compound and spiny toothed. Flowers yellow, in racemes; berries bluish. **BERBERIS**

1   Bud scales persistent, hardened, pointed, 15–40 mm long. Leaflets 7–23. Racemes simple, erect, elongated, 7–20 cm long. Filaments of stamens smooth, without teeth.   **BERBERIS NERVOSA**

1   Bud scales deciduous, 2–5 mm long. Leaflets (3)5–9(11). Racemes compound, more clustered, dense and short, 3–8 cm long. Filaments of stamens with a distinct pair of recurved teeth or lobes near the middle.   **BERBERIS AQUIFOLIUM**

044   **BERBERIS AQUIFOLIUM**   Pursh.
Holly-Leaved Barberry

Perennial, erect, woody shrub with well-developed rhizomes and evergreen, pinnately divided, spiny foliage. Stem stiff branched, ascending, 10–450 cm tall. Leaves 10–25 cm long, spiny, tufted along stems, odd-pinnate with 3–9(11) leaflets. Leaflets broad, oblong-lance shaped, leathery, thin, glossy green on both sides, 2.5–8 cm × 2–5 cm. Clustered racemes in leaf axils or terminal. Perianth in 5 whorls of 3, the smaller, outer whorl considered bracts. Stamens white, swollen in middle and partly lobed or toothed. Fruit a berry, 7–14 mm, deep blue with bluish white bloom. *Flowering:* February–May. *Fruiting:* September–November.

Prefers dry, rocky sites in the redwood region. Generally flowering only in open clearings of the forest or following timber harvest on exposure to fall sunlight. From southern British Columbia to northeastern Idaho on both sides of the Cascades to the Santa Cruz Mountains and Modoc County, California, below 2300 m elevation.

045   **BERBERIS NERVOSA**   Pursh.
Oregon Grape

Perennial, woody herb with short stems, 10–90 cm tall, covered with persistent bud scales 2–4 cm long, with developed rootstock. Woody stem, erect to prostrate, with inner bark yellow. Leaves more or less whorled, mostly basal, odd-pinnate with 7–23 leaflets. Leaflets leathery, 3–8 palmately nerved, 2–10 cm × 2–4 cm, with 6–12 bristlelike teeth along each margin. Simple, unbranched, much elongated raceme, 7–20 cm long, mostly solitary and terminal. Perianth in 5 whorls of 3, the smaller outer whorl considered bracts. Sepals in 2 whorls of 3, yellow. Petals in 2 whorls of 3, yellow, with 2 glands at their bases. Stamens 2 whorls of 3, opposite and attached to base of petals, swollen but not toothed or lobed. Fruit a berry, 8–11 mm, blue with light bluish bloom. *Flowering:* March–June. *Fruiting:* October–November.

In shaded, coniferous woods below 2000 m elevation. From southern British Columbia to the Santa Cruz Mountains, California, along the coast, inland to Shasta and Siskiyou counties, California, and in northwestern Idaho.

BETULACEAE
Birch Family

Habit	Trees or shrubs, deciduous.
Stem	Trunk much branched with thin, peeling bark.
Leaves	Alternate, pinnately veined, mostly sawtoothed. Stipules free, often deciduous.
Inflorescence	Male and female flowers borne separately on the same plant. Male inflorescence a pendulous catkin, terminal or lateral. Female flowers in cylindrical conelike spikes with overlapping bracts, 2 or 3 per bract. Both male and female catkins appearing before the leaves or with very young leaves. Fruiting spikes cylindrical or ovoid, the bracts falling off or persisting.
Male Flowers	Flowers 2–5 subtended by small bracts within each scale. Calyx membranous, usually 4-parted, slightly overlapping. Stamens 2 or 4, filaments very short. Anthers 2-celled, cells united or separate, opening lengthwise.
Female Flowers	Perianth absent, ovary naked, compressed, 2-celled, styles 2, free, linear. Ovules solitary and attached near the apex of each cell.
Fruit	Conelike or cylindrical, catkin with woody scales, solitary or clustered, erect or hanging.
Seeds	Nutlet, small, winged or unwinged, often crowned by persistent styles. Solitary, hanging without endosperm, with straight embryo and flat cotyledons.
Distribution	Distributed over mostly temperate to arctic regions of the Northern Hemisphere, 5 genera and 100+ species.
Ecology	Most species requiring moist soils.
Phenology	Flowering very early in the spring before the leaves or with very young leaves (*Betula*).
Uses	Shrubs, dwarf shrubs, or commercial forest trees, some especially valuable for their timber or veneer quality; others used as ornamentals and shade trees.

Key to BETULACEAE

Only 1 genus, *Alnus,* is represented.

Tall trees, 5–35 m high with large boles and smooth, often light gray bark. Leaves with wedge-shaped leaf base, with conspicuously pinnate veins, often with a more finely sawtoothed margin. Male flowers in large, elongated catkins usually clustered on leafless branches, hanging. Anthers 2-celled. Female flowers in short, ascending catkins, clustered near lip of leafless, 1-year-old branches. Fruit a conelike woody structure, clustered, often more or less drooping. Seed a small, flattened, winged or wingless nutlet.
ALNUS

1 Leaves rusty-hairy beneath and with distinctly rolled leaf margins. Bark thin, smooth, light ashy gray, inner bark when freshly exposed

deep red. Seed a small nutlet, distinctly winged. Species always near the Pacific coast.　**ALNUS OREGONA**

1　Leaves without hairs, light green beneath and with thin, not rolled margins. Bark thin, conspicuously scaly, brown, inner bark when freshly exposed not deep red. Seed small nutlet without wings. Species more frequent in the interior of the Coast Ranges. **ALNUS RHOMBIFOLIA**

046　ALNUS OREGONA　Nutt.
Red Alder, Oregon Alder

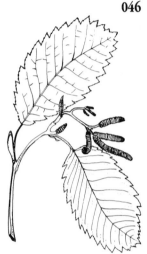

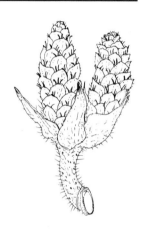

Deciduous trees, 15–45 m tall, with large bole. Trunks straight, clear of branches for one-half to two-thirds of their height. Bark thin, smooth, and light ashy gray to whitish, inner bark dark red. Branches ascending in young trees, drooping and forming a rounded crown in mature trees. Leaves simple, alternate, broadly elliptic-ovate, coarsely toothed, 6–12 cm long. Male catkins 2–4 per cluster at the ends of branchlets, drooping, cylindrical, 10–15 cm long. Female catkins 3–5 per cluster, terminal, erect, on stout stalks. Fruit woody, conelike, 3–5 cones per cluster. Seed a small but distinctively winged nutlet. *Flowering:* March–April. *Fruiting:* September–December.

Common on stream banks and marshy places below 400 m along the Pacific coast from Santa Cruz, California, to Alaska. A significant pioneer species following logging or other disturbance; often the dominant tree cover on seepage slopes.

047   **ALNUS RHOMBIFOLIA**   Nutt.
White Alder

Deciduous trees, 10–35 m tall. Trunks straight, clear of branches for one-half to two-thirds of their height, crown rounded. Bark scaly, whitish gray brown, inner bark gray brown. Leaves ovate, rounded or pointed at tip, doubly sawtoothed, 5–11 cm long. Male catkins 2–4 per cluster, drooping, cylindrical, 4–8 cm long. Female catkins erect, 1–2 cm long on stout stalks. Fruit woody, conelike, 1–3 cones per cluster terminally on branches. Seeds ovate, brown, without wings. *Flowering:* January–April. *Fruiting:* April–September.

Common inland and never near the Pacific coast in gravelly flood plains from southern British Columbia and northern Idaho south through Pacific states to northern California and southern California to Baja California below 1700 m elevation.

BLECHNACEAE
Deer Fern Family

Habit	Terrestrial ferns, often evergreen, with large, coarse, pinnatifid fronds.
Life Form	Hemicryptophyte.
Roots	Rootstocks creeping or erect, with thin, dry scales.
Fronds	Large and coarse, mostly pinnately lobed or cleft, sometimes compound. Veinlets branching and interwoven.
Sori	Parallel to the midrib of the pinna, separate or united.
Indusium	Opening toward the midrib of the pinna.
Sporangia	Large, with a lengthwise, interrupted ring (annulus) of cells with reinforced walls, stalked, as long as the sporangium.
Spores	Two-sided.
Distribution	In North America, Eurasia, and the Southern Hemisphere, 8 genera.

Key to BLECHNACEAE

1 Fronds once pinnate. Sterile and fertile fronds conspicuously of 2 types. Sori borne in continuous bands parallel to the midribs of the pinnae. **BLECHNUM**

Sterile fronds evergreen, 10–80(100) cm long. Fertile fronds deciduous, 40–150 cm long. Pinnae mostly in 35–70 pairs, entire, more or less linear-oblong, united at the slightly flaring base. Fertile pinnae much narrower and more widely spaced. **BLECHNUM SPICANT**

1 Fronds twice pinnate. Sterile and fertile fronds not conspicuously dissimilar. Sori in separate, elongate patches along each side of the pinnae midrib. **WOODWARDIA**

Fronds almost erect, 1–2 m long. Main pinnae divided into 10–20 pairs of smaller pinnae, which are finely sawtoothed. The main pinnae segments 2–5(10) cm long and up to 1 cm wide. **WOODWARDIA FIMBRIATA**

048 BLECHNUM SPICANT (L.) With.
Deer Fern

Perennial fern, 10–150 cm high, with black, shiny stalks, and 2 distinct types of fronds. Short-creeping, woody rootstock, 1–2 cm thick, covered with brownish linear to lance-shaped scales, 5–10 mm long. Fronds linear to somewhat lance shaped, 10–80(100) cm × 2–9 cm, pinnate to pinnately cleft. Pinnae entire or occasionally toothed or cleft. Largest pinnae born near or above middle of frond, 15–50 mm × 3–7(10) mm. Fertile fronds dissimilar and usually longer than sterile fronds, deciduous. Fertile pinnae much narrower, 1.5–2 mm wide, the back nearly covered with sporangia. *Spore production:* August–January. (See Plate II.)

Found in wet, sheltered places from Santa Cruz County, California, to Alaska and northern Idaho; and Eurasia. From near sea level to middle altitudes in the mountains.

049 WOODWARDIA FIMBRIATA Sm. in Rees.
Giant Chain Fern

Large, almost erect, leathery, deciduous, perennial fern, 1–2 m high, from a woody, scaly rootstock. Scales of rootstock taper to a point, 1–3 cm long. Fertile and sterile fronds very similar. Fronds somewhat oblong, 40–150 cm × 20–50 cm, twice pinnate. Pinnae alternate along the coarse midrib of the blade, pinnately cleft, tending to be hairy on midvein beneath. Segments of pinnae pointed at tip, sharply or finely sawtoothed, mostly 2–5(10) cm long and up to 1 cm wide. Largest pinnae near or below middle of the frond. Sori set in shallow depressions. Sorus cover 1.5–6 mm long. *Spore production:* November–June.

Found on stream banks and in other moist, wet places, from southern British Columbia to southern California, chiefly near the coast; Arizona and southern Nevada. Below 2500 m elevation.

BRASSICACEAE
Mustard Family

Habit	Annual to perennial herbs or rarely with a somewhat woody base, often with a rather pungent, watery juice.
Leaves	Alternate, entire, lobed, dissected or pinnate, without stipules.
Inflorescence	Flowers in terminal racemes or corymbs, rarely solitary and terminal.
Flowers	Bisexual, regular to slightly irregular. Sepals 4, erect or somewhat spreading, rather alike, deciduous, greenish to colored. Petals 4, rarely 2 or lacking, commonly clawed, the blades spreading in the form of a cross, yellow, white or pink to blue or purple. Stamens 6, rarely 4 or 2, 2 of them inserted lower and shorter. Ovary superior, usually 2-celled by a thin partition stretched between the 2 marginal carpels, from which, when ripe, the valves usually separate. Style 1, stigma 2-lobed or entire.
Fruit	Capsule 2-celled, narrow and long (silique) or short (silicle), many-seeded, with 2 valves, splitting from the bottom and leaving the carpels with the false partition between them intact.
Seeds	Without endosperm, filled with large embryo, smooth, lined, or pitted; plump to flattened or even wing margined.
Distribution	A large family, widely distributed.
Uses	Many plants of economic or horticultural value (cabbage, mustard, radish, turnip, rutabaga, cauliflower, and stock).

050   DENTARIA CALIFORNICA   Nutt.
California Toothwort

Perennial herb with deep-seated rootstalks arising from a bulb. Stems slender, 10–40 cm tall. Leaves from rootstalks long stalked, simple or compound with 3(5) broad leaflets, often heart shaped. Leaflets 2–5 cm. Stem leaves 2–5 with 3–5 leaflets or lobes, lance shaped to ovate. Racemes with many flowers, flowering stalks 1–3 cm long. Petals pale rose to white, 9–14 mm long. Fruit a silique, 2–5 cm × 1–2 mm. Seeds ovoid. *Flowering:* February–May. *Fruiting:* May–June.

Found on shady banks and slopes. San Diego County through the Coast Ranges to southwestern Oregon, occasionally in the Sierra Nevada, lower California, below 850 m elevation.

Brassicaceae = Cruciferae.

CAMPANULACEAE
Bellflower (Bluebell, Harebell) Family

Habit Annual, biennial, or perennial herbs, or sometimes shrubs or trees, with bitter-sharp or milky juice and mostly alternate (or all basal), simple leaves without stipules.

Inflorescence Diverse types.

Flowers Bisexual, regular or irregular. Perianth 5-parted except for carpels. Sepals separate or united at the base, persistent. Petals united, blue or white. Stamens generally free from and alternate with the petals. Anthers facing inward, 2-celled. Ovary inferior or partly so, 2–5-celled. Style 1, stigma lobes usually as many as the carpels, usually distinct.

Fruit A single capsule, usually opening by valves or pores, or sometimes a berry.

Seeds Minute, numerous.

Distribution About 60 genera and 1600 species throughout the world.

051 CAMPANULA PRENANTHOIDES Durand
California Harebell

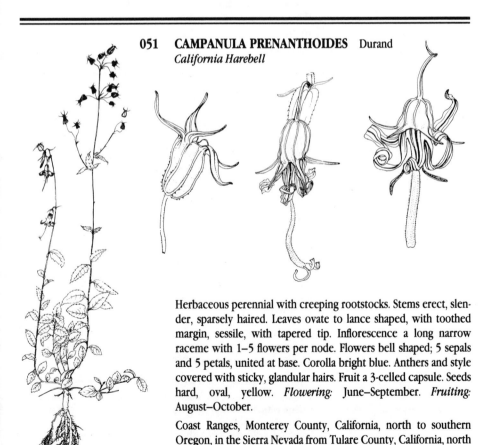

Herbaceous perennial with creeping rootstocks. Stems erect, slender, sparsely haired. Leaves ovate to lance shaped, with toothed margin, sessile, with tapered tip. Inflorescence a long narrow raceme with 1–5 flowers per node. Flowers bell shaped; 5 sepals and 5 petals, united at base. Corolla bright blue. Anthers and style covered with sticky, glandular hairs. Fruit a 3-celled capsule. Seeds hard, oval, yellow. *Flowering:* June–September. *Fruiting:* August–October.

Coast Ranges, Monterey County, California, north to southern Oregon, in the Sierra Nevada from Tulare County, California, north to British Columbia. Dryish woods, below 2000 m in elevation.

CAPRIFOLIACEAE
Honeysuckle Family

Habit   Shrubs or woody vines, less often herbs or trees.

Leaves   Opposite, rarely alternate or whorled, simple or pinnate. Stipules absent (rarely present in *Sambucus*).

Inflorescence   Various, mostly cymes or panicles.

Flowers   Bisexual, regular or irregular. Calyx of 3–5 united or separate sepals, joined to the ovary, or calyx absent. Corolla of 5 united petals, or 2-lipped, the tube sometimes spurred or swollen with a pouch on one side. Stamens 5 (only 4 in *Linnaea*), inserted on the corolla tube and alternate with its lobes. Anthers free moving, 2-celled, splitting lengthwise. Ovary inferior, 1–6-celled, with 1 to several hanging ovules per cell, the placentae on its axis. Style slender to obsolete. Stigma headlike or 2–5-lobed.

Fruit   Usually a berry or drupe, sometimes a capsule or achene.

Seeds   Seed coat adherent to the fleshy endosperm. Embryo small.

Distribution   About 12 genera and 400 species, of wide distribution, chiefly in the northern temperate zone or in mountainous areas in the tropics.

Uses   Many of ornamental use.

Key to CAPRIFOLIACEAE

1 Leaves pinnately compound. Inflorescence a compoundly branched panicle. Corolla tube very short, round in top view, the free lobes flattened. Style short, stigma 3–5-lobed.   **SAMBUCUS**

   Leaflets 5–7(9), the margins finely and sharply toothed. Inflorescence a dense panicle. Berry bright scarlet (rarely chestnut brown or yellowish).   **SAMBUCUS CALLICARPA**

1 Leaves simple. Inflorescence of small terminal clusters or paired flowers. Corolla elongate or bell shaped, sometimes with a basal pouch; if round in top view, the free lobes not flattened. Style slender, stigma headlike or 2-lobed.   **2**

2 Sepals fused into a nearly spherical tube. Corolla about as wide as long, densely white hairy within. Fruit a white berrylike drupe. **SYMPHORICARPOS**

   Erect, branching shrub with pink to white flowers in terminal racemes. Leaves oval to elliptic-ovate, entire or with a few coarse, irregular teeth.   **SYMPHORICARPOS ALBUS**

2 Sepals reduced to teeth or absent. Corolla longer than wide, not densely white hairy within. Fruit a red or black juicy berry. **LONICERA**   **3**

3 Corolla usually yellow, sometimes tinged with red. Terminal corolla lobes 5, equal. Flowers always in pairs, subtended by 2 large

green purple dark red bracts, and 2 smaller bracts. Sepals absent. Fruit a black berry. **LONICERA INVOLUCRATA**

3 Corolla usually whitish, purple, or pink. Terminal corolla lobes 5, unequal. Flowers in many whorls forming spikes or loose panicles. Sepals reduced to teeth. Fruit a red berry. **LONICERA HISPIDULA**

052 LONICERA HISPIDULA Dougl.
Hairy Honeysuckle

Woody vine or climbing shrub, 2–6 m high. Stems slender, branched, with interspersed long and short hairs. Leaves elliptic to oblong-ovate, 2–8 cm × 1.5–5 cm, the uppermost pair fused around the stem. Flowers in many whorls forming spikes or loose panicles. Sepals 5, reduced to teeth. Corolla mostly pink, purple, or whitish, unequally 5-lobed, 2-lipped. Ovary 3-celled. Stamens and style protruding from the corolla tube. Fruit a red berry, 5–10 mm in diameter. Seed yellow orange with jellylike coating. *Flowering:* April–August. *Fruiting:* September–December.

Below 800 m elevation from southern British Columbia to southern California. Along streams, on wooded slopes, and in thickets; dry to medium-wet sites along the forest edge.

053 LONICERA INVOLUCRATA (Richards.) Banks
Black Twinberry

Erect shrub, .5–4 m high. Bark freely peeling. Branches leafy, young twigs 4-angled. Leaves variable in shape, usually with a pointed tip, 3–14 cm long, 2–8 cm wide. Flowers axillary, in pairs, subtended by 2 large, green purple red bracts 1–2 cm long and 2 shorter bracts that eventually enlarge to nearly the same size. Sepals absent, corolla yellow and elongate with a basal pouch on one side; terminal corolla lobes equal, short, and rounded. Fruit a black berry, almost enclosed in the bractlets. Seed black with juicy flesh. *Flowering:* March–August. *Fruiting:* May–September. (See Plate II.)

Found in woodlands, forests, and thickets, mostly in fairly moist or wet soil. Below 3000 m elevation from Alaska to Santa Barbara County, California.

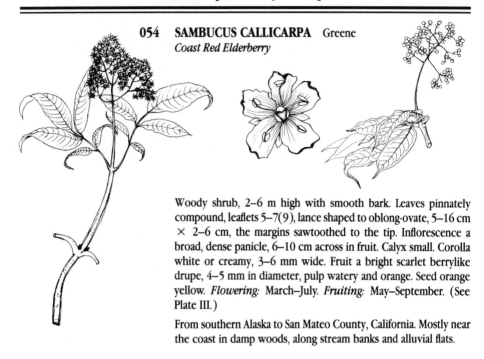

054   SAMBUCUS CALLICARPA   Greene
Coast Red Elderberry

Woody shrub, 2–6 m high with smooth bark. Leaves pinnately compound, leaflets 5–7(9), lance shaped to oblong-ovate, 5–16 cm × 2–6 cm, the margins sawtoothed to the tip. Inflorescence a broad, dense panicle, 6–10 cm across in fruit. Calyx small. Corolla white or creamy, 3–6 mm wide. Fruit a bright scarlet berrylike drupe, 4–5 mm in diameter, pulp watery and orange. Seed orange yellow. *Flowering:* March–July. *Fruiting:* May–September. (See Plate III.)

From southern Alaska to San Mateo County, California. Mostly near the coast in damp woods, along stream banks and alluvial flats.

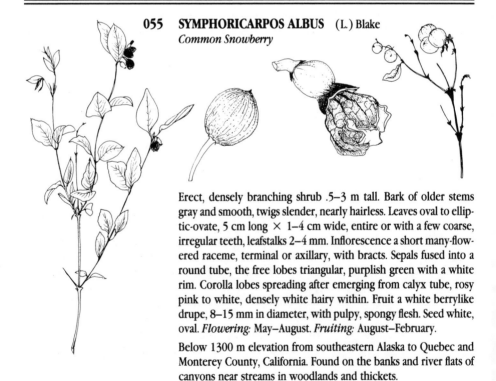

055   SYMPHORICARPOS ALBUS   (L.) Blake
Common Snowberry

Erect, densely branching shrub .5–3 m tall. Bark of older stems gray and smooth, twigs slender, nearly hairless. Leaves oval to elliptic-ovate, 5 cm long × 1–4 cm wide, entire or with a few coarse, irregular teeth, leafstalks 2–4 mm. Inflorescence a short many-flowered raceme, terminal or axillary, with bracts. Sepals fused into a round tube, the free lobes triangular, purplish green with a white rim. Corolla lobes spreading after emerging from calyx tube, rosy pink to white, densely white hairy within. Fruit a white berrylike drupe, 8–15 mm in diameter, with pulpy, spongy flesh. Seed white, oval. *Flowering:* May–August. *Fruiting:* August–February.

Below 1300 m elevation from southeastern Alaska to Quebec and Monterey County, California. Found on the banks and river flats of canyons near streams in woodlands and thickets.

CORNACEAE
Dogwood Family

Habit	Trees, shrubs, or perennial herbs.
Leaves	Usually opposite or, less commonly, alternate, rarely whorled, simple, stalked, entire, without stipules.
Inflorescence	Panicles, cymes, or heads conspicuously surrounded by a whorl of showy bracts. Male and female flowers borne on the same plant or on separate plants.
Flowers	Bisexual or unisexual. Sepals 4 or 5, usually very small. Petals 4 or 5 or missing. Male flower stamens usually as many as the petals and alternate with them but sometimes twice as many. Female flower pistil 1, carpels 2–4, ovary inferior, 1–4-celled, each cell with 1 hanging ovule, style usually 1.
Fruit	Berry or fleshy, 1-seeded, nonsplitting fruit containing a 1- or 2-celled stone.
Seeds	Endosperm present.
Distribution	About 16 genera and 80 species mostly of the Northern Hemisphere.

056   CORNUS NUTTALLII Aud.
Pacific Dogwood

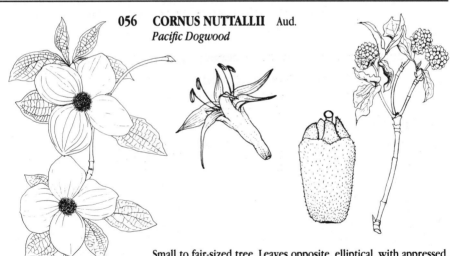

Small to fair-sized tree. Leaves opposite, elliptical, with appressed, straight hairs. Foliage deciduous, changing to a red color in the fall. Young twigs with appressed hairs, becoming hairless and dark red. Flowers small, crowded in a head that is subtended by 4–7 large, showy, pinkish or white petallike bracts. Fruit a cluster of sessile red drupes, minutely hairy and elliptical. *Flowering:* April–July. *Fruiting:* July–September.

Prefers moist, hilly areas and valleys. From the Coast Ranges north of the Santa Lucia Mountains, California, the Sierra Nevada north of Tulare and San Diego counties, California, north to the mountains of Idaho and British Columbia.

CORYLACEAE
Hazelnut (Filbert) Family

Habit	Shrubs or small trees, deciduous.
Stems	Trunk ascending, much branched.
Leaves	Alternate, prominently pinnately veined, mostly sawtoothed. Stipules present.
Inflorescence	Male and female flowers borne separately on the same plant. Male flowers in catkins. Female flowers in pairs in a short spike, surrounded with bracts.
Male Flowers	Calyx absent. Stamens several, inserted on the bract, filaments often deeply divided. Anther cells often hairy at the apex, separate, solitary on each split or divided filament.
Female Flowers	Calyx present, fused to the ovary, irregularly lobed at the top. Ovary inferior, rather imperfectly 2-celled. Ovules 2 or 1 by abortion, hanging from apex. Styles 2, free or nearly so, linear.
Fruit	Nutlet, enclosed in a leafy involucre, the involucre increasing in size with age.
Seeds	Solitary, without endosperm, embryo straight, with fleshy cotyledons much longer than the small embryonic root tip.
Distribution	Temperate Northern Hemisphere to Central America, 4 genera.
Uses	Some useful products: hornbeam (wood), filberts, and barcelona nuts.

057   **CORYLUS CORNUTA**   Marsh.
var. CALIFORNICA   Sharp
California Hazelnut

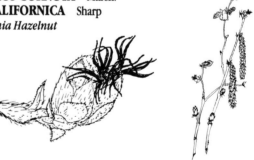

Deciduous shrub, densely branched to open-spreading, 1–6 m high. Leaves oval to oblong to inversely ovate, doubly sawtoothed, sometimes 3-lobed, 4–8 cm long. Male catkins drooping, cylindrical, 3–6 cm long. Female catkins showy, deep rose, erect, conelike, terminal, 6–8 mm long. Basal bracts stiffly haired, clasping into a tube 15–25 mm long. Fruit brown, hard-shelled nut, 12–15 mm long. *Flowering:* January–March. *Fruiting:* October–December.

Widespread in North America from Newfoundland to the Pacific coast excluding Montana, but present in Idaho, Washington, and Oregon to coastal and Sierran California (var. *californica*) below 2500 m elevation.

CRASSULACEAE
Stonecrop (Orpine) Family

Habit   Succulent herbs and small somewhat woody shrubs.
Leaves   Alternate or opposite, simple, entire, stipules absent.
Inflorescence   Flowers in panicle or cymes, rarely solitary.
Flowers   Usually bisexual, regular. Calyx consisting of 4 or 5 united sepals, free from ovary, mostly persistent. Petals 4 or 5, distinct or united, usually persistent. Stamens as many or twice as many as petals. Carpels as many as calyx segments, distinct or united below, usually with a scale at base of each. Styles filiform or awl shaped.
Fruit   Follicles (1-celled, splitting along ventral seam).
Seeds   Minute, mostly narrow, pointed at both ends. Endosperm fleshy, embryo rounded, with short cotyledons.
Distribution   Widely distributed, 25 genera and 1000 species.
Uses   Some valuable ornamentals used in rock gardens.

058   SEDUM SPATHULIFOLIUM Hook.
Pacific Stonecrop

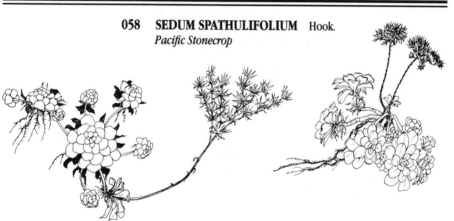

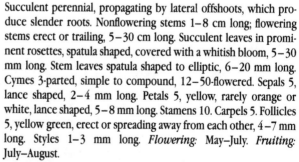

Succulent perennial, propagating by lateral offshoots, which produce slender roots. Nonflowering stems 1–8 cm long; flowering stems erect or trailing, 5–30 cm long. Succulent leaves in prominent rosettes, spatula shaped, covered with a whitish bloom, 5–30 mm long. Stem leaves spatula shaped to elliptic, 6–20 mm long. Cymes 3-parted, simple to compound, 12–50-flowered. Sepals 5, lance shaped, 2–4 mm long. Petals 5, yellow, rarely orange or white, lance shaped, 5–8 mm long. Stamens 10. Carpels 5. Follicles 5, yellow green, erect or spreading away from each other, 4–7 mm long. Styles 1–3 mm long. *Flowering:* May–July. *Fruiting:* July–August.

Found on rocky ledges and slopes, below 2500 m elevation. Coast Ranges from Santa Cruz County, California, north, and the Sierra Nevada from Eldorado County, California, north to British Columbia.

CUCURBITACEAE
Gourd Family

Habit	Mostly herbaceous annual or perennial vines, trailing or climbing by means of tendrils.
Leaves	Usually simple, alternate, palmately veined or lobed, with or without hairs, stalked. Tendrils simple or branched, opposite the leaves.
Flowers	Flowers unisexual, on the same or separate plants, regular. Calyx usually 5-lobed, united to ovary. Petals usually 5, separate or united, inserted onto calyx tube. Stamens usually 5, with 2 pairs united, and remaining anther free. Ovary inferior, 1–4-celled with placentation along the side walls. Style simple or lobed.
Fruit	Gourd, with hard rind, fleshy or sometimes dry interior, usually relatively large, usually not splitting, many-seeded.
Seeds	Large, commonly flat, endosperm lacking.
Distribution	Chiefly in tropical and subtropical regions, 90 genera and 900 species.
Uses	Watermelons, cantaloupes, cucumbers, gourds, squashes, and pumpkins cultivated for their food value.

059   MARAH OREGANUS   (T. & G.) Howell
Coastal Manroot, Western Wild Cucumber

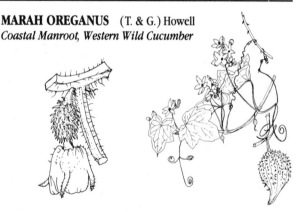

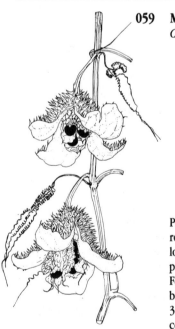

Perennial herb, vines arising annually from very massive tuberous root, stems up to 90 cm long. Leaves palmately lobed with 5–7 lobes, stiff hairs on upper surface, sparsely hairy beneath; tendrils present in leaf axils. Inflorescence an open raceme of male flowers. Female flowers solitary in leaf axils. Perianths white, united into bell-shaped corolla, mostly 5-parted. Male flowers smaller, stamens 3 or 4, curved tip. Female flowers with inferior ovary, mostly 4-celled (2–8). Fruit a pointed gourd with fleshy spines with light and dark stripes. Seeds 5 or 6, smooth, black, disk shaped. *Flowering:* March–August. *Fruiting:* July–October. (See Plate III.)

From Santa Clara County, California, to southern British Columbia west of the Cascades. Below 2000 m elevation. Grows at edge of forests and on hillsides, more abundant on alluvial flats.

CUPRESSACEAE
Cedar (Cypress) Family

Habit   Coniferous, evergreen trees or shrubs, erect or prostrate.

Leaves   Opposite or whorled, scalelike or sometimes linear and needlelike, densely covering the branchlets or jointed at the base.

Cones   Staminate and pistillate cones together on the same plant or on separate plants.

Staminate Cones   Small, mostly terminal on the short branchlets, consisting of opposite, fleshy, overlapping, whorled scales. Stamens with 2–6, commonly 4, pollen sacs attached to the lower half of the thin, shieldlike, expanded portion of the scale and at maturity, pollen sacs are well exposed and exceeding the scale.

Pistillate Cones   Small, terminal, greenish or purplish, and somewhat fleshy, becoming woody at maturity. Scales 2–12, opposite or in whorls of 3, flattened, shieldlike, woody or fleshy, overlapping and grown together, mostly 10–25 mm long, bearing 1–several erect ovules near the base. Maturing at end of first or second season.

Seeds   Angled or winged, cotyledons mostly 2, but sometimes 5 or 6.

Distribution   About 20 genera in both hemispheres, perhaps 150 species.

Uses   Strongly aromatic wood, durable, yet of little commercial value. Used to form protective covers on wind-swept, sandy coasts or arid slopes.

Key to CUPRESSACEAE

1   Cones oblong, their scales oblong-elongated, each bearing 2 ovules. Trees with an erect or drooping leader, top leader needles in whorls of 4 or 2, the opposite needles with visible parallel or joined margins and not obscured by the lower needle.   **2**

1   Cones nearly spherical, their scales shield shaped, each bearing 2–5 ovules. Trees with a drooping top leader. Needles in whorls of 2, the opposite needles without visible parallel or joined margins, directly separating and spreading beyond the tip of the lower needle. **CHAMAECYPARIS**

    Bark dark reddish brown, smooth on young trees, on the older 15–20 cm thick, separating into large, thin shreds and becoming divided into broad, round ridges. Leaves bright green above, whitish beneath, about 1.5 mm long. Stamens of male cones with red expanded part. Female cones reddish brown with a slight whitish bloom, 8 mm in diameter. **CHAMAECYPARIS LAWSONIANA**

2   Leaves appearing to be in whorls of 4. Cone scales 6, only the middle pair fertile. Seeds unequally 2-winged. Male cones with 6–18 stamens. **CALOCEDRUS**

    Bark bright cinnamon brown, fibrous. Branchlet foliage often vertically oriented, needles 4–6 mm long, the tips usually incurved rather than spreading. Male cones yellow, ovate, 5–7 mm long. Female cones deep reddish brown, 20–25(28) mm long.   **CALO-CEDRUS DECURRENS**

2   Leaves clearly in pairs or whorls of 2. Cone scales 8–12, only the 2 or 3 middle pairs fertile. Seeds equally 2-winged. Male cones with 4–6 stamens.   **THUJA**

Trunk tapering and strongly buttressed at base. Bark thin, reddish brown, divided into broad, rounded ridges, separating into fibrous shreds. Branches tending to droop slightly and then turn upward at the tip. Leaves about 3 mm long, on the leading shoots conspicuously glandular. Male cones brownish, about 2 mm long. Female cones 8–12 mm long, at first brownish, later turning brown. **THUJA PLICATA**

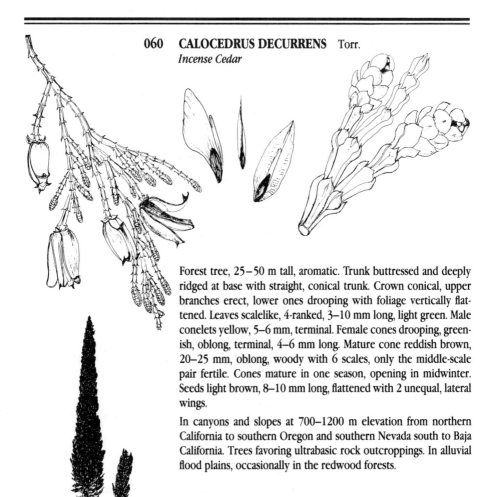

060   CALOCEDRUS DECURRENS Torr.
Incense Cedar

Forest tree, 25–50 m tall, aromatic. Trunk buttressed and deeply ridged at base with straight, conical trunk. Crown conical, upper branches erect, lower ones drooping with foliage vertically flattened. Leaves scalelike, 4-ranked, 3–10 mm long, light green. Male conelets yellow, 5–6 mm, terminal. Female cones drooping, greenish, oblong, terminal, 4–6 mm long. Mature cone reddish brown, 20–25 mm, oblong, woody with 6 scales, only the middle-scale pair fertile. Cones mature in one season, opening in midwinter. Seeds light brown, 8–10 mm long, flattened with 2 unequal, lateral wings.

In canyons and slopes at 700–1200 m elevation from northern California to southern Oregon and southern Nevada south to Baja California. Trees favoring ultrabasic rock outcroppings. In alluvial flood plains, occasionally in the redwood forests.

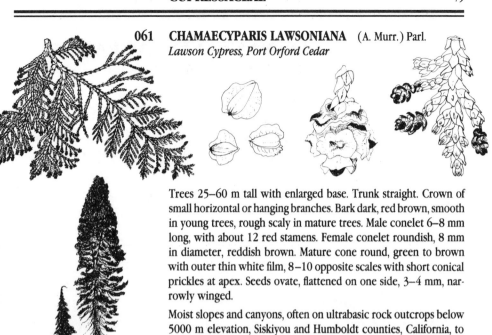

061 CHAMAECYPARIS LAWSONIANA (A. Murr.) Parl.
Lawson Cypress, Port Orford Cedar

Trees 25–60 m tall with enlarged base. Trunk straight. Crown of small horizontal or hanging branches. Bark dark, red brown, smooth in young trees, rough scaly in mature trees. Male conelet 6–8 mm long, with about 12 red stamens. Female conelet roundish, 8 mm in diameter, reddish brown. Mature cone round, green to brown with outer thin white film, 8–10 opposite scales with short conical prickles at apex. Seeds ovate, flattened on one side, 3–4 mm, narrowly winged.

Moist slopes and canyons, often on ultrabasic rock outcrops below 5000 m elevation, Siskiyou and Humboldt counties, California, to southwestern Oregon. In the redwood forests only irregularly in alluvial flood plains of Del Norte and northern Humboldt counties, California.

062 THUJA PLICATA Donn.
Giant Cedar

Large forest trees up to 70 m tall, bole strongly fluted and buttressed at base. Bark relatively thin, reddish brown, peeling in long, fibrous strips. Leader drooping. Branches ascending at tips, branchlets pendulous distinctly flattened, spraylike. Needles scalelike, opposite, flattened in 4 rows. Male conelets globose, 2 mm long, terminal, brownish. Female conelets solitary, terminal at short branchlets, bluish green. Mature cone brown, ovoid-elliptical 8–12 mm long. Seeds winged, yellow brown, 6–7 mm.

Moist to swampy soil, southern Alaska to Humboldt County, California, along the coast, inland up to 4500 m elevation in British Columbia, northern Idaho, northwestern Montana. In Del Norte and Humboldt counties, California, not commonly associated with redwoods, limited to sheltered valleys.

DENNSTAEDTIACEAE
Bracken Fern Family

Habit	Large, terrestrial ferns with hairy rootstocks.
Fronds	Pinnately compound, not jointed to the rootstock.
Sori	Continuous along the pinnae margins.
Indusium	Double, the outer (false) cover formed by the reflexed leaf margin, the inner (true) cover minute and nearly concealed by the sporangia.
Sporangia	Long and slender stalked.
Spores	Tetrahedral or spherical-tetrahedral.
Distribution	Worldwide, about 20 genera.

063 PTERIDIUM AQUILINUM (L.) Kuhn
Western Bracken Fern

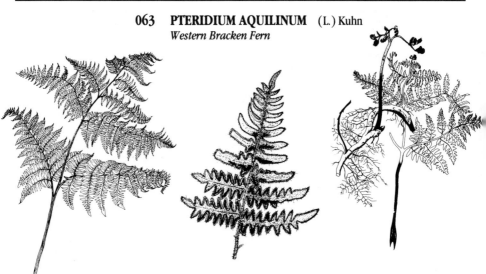

Tall fern, 25–200 cm, the fronds erect or arching, arising singly from a deep-seated rootstock. Rootstocks hairy, without scales. Fronds usually thrice pinnate in the lower part, inconspicuously or not at all hairy above, usually densely hairy beneath and on the inrolled margins. Pinnae linear-oblong, 5–25 mm. Indusium narrow, whitish, with long, soft hairs, almost totally hidden. *Spore production:* September–January. (See Plate III.)

In a wide variety of habitats with a moderate amount of water available, wooded sites to clearings and disturbed sites. Quickly regenerating after fire. Widely distributed in California; to Alaska; South Dakota; northwestern Mexico; Texas; scattered to eastern Canada. Up to 3300 m elevation.

EQUISETACEAE
Horsetail Family

Habit   Rushlike, often branching plants. Plants with 2 different forms: the sexual (gametophyte) and nonsexual (sporophyte) generation, both generations physiologically independent at maturity.

Gametophyte   Sexual generation, tiny, photosynthetic, not differentiated into roots, stem and leaves.

Sporophyte   Nonsexual generation, well differentiated into rootstocks, stems, leaves, and sporangia, the most conspicuous and usually observed form of the plant. The sporangia usually clustered into a terminal cone structure with many whorls of shield-shaped, scalelike bracts to which the sporangia are attached.

Rootstock   Perennial, creeping, branching, rooting at nodes.

Stems   Aerial stems, perennial or annual, cylindrical, fluted or grooved, simple or with whorled branches at the solid, sheathed nodes, the internodes generally hollow. Stem surfaces usually overlaid with silica. Stomates arranged in bands or rows in the grooves.

Leaves   Scalelike, nodal, minute, united lengthwise to form cylindrical or loose, expanded sheaths at each node, their tips converging or free, persistent or deciduous, often not photosynthetic.

Cones   Terminal, formed of stalked, shield-shaped bracts (sporophylls), arranged in closely set whorls around a central axis, these bearing a circle of sporangia beneath. Spores uniform, green, provided with 4 elongated, outer bands that spirally curl and expand according to moisture conditions.

Distribution   Worldwide, 1 genus and 25 species.

Key to EQUISETACEAE

Only 1 genus, *Equisetum,* is represented.

1   Rushlike, often branching plants with creeping rootstocks branching and rooting at internodes. Aerial stems cylindrical, fluted, hollow, sheathed at the nodes by means of minute, whorled leaves that may be free at the tips. Cones terminal. **EQUISETUM**

Aerial stems persistent in winter, all green, of 1 kind, often branched, the branches arising from between the nodes. Stomates in 2 longitudinal rows. Cones oval, rigidly pointed, short, 10–25 mm long. Blackish, distinctly pointed. Base of cone enclosed by a dense row of pointed blackish bracts. **EQUISETUM HYEMALE**

1   Aerial stems not persistent in winter, of 2 kinds, the fertile ones yellowish to whitish, not branched, the sterile green, with many slender branches, these arising from the nodes. Stomates scattered. Cones oval-elongate, blunt, rounded, long, 40–100 mm long, never distinctly pointed, no bracts at base of cone. **EQUISETUM TELMATEIA**

064   **EQUISETUM HYEMALE** L.
Common Scouring Rush

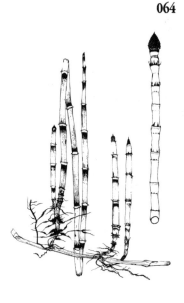

Evergreen, perennial, unbranched herbs with dark green stems. Rootstocks thin, blackish, creeping. Stems all alike, fertile stems sometimes irregularly branched in a whorl near the upper third of the stem. Leaves whorled, reduced to a sheath 5–15 mm long, ending in 10 free teeth that break off readily. Teeth 2–4 mm long, dry, dark brown black. Short, oval cone, 10–25 mm long, sharply terminated in a fine point. *Spore production:* April–September.

Found on stream banks and other moist or wet places. From west of the Sierra Nevada, California, to British Columbia, Quebec, and most of the United States below 2800 m elevation.

065   **EQUISETUM TELMATEIA** Ehrh.
Giant Horsetail

Herbs, usually occurring in groups, from a thickened, perennial rootstock, often 1 m or more deep. Rootstock cross section with a dark brown outer layer, a solid center, and divided into about 15 hollow compartments between. Erect, annual stem, with longitudinal ridges and grooves. Sterile stems 50–300 cm tall, 5–20 mm thick, green and branched. Branches whorled and regularly spaced, solid, 4- to 6-angled nodes. A cylindrical leaf sheath mostly 10–25 mm long with slender, sharp-pointed teeth, 3–8 mm, whorled. Fertile stems 25–80 cm tall, 10–25 mm thick, whitish or brownish, with sheaths 20–50 mm long, with 20–30 teeth united basally in groups of 2–4. Cones 4–10 cm long, terminal, blunt, and stoutly stalked. *Spore production:* March–May. (See Plate III.)

Common in moist low places. From west of the Sierra Nevada, California, to British Columbia; also in Michigan. Below 1500 m elevation.

ERICACEAE
Heath Family

Habit	Trees, shrubs, or woody herbs, often densely clumped or matting and dominant.
Leaves	Simple, alternate or opposite, persistent or deciduous, without stipules, usually thick and leathery when evergreen, or thin and soft when deciduous. Often with spectacular red to yellow coloration before they drop in the fall.
Inflorescence	Various types of clusters or (rarely) solitary flowers.
Flowers	Bisexual, regular or slightly irregular, sepals 4–7, usually united, persistent. Petals united, except in 2 genera. Stamens usually twice as many as petals, alternate with them when equal in number. Filaments occasionally slightly joined. Anthers 2-celled, opening with terminal pores or short tubes. Ovary superior, 2–4 lobed, several-celled, with the placentae on its central axis. Style simple, cylindrical to ovate. Stigma club shaped or shallowly lobed.
Fruit	Capsule or berry or drupe, many-seeded.
Distribution	Throughout the world, about 55 genera and over 1100 species.

Key to ERICACEAE

1   Stamens 8, corolla lobes 4, yellow tinged with red.   **MENZIESIA**

     Leaves oblong to elliptic, 3–6 cm long, obscurely sawtoothed and hairy on the margins. Flower stalks glandular-hairy, the hairs matted, red brown. Filaments light orange.   **MENZIESIA FERRUGINEA**

1   Stamens 5 or 10, corolla lobes 5, pink, white, or reddish pink, or white with yellow blotch.   **2**

2   Flowers large and showy, 3–5 cm long. Corolla funnel shaped, flaring widely, with 5 large, free lobes.   **RHODODENDRON 3**

2   Flowers small, at the most 1 cm long. Corolla urn shaped, fused almost the entire length, with 5 small, free lobes.   **4**

3   Stamens 5, protruding from the corolla along with the stigma. Corolla white or with a pink tinge, upper lobe with yellowish blotch.   **RHODODENDRON OCCIDENTALE**

3   Stamens 10, included in the corolla. Corolla pink or pinkish purple, rarely white, upper lobe spotted.   **RHODODENDRON MACROPHYLLUM**

This family, Ericaceae, is sometimes taken to include the Vacciniaceae, Monotropaceae, and Pyrolaceae. They are treated in this flora as families separate from the Ericaceae.

4   Upper and lower leaf surfaces appearing very similar, leafstalks hairy. **ARCTOSTAPHYLOS**

Shrub with dark reddish purple, peeling bark. Flowers white, sometimes tinged with pink. Anthers with 2 linear appendages, filaments hairy. Fruit a round, berrylike drupe, red to brown in color. **ARCTOSTAPHYLOS COLUMBIANA**

4   Upper leaf surface glossy green, the lower surface paler, leafstalks without hairs.   **5**

5   Large much-branched tree with orange brown peeling bark, exposing a smooth surface.   **ARBUTUS**

Flowers pink or white, 6–8 mm long. Anthers with 2 linear appendages, filaments hairy at the base. Leaves large, 5–15 cm long, oblong to elliptic. Fruit a red or orange berry.   **ARBUTUS MENZIESII**

5   Diffusely branching shrub or almost herbaceous.   **GAULTHERIA**

Leaves leathery, 3–10 cm, oval or ovate, on short stalks, 2–4 mm. Flowers white or pink, 8–10 mm. Anthers with 2 linear appendages, filaments hairy. Fruit a dark purple to blackish capsule enclosed by the fleshy calyx, tipped with the persistent style and stigma. **GAULTHERIA SHALLON**

---

066   **ARBUTUS MENZIESII**   Pursh.
Madrone

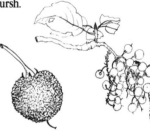

Evergreen tree 3–40 m high, crown widely spreading. Bark thin and smooth, brown red, peeling, leaving a smooth surface, colored with blends of green, brown, and red; basally the bark is furrowed and persistent. Leaves leathery, ovate-oblong to elliptic, dark glossy green above, paler beneath, 5–15 cm long, on 2–5 cm long stalks. Inflorescence a terminal panicle 5–15 cm long, with hairy stalks. Sepals 5, somewhat united, the lobes ovate, thin, fringed with hairs, about 1 mm long. Corolla white to pink, 6–8 mm long. Berry fruit red to orange, 8–12 mm in diameter. Seed thick and hard, light brown, about 3 mm long. *Flowering:* March–May. *Fruiting:* October–January. (See Plate IV.)

Wooded slopes and canyons up to 1700 m elevation, chiefly in drier areas. From British Columbia south to Baja California, west of the Cascades and the Sierra Nevada.

067 ARCTOSTAPHYLOS COLUMBIANA Piper
Columbia Manzanita

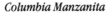

Erect or spreading, much-branched shrub, 1–3(4) m high. Old branches with purplish red, peeling bark. Leaves evergreen and leathery, entire, usually similar on both surfaces, oblong to elliptic or ovate, with a pointed tip and rounded base, 2–5(6) cm long, 1–3 cm wide. Panicle inflorescence compact and hairy. Flowers pink or white, 5-parted, 6–7 mm long on stalks 3–4 mm long. Drupe fruit a flattened sphere, red to brown, 6–10 mm wide, 3–6 mm long, lightly hairy and often sticky. Stones coarsely veined or pitted. *Flowering:* March–July. *Fruiting:* June–October.

Dry rocky or clay slopes below 800 m elevation. From southern British Columbia south along the coast to Sonoma County, California.

068 GAULTHERIA SHALLON Pursh.
Salal

Branching shrub 60–200 cm tall with erect or spreading stems. Leaves oval, tapering to a point at the tip, round to heart shaped at base, finely sawtoothed, glossy, hairless, 3–10 cm long. Leafstalks 2–4 mm long. Inflorescence a panicle 3–15 cm long with conspicuous reddish bracts subtending each flower. Calyx 6–8 mm long, lobes triangular. Corolla white to pink, urn shaped 8–11 mm long, lobes recurved. Anthers with 2 long, forked awns. Fruit a capsule, enclosed when ripe in the hairy calyx or its fleshy base so as to appear a berry and tipped with persistent style and stigma. Seeds brown, 1 mm long. *Flowering:* April–July. *Fruiting:* July–October. (See Plate IV.)

Found in woods or brushy places and in coniferous forest, from southern Alaska south to southern California, west of the Cascades and the Sierra Nevada below 800 m elevation.

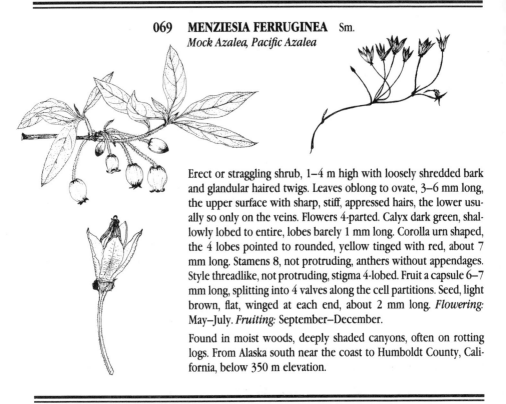

069   MENZIESIA FERRUGINEA Sm.
Mock Azalea, Pacific Azalea

Erect or straggling shrub, 1–4 m high with loosely shredded bark and glandular haired twigs. Leaves oblong to ovate, 3–6 mm long, the upper surface with sharp, stiff, appressed hairs, the lower usually so only on the veins. Flowers 4-parted. Calyx dark green, shallowly lobed to entire, lobes barely 1 mm long. Corolla urn shaped, the 4 lobes pointed to rounded, yellow tinged with red, about 7 mm long. Stamens 8, not protruding, anthers without appendages. Style threadlike, not protruding, stigma 4-lobed. Fruit a capsule 6–7 mm long, splitting into 4 valves along the cell partitions. Seed, light brown, flat, winged at each end, about 2 mm long. *Flowering:* May–July. *Fruiting:* September–December.

Found in moist woods, deeply shaded canyons, often on rotting logs. From Alaska south near the coast to Humboldt County, California, below 350 m elevation.

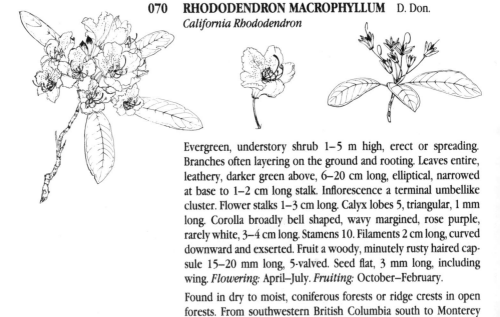

070   RHODODENDRON MACROPHYLLUM D. Don.
California Rhododendron

Evergreen, understory shrub 1–5 m high, erect or spreading. Branches often layering on the ground and rooting. Leaves entire, leathery, darker green above, 6–20 cm long, elliptical, narrowed at base to 1–2 cm long stalk. Inflorescence a terminal umbellike cluster. Flower stalks 1–3 cm long. Calyx lobes 5, triangular, 1 mm long. Corolla broadly bell shaped, wavy margined, rose purple, rarely white, 3–4 cm long. Stamens 10. Filaments 2 cm long, curved downward and exserted. Fruit a woody, minutely rusty haired capsule 15–20 mm long, 5-valved. Seed flat, 3 mm long, including wing. *Flowering:* April–July. *Fruiting:* October–February.

Found in dry to moist, coniferous forests or ridge crests in open forests. From southwestern British Columbia south to Monterey County, California, below 1400 m elevation.

071   RHODODENDRON OCCIDENTALE   (T. & G.) Gray
Western Azalea

Loosely branching, deciduous shrub 1–4(5) m high with shredding bark. Leaves light green, thin, 3–9 cm long, elliptical, entire, fringed with stiff hairs, changing to pale yellow in the fall. Leafstalks 4–8 mm long. Terminal umbel or corymb sticky. Flower stalks 1–3 cm long. Calyx lobes 5, 2–5 mm long, fringed with hairs. Corolla funnel shaped, 30–50 mm long, deeply and slightly irregularly lobed, white or tinged with pink, the upper lobes often with a yellow patch. Stamens 5, protruding. Fruit a brown, hairy capsule, 10–20 mm long. Seed flat, 3 mm long, including wing. *Flowering:* April–August. *Fruiting:* October–January.

Found in moist meadows and flats, limited to contact with flowing surface water in the mountains of southern California through the Sierra Nevada and Coast Ranges to southwestern Oregon as far as the Umpqua Valley below 2500 m elevation.

FABACEAE
Pea Family

Habit	Herbs or woody plants with alternate, usually compound leaves, with stipules and often tendrils.
Inflorescence	Racemes, spikes, heads, or single flowers, on stalks.
Flowers	Usually bisexual, irregular in flower structure and shape. Sepals usually 5, at least partially joined. Petals consisting of 1 (usually the largest) upper petal (banner) and 2 lateral, horizontal petals (wings) that are usually stuck to the 2 lower more or less joined petals (the keel), which enclose the stamens and pistil. Petals sometimes reduced to 3 or 1. Stamens 10, all united into 1 group or divided into 2 groups, 1 consisting of 9 united stamens plus 1 free stamen. Pistil 1, 1-carpelled. Ovary superior, 1-celled, with the placentae on its wall, or sometimes 2-celled by the intrusion of the seams. Ovules 1 to many.
Fruit	A pod, usually opening by 2 valves lengthwise or, less frequently, nonsplitting and breaking off crosswise into 1-seeded segments.
Seeds	Seeds 1 to several, generally with thick cotyledons and no endosperm.
Distribution	Widely distributed, 500–600 genera and 5000+ species.
Uses	Food, dyes, resins, valuable wood, oils, forage, ornamentals.

Key to FABACEAE

1   Leaflets 3, shallowly sawtoothed. Stamens in 2 groups of 5.   **2**

1   Leaflets usually more than 3, entire, sometimes partly replaced by tendrils. Filaments 9, united into a column, the tenth filament free.   **5**

2   Flowers in long, narrow racemes, white or yellow. Petals free of the stamens, deciduous. Leaves compound, the leaflets short stalked.   **MELILOTUS**   **3**

2   Flowers in ovoid to oblong heads, commonly pink to purplish. Petals more or less joined by their claws to the column of stamens, persistent when withering. Leaves compound, the leaflets not stalked.   **TRIFOLIUM**   **4**

3   Flowers white, 4–6 mm. Pods not hairy.   **MELILOTUS ALBA**

3   Flowers yellow, 4–6 mm. Pods hairy.   **MELILOTUS OFFICIN-ALIS**

4   Flowers white or cream to pink tinged, 5–10 mm long, in long-stalked axillary heads. Leaflets 8–20 mm long. Stipules membranous, 3–10 mm long. Seed light yellow brown.   **TRIFOLIUM REPENS**

Fabaceae = Leguminosae.

4   Flowers dark rose to red, 10–20 mm long, in sessile or short-stalked terminal heads. Leaflets 20–60 mm long. Stipules leafy, 10–30 mm long, with conspicuous green veins. Seeds light gray green.   **TRIFOLIUM PRATENSE**

5   Leaves not bearing tendrils. Plant not vinelike. Inflorescence an umbel, or flowers solitary. Banner petal ovate or round, entire. Alternate filaments with the free portion considerably widened.   **LOTUS**   6

5   Leaves tendril bearing. Plants vinelike. Inflorescence a raceme, or flowers solitary. Banner petal distinctly clawed, or asymmetric, oblong, and notched at the tip. Filaments not widened.   7

6   Leaflets mostly 3. Flowers solitary, axillary, 4–8 mm long, on a 5–30 mm long stalk. Floral bract small, simple. Seed 2–3 mm long.   **LOTUS PURSHIANUS**

6   Leaflets 7–19. Flowers in 4–20-flowered umbels, on 1–3 mm long stalks, the umbel on a 3–6 cm long stalk, which often bears a compound leaflike floral bract at about its middle. Seed about 3.5 mm long.   **LOTUS STIPULARIS**

7   Wings of corolla fitting with a small, lengthwise, basal ridge into a fold along the upper margin of the keel. Wings are essentially free from the keel. Style usually sharply upturned from the ovary at about a right angle, flattened, long, hairy only along its inner side for about half its length.   **LATHYRUS**

     Leaflets mostly 10, 2–6 cm long, 5–30 mm broad. Stipules lance shaped, .5–3 cm long, toothed. Tendrils well-developed. Flowers in 5–20-flowered racemes, cream colored, tinged with pink or purple, 15–20 mm long. Pods 4–6 cm long, the valves twisting as they open, 5–12-seeded.   **LATHYRUS VESTITUS**

7   Wings of corolla without a basal ridge, sticking to or clasping around at least the middle of the keel, covering the keel. Style slender, not sharply upturned or flattened, densely bearded on all sides beneath the stigma.   **VICIA**   8

8   Raceme 7–20-flowered. Leaflets 16–29, close together, blunt or rounded at the tip. Petals yellowish white to orange or reddish purple. Pods 3–4 cm long, light green, discoloring to blackish when ripe. Succulent, climbing perennial, .6–2 m tall, the whole plant turning dark when dry.   **VICIA GIGANTEA**

8   Raceme 1–6-flowered. Leaflets 6–12, spine tipped. Petals violet or bluish. Pods black or brownish, less than 1.5 cm long or longer than 4 cm. Annual or winter annual, 30–70 cm high.   9

9   Flowers 10–18 mm long, 1 or 2 in the leaf axils, sessile, corolla purple violet, conspicuous. Pods 4–6 cm long, black. Tendrils well-developed, branched. Stipules 3–8 mm long, usually deeply toothed.   **VICIA ANGUSTIFOLIA**

9   Flowers 5–6 mm long, 1–6 in a raceme on a threadlike stalk, corolla bluish white, inconspicuous. Pods 8–15 mm long, brownish. Tendrils simple or branched. Stipules small, about 1 mm, entire. **VICIA TETRASPERMA**

072   **LATHYRUS VESTITUS**   Nutt.
Common Pacific Pea

Mostly whitish hairy, sometimes hairless, perennial seldom over 40 cm tall with slender rootstocks and angled but not winged, 30–100 cm long stems. Leaves even-pinnately compound with 10 imperfectly paired or scattered leaflets. Leaflets 2–6 cm long, .5–3 cm wide. Tendrils well-developed. Stipules .5–3 cm long and toothed. Inflorescence a 5–20-flowered raceme. Flowers 15–20 mm long. Calyx 12–15 mm long, hairy, the lower lobes longer than the upper. Banner 17–22 mm long, narrow, reversed heart shaped. Wings shorter than banner. Keel equaling wings. Petals white to cream tinged with rose or tan. Fruit a pod, 4–6 mm long, 5–12 seeded, brown, valves twisting as they open. *Flowering:* April–June. *Fruiting:* May–August. (See Plate IV.)

Found in open or brushy places along the coast below 1300 m elevation from Washington to southern California.

073   **LOTUS PURSHIANUS**   (Benth.) Clem. & Clem.
Lotus

Erect, branched annual 10–80 cm tall, sparsely to strongly hairy. Leaflets usually 3, stalked, lance shaped to oblong-obovate, 6–30 mm long, 3–10(15) mm broad. Flowers 4–8 mm long, solitary in the axils on 5–30 mm long stalks with a small, simple floral bract just below the flower. Calyx tube 1.5 mm long, the narrow calyx lobes 1.5–4 mm long. Banner light rose with purplish veins. Other petals yellow or creamy white. Fruit a pod 15–35 mm × 2–3 mm, not hairy, slightly flattened, smooth, brownish with darker mottling. *Flowering:* April–October. *Fruiting:* May–November.

Found in sandy or rocky exposed or wooded areas, common in disturbed areas. From British Columbia to California and east through Montana to the central states; south to Mexico below 2300 m elevation.

074 LOTUS STIPULARIS (Benth.) Greene
Stipulate Lotus

Perennial herb 20–50 cm tall, with long, soft hairs or the leaflets nearly hairless. Stems unbranched or with a few branches near the base. Leaves odd-pinnately compound. Leaflets 7–19, 6–25 mm long. Stipules leafy, lance shaped, with an arrow-shaped base. Umbel 4–10-flowered on 3–6 mm long stalks. Floral bract borne on the middle of the flower stalk, compound or simple or reduced to a scale. Flower stalks 1–3 mm long, flowers 8–13 mm long. Banner and keel red purple, with white, rose-veined tips, wings white with rose veins. Pod 2–4 mm long, 4–10 seeded. Seeds 3–4 mm long, ovoid. *Flowering:* April–June. *Fruiting:* May–August.

Found on dry, wooded slopes to moist stream banks. From Monterey County, California, north through the Coast Ranges and Tulare County, California, to northwestern Washington below 1400 m elevation.

075 MELILOTUS ALBA Desr.
White Melilot, White Sweet Clover

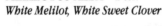

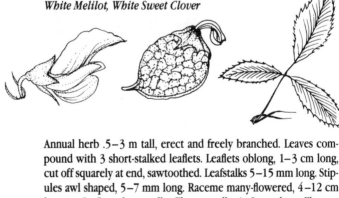

Annual herb .5–3 m tall, erect and freely branched. Leaves compound with 3 short-stalked leaflets. Leaflets oblong, 1–3 cm long, cut off squarely at end, sawtoothed. Leafstalks 5–15 mm long. Stipules awl shaped, 5–7 mm long. Raceme many-flowered, 4–12 cm long on 3–5 cm long stalks. Flower stalks 1–2 mm long. Flowers 3–5 mm long. Calyx teeth narrowly lance to awl shaped. Petals white, 4–6 mm. Fruit a pod, 3–4 mm long, 2-valved, not hairy. Seed light olive brown. *Flowering:* May–October. *Fruiting:* July–November.

Naturalized in damp waste places and alluvial flats over most of the United States and Canada. Native of Eurasia.

076   MELILOTUS OFFICINALIS   (L.) Lam.
Yellow Melilot, Yellow Sweet Clover

Annual or biennial herb, .5–3 m tall, with erect stems and a strong taproot. Leaves compound with 3 stalked leaflets. Leaflets lance shaped, 10–25 mm long, sawtoothed. Leafstalks .5–2 cm long. Stipules lance to awl shaped, 4–6 mm long. Raceme many-flowered, 3–10 cm long, including stalks. Flower 4–6 mm long. Calyx teeth narrowly awl to lance shaped, not hairy, corolla yellow. Fruit a 2-valved, strongly wrinkled pod, 3 mm long. *Flowering:* May–September. *Fruiting:* June–October.

Found in open river bars and waste places throughout the Rocky Mountains; less frequently farther west in alluvial flats.

077   TRIFOLIUM PRATENSE   L.
Red Clover

Sparsely soft, hairy, short-lived, taprooted perennial with erect or trailing, branching stems 30–100 cm tall. Leaves compound with 3 unstalked leaflets. Leaflets 2–6 cm long, hairy, oblong to lance shaped, often with a large, dark spot near the middle. Stipules 1–3 cm long, joined to the leaf base, with conspicuous green veins. Compact raceme or terminal head, 50–200-flowered, spherical to ovoid, sessile or short stalked. Flower, sessile, 10–20 mm long. Calyx 5–8 mm long, the lobes needlelike, the lower lobes longer than the upper. Corolla 10–20 mm long, petals deep rose to red. Pod 2-seeded, red brown and papery. *Flowering:* April–November. *Fruiting:* April–November.

Found in fields and meadows throughout the United States.

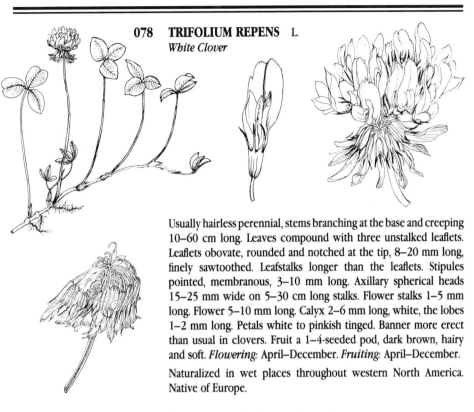

078   TRIFOLIUM REPENS L.
White Clover

Usually hairless perennial, stems branching at the base and creeping 10–60 cm long. Leaves compound with three unstalked leaflets. Leaflets obovate, rounded and notched at the tip, 8–20 mm long, finely sawtoothed. Leafstalks longer than the leaflets. Stipules pointed, membranous, 3–10 mm long. Axillary spherical heads 15–25 mm wide on 5–30 cm long stalks. Flower stalks 1–5 mm long. Flower 5–10 mm long. Calyx 2–6 mm long, white, the lobes 1–2 mm long. Petals white to pinkish tinged. Banner more erect than usual in clovers. Fruit a 1–4-seeded pod, dark brown, hairy and soft. *Flowering:* April–December. *Fruiting:* April–December.

Naturalized in wet places throughout western North America. Native of Europe.

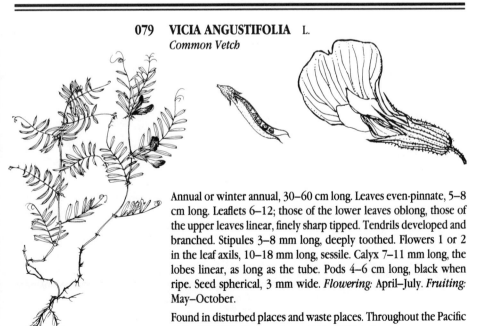

079   VICIA ANGUSTIFOLIA L.
Common Vetch

Annual or winter annual, 30–60 cm long. Leaves even-pinnate, 5–8 cm long. Leaflets 6–12; those of the lower leaves oblong, those of the upper leaves linear, finely sharp tipped. Tendrils developed and branched. Stipules 3–8 mm long, deeply toothed. Flowers 1 or 2 in the leaf axils, 10–18 mm long, sessile. Calyx 7–11 mm long, the lobes linear, as long as the tube. Pods 4–6 cm long, black when ripe. Seed spherical, 3 mm wide. *Flowering:* April–July. *Fruiting:* May–October.

Found in disturbed places and waste places. Throughout the Pacific states from Washington to southern California.

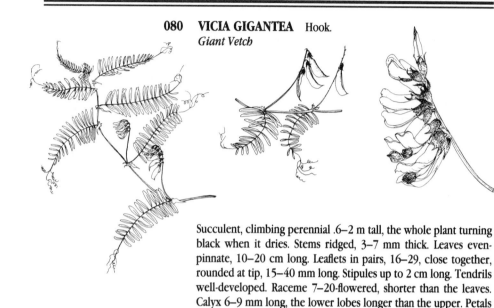

080   VICIA GIGANTEA   Hook.
Giant Vetch

Succulent, climbing perennial .6–2 m tall, the whole plant turning black when it dries. Stems ridged, 3–7 mm thick. Leaves even-pinnate, 10–20 cm long. Leaflets in pairs, 16–29, close together, rounded at tip, 15–40 mm long. Stipules up to 2 cm long. Tendrils well-developed. Raceme 7–20-flowered, shorter than the leaves. Calyx 6–9 mm long, the lower lobes longer than the upper. Petals whitish to red purple, 12–18 mm long. Pods oblong 3–4 cm long, 1–1.5 cm long, several-seeded. *Flowering:* March–July. *Fruiting:* April–August.

Found in moist places from southern Alaska to Monterey County, California, and inland to the Willamette valley, Oregon.

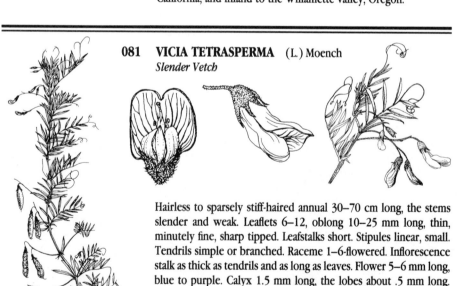

081   VICIA TETRASPERMA   (L.) Moench
Slender Vetch

Hairless to sparsely stiff-haired annual 30–70 cm long, the stems slender and weak. Leaflets 6–12, oblong 10–25 mm long, thin, minutely fine, sharp tipped. Leafstalks short. Stipules linear, small. Tendrils simple or branched. Raceme 1–6-flowered. Inflorescence stalk as thick as tendrils and as long as leaves. Flower 5–6 mm long, blue to purple. Calyx 1.5 mm long, the lobes about .5 mm long. Banner bluish. Wings white. Keel white. Pods oblong, 8–15 mm long, not hairy, 3–6-seeded. Seeds about 2 mm wide. *Flowering:* May–August. *Fruiting:* May–October.

Found in meadows and waste places from Portland, Oregon, to Humboldt County, California.

FAGACEAE
Beech Family

Habit	Deciduous or evergreen trees and shrubs with often very large, rounded crowns.
Roots	Usually very large; long taproots especially in seedlings.
Stems	Heavy, massive bole with heavy arching and spreading branches.
Leaves	Alternately stalked leaves and small, usually deciduous stipules.
Inflorescence	Male and female catkins separate on same plant, flowers with 4–8 minute perianth segments. Male catkins or spikes hanging or erect to drooping, mostly clustered or sometimes in stalked heads. Female inflorescence an erect small catkin or conelike with a solitary flower or with clusters of 2 or 3 flowers. Female flower with a single ovary surrounded by whorls of bracts, initially erect to spreading but which later overlap or fuse, forming a burr or a cup surrounding the nut or acorn.
Flowers	Male flowers with 4–7 small perianth segments and 4–20 or more stamens, a remnant pistil sometimes present. Female flowers 4–8 perianth segments adhering to the ovary. Ovary inferior, 3–7-celled, and 1 or 2 ovules per cell with only 1 ovule in each ovary maturing, styles as many as the cells of the ovary.
Fruit	Nut, 1-seeded with hard, bony fruit wall. Embryo small, without endosperm. Cotyledons large, fleshy.
Distribution	Perhaps 500 species in 7 genera of temperate to subtropical (tropical) regions, mainly in the Northern Hemisphere, absent from Africa except in the northern part. *Nothofagus* the only representative in the Southern Hemisphere.
Phenology	Flowering in the spring when young leaves appear or after leaves have fully developed in late summer.
Uses	Fruits (beechnuts, chestnuts, acorns) of considerable economic importance, also important in the diet of the American Indian and as food for wildlife. A source of tannin, cork, and lumber.

Key to FAGACEAE

1   Leaves alternate, entire. Male flowers in erect, dense catkins with persistent bracts, stamens 10. Female flowers conelike, solitary, erect, at the base of the male catkins. Fruit an acorn, with a shallow cup surrounding it for less than one-fifth its entire length. Cup with linear, stiff, spreading, fleshy scales.   **LITHOCARPUS**

Leaves oblong, pointed or sometimes rounded at both ends. Fruit woolly-hairy on inner surface surrounding the nutlet.   **LITHO-CARPUS DENSIFLORA**

1   Leaves alternate and sometimes opposite, entire or variously lobed. Male catkins drooping, lax, with deciduous bracts, stamens 5–12. Female flowers in axillary clusters. Fruit an acorn, usually with a

deeper cup surrounding it for more than one-fifth its entire length. Cup with nonspreading, more rounded scales.   **QUERCUS**   **2**

2   Leaves soft, dull green, deciduous, deeply lobed or incised, incisions for at least one-third to one-fourth the leaf blade. Acorn surrounded by a cup with closely overlapping bracts, cup about one-fifth the acorn length.   **3**

2   Leaves leathery, often glossy green, evergreen, not deeply lobed or incised, often irregularly toothed or scalloped along leaf margins. Acorn mostly with a longer cup deeper than one-fourth to one-fifth the acorn length. When cut open shell of nut sometimes sparsely woolly haired on inner surface.

Leaves flat, 20–60 mm long × 15–25 mm wide, oblong to ovate, with entire margins, or often spiny toothed on vigorous shoots of young trees. Leaves glossy green above, grayish yellow below. Leafstalks 3–8 mm long. Acorn 25–30 mm long × 20–25 mm wide. **QUERCUS CHRYSOLEPIS**

3   Leaves 8–20 cm long with deeply incised, large, bristle-tipped lobes. Acorn shell when cut open minutely hairy on inner surface. Female flowers with 3 long, slender styles, stigmas flattened. Large trees with dark, smooth bark. In mature trees the bark is broken into broad ridges at the base and broken above into thick, irregular plates or smooth.   **QUERCUS KELLOGGII**

3   Leaves usually smaller, 8–15 cm long, with shallow, rounded lobes and no bristles on the lobes. Acorn shell not woolly-hairy on inner surface when cut open. Female flowers with 3 broad-lobed stigmas, styles short. Large trees with grayish white, scaly bark, with large ridges and shallow furrows.   **QUERCUS GARRYANA**

082   LITHOCARPUS DENSIFLORA   (H. & A.) Rehd.
Tan Oak, Tanbark Oak

Evergreen tree 20–45 m tall with a narrow, conical crown. Trunk 1–2 m in diameter, bark thick and fissured. Leaves alternate, 4–12 cm long, oblong, entire or slightly toothed. Male flowers yellowish white, in erect, densely flowered, 5–10 cm long catkins. Female flowers brownish green, with yellowish styles, at the base of the male catkins. Acorn short, 2–4 cm long, the shallow cup surrounding it with linear, stiff, spreading scales. *Flowering:* June–October. *Fruiting:* September–November. (See Plate IV.)

Found on wooded slopes below 1500 m in the Coast Ranges from Ventura County, California, to southern Oregon.

083 QUERCUS CHRYSOLEPIS Liebm.
Canyon Live Oak

Evergreen tree 6–20 m high with spreading or roundish crown. Bark pale gray and scaly. Leaves leathery, oblong, entire or spiny toothed on young and sucker shoots, 2–6 cm long, hairy beneath when young, later hairless and covered with a whitish bloom. Male flowers brownish, in loosely flowered, drooping catkins, 2–6 cm long. Female flowers light green with silvery hairs, solitary or clustered in axils of leaves. Acorn 25–30 mm, oblong to ovoid, the cup deeper than one-fourth to one-fifth the acorn length. *Flowering:* April–May. *Fruiting:* August–December.

Found in canyons and on steep slopes from southern Oregon south along the western slopes of the Sierra Nevada and the Coast Ranges to Baja California, Arizona, and New Mexico. Below 2200 m elevation.

084 QUERCUS GARRYANA Dougl.
Oregon White Oak

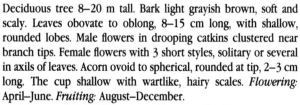

Deciduous tree 8–20 m tall. Bark light grayish brown, soft and scaly. Leaves obovate to oblong, 8–15 cm long, with shallow, rounded lobes. Male flowers in drooping catkins clustered near branch tips. Female flowers with 3 short styles, solitary or several in axils of leaves. Acorn ovoid to spherical, rounded at tip, 2–3 cm long. The cup shallow with wartlike, hairy scales. *Flowering:* April–June. *Fruiting:* August–December.

Associated within the conifer region with open grassy prairies, where it forms dominant patches. From British Columbia south along the coast and in the Coast Ranges to Marin County, California. Mostly 300–1700 m elevation.

085   QUERCUS KELLOGGII   Newb.
California Black Oak

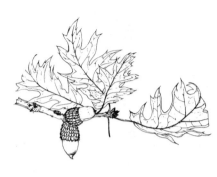

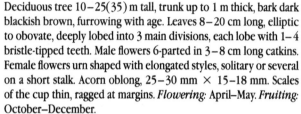

Deciduous tree 10–25(35) m tall, trunk up to 1 m thick, bark dark blackish brown, furrowing with age. Leaves 8–20 cm long, elliptic to obovate, deeply lobed into 3 main divisions, each lobe with 1–4 bristle-tipped teeth. Male flowers 6-parted in 3–8 cm long catkins. Female flowers urn shaped with elongated styles, solitary or several on a short stalk. Acorn oblong, 25–30 mm × 15–18 mm. Scales of the cup thin, ragged at margins. *Flowering:* April–May. *Fruiting:* October–December.

Favors rocky knolls and moisture drains. From Oregon south through the Coast Ranges and the Sierra Nevada to San Diego County, California.

FUMARIACEAE
Fumitory (Fumewort) Family

Habit Annual or perennial herbs with watery juice.

Stems Brittle.

Leaves Basal or alternate, dissected, having a bluish hue, hairy or without hairs.

Inflorescence Flowers usually in small-bracted racemes, or panicles, rarely solitary.

Flowers Bisexual, irregular. Sepals 2, small and bractlike, deciduous. Petals 4, somewhat united into 2 dissimilar pairs, the 2 outer ones spreading at the tip and 1 or both furnished with a sac or pouch at the base, the 2 inner smaller and narrower, their tips thickened and united over the stigma. Stamens 4, free and opposite the petals, or 6 and divided into 2 sets of 3 each. Pistil of 2 carpels. Ovary superior, 1-celled, ovules 1 to several, the placentae 2, along the walls. Style slender, stigma 2-lobed.

Fruit Capsule, 2-valved, several-seeded; or a 1-seeded nut.

Seeds Shining, with a conspicuous arillus, the minute embryo embedded in a fleshy endosperm.

Distribution About 200 species in 5 genera, natives of the North Temperate Zone.

---

086 DICENTRA FORMOSA (Andr.) Walp.
Pacific Bleeding Heart

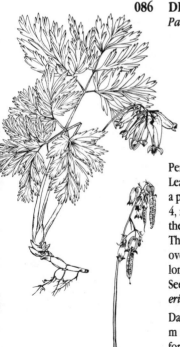

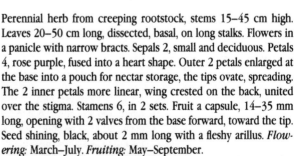

Perennial herb from creeping rootstock, stems 15–45 cm high. Leaves 20–50 cm long, dissected, basal, on long stalks. Flowers in a panicle with narrow bracts. Sepals 2, small and deciduous. Petals 4, rose purple, fused into a heart shape. Outer 2 petals enlarged at the base into a pouch for nectar storage, the tips ovate, spreading. The 2 inner petals more linear, wing crested on the back, united over the stigma. Stamens 6, in 2 sets. Fruit a capsule, 14–35 mm long, opening with 2 valves from the base forward, toward the tip. Seed shining, black, about 2 mm long with a fleshy arillus. *Flowering:* March–July. *Fruiting:* May–September.

Damp, shaded places, moist woods, and stream banks, below 200 m elevation, from western British Columbia south to central California.

GROSSULARIACEAE
Gooseberry (Currant) Family

Habit Deciduous shrubs with simple, alternate, palmately veined and usually lobed leaves, often resinous or sticky.

Inflorescence Racemes mostly 2–several-flowered, on 1- or 2-leaved axillary shoots.

Flowers Flower stalks subtended by a bract and usually bearing 2 bractlets. Flowers rarely solitary, usually bisexual, but sometimes male and female flowers occur on separate plants. Sepals 5 (rarely, 4), partially united to the ovary, mostly larger and showier than the petals. Stamens 5, alternate with the 5 petals. Styles 2, more or less united. Ovary inferior, 1-celled with 2 placentae along its walls.

Fruit Berry crowned with the withering remains of the flower.

Seeds Several to many, with abundant, fleshy endosperm.

Distribution About 120 species in 1 genus, natives of the North Temperate Zone and of the Andes in South America.

Key to GROSSULARIACEAE

Leaves palmately 3–5(7) lobed, variously toothed. Sepals larger than petals, colored, erect or spreading to reflexed. Petals smaller, often differently colored, generally erect, narrowed to a clawlike base. Berry spherical or nearly so, smooth or spiny. **RIBES** **1**

1 Large, stout spines, 1–3 at each node. Racemes 1–6-flowered. Styles slender, equaling or exceeding the extended petals. **2**

1 Nodal spines lacking. Racemes with more than 6 flowers. Styles shorter, not quite as long as the extended petals. **3**

2 Branches with many small, slender, weak spines between the nodes, prominent, stout, nodal spines, usually 3. Sepals dark crimson, 7–11 mm long. Petals white, 3–4 mm long, often with inrolled margins. Stamens shorter than style. Ovary fused with floral tube, not free. Berry reddish purple, spiny. **RIBES MENZIESII**

2 Branches without small spines between the nodes, 1–3 prominent, stout, white nodal spines only. Sepals 5–7 mm, greenish or purplish. Petals white to red, 1–3 mm long. Stamens about equaling the length of the style. Ovary free, hairy, slender. Berry purple black, smooth. **RIBES DIVARICATUM**

3 Sepals 3–4 mm, greenish or brownish purple to nearly white. Petals white, reduced, only .5 mm long. Anthers nearly spherical with glandular hairs on short, stout filaments. Ovary totally submerged by a thick, glandular disk, not free, styles 2, short. Base of leafstalk with fleshy, soft, spinelike hairs. Plant with small glands excreting a characteristic pungent but somewhat disagreeable odor, especially the foliage. **RIBES BRACTEOSUM**

3   Sepals 3–5 mm, pale to deep rose. Petals white to light rose, 2–5
    mm long. Anthers ovate, on slender filaments. Ovary fused with the
    floral tube over half its length without a distinct, glandular disk.
    Base of leafstalk without fleshy spinelike hairs. No disagreeable
    odor.   **RIBES SANGUINEUM**

087   RIBES BRACTEOSUM   Dougl.
Stink Currant

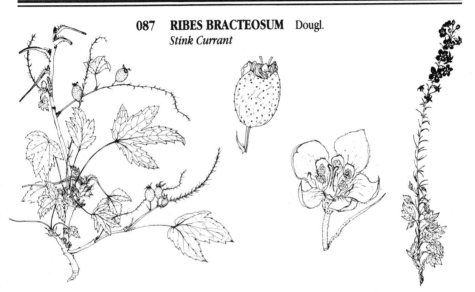

Erect, often straggly shrub, 1–4 m tall with numerous glands
excreting a characteristic pungent, disagreeable odor. Leaves
deeply 5–7-lobed mostly over one-half their length; main segments
shallowly lobed, toothed. Leafstalks 2–10 cm long, sparsely hairy
with several fleshy, spinelike hairs near the base. Racemes many-
flowered. Flower tube flared and saucer shaped, 1–2 mm long.
Sepals 3–4 mm, greenish or purple black to white. Petals much
reduced, .5 mm, white wedge to fan shaped. Stamens very short,
anthers somewhat spherical on stout filaments. Ovary hairy, styles
2, joined for one-fourth to one-half their length. Berry spherical, 10
mm, black with numerous white dots or glands and a disagreeable
taste. *Flowering:* February–June. *Fruiting:* June–October.

Found along stream banks or in moist shaded woods, usually along
creeks. From Alaska south along the Pacific coast to Mendocino
County, California.

088   RIBES DIVARICATUM   Dougl.
Straggly Gooseberry

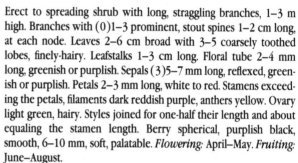

Erect to spreading shrub with long, straggling branches, 1–3 m high. Branches with (0)1–3 prominent, stout spines 1–2 cm long, at each node. Leaves 2–6 cm broad with 3–5 coarsely toothed lobes, finely-hairy. Leafstalks 1–3 cm long. Floral tube 2–4 mm long, greenish or purplish. Sepals (3)5–7 mm long, reflexed, greenish or purplish. Petals 2–3 mm long, white to red. Stamens exceeding the petals, filaments dark reddish purple, anthers yellow. Ovary light green, hairy. Styles joined for one-half their length and about equaling the stamen length. Berry spherical, purplish black, smooth, 6–10 mm, soft, palatable. *Flowering:* April–May. *Fruiting:* June–August.

Found in open woods and shaded canyons and on prairies and moist hillsides, especially along stream banks from British Columbia south to Santa Barbara County, California.

089   RIBES MENZIESII   Pursh.
Canyon Gooseberry

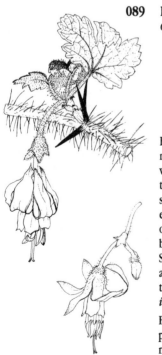

Erect, loosely branched shrub 1–2 m tall. Branches with 3 prominent, stout spines 1–2 cm long, at each node, and many slender, weak spines along the branches. Leaves 2–4 cm wide, 3–5-lobed, the lobes scalloped, deep green above, grayish velvety below. Leafstalks 1–3 cm long, glandular-hairy. Racemes hanging, 1 or 2-flowered. Floral tube 2–4 mm long. Sepals dark crimson, the lobes oblong, 7–11 mm long, reflexed. Petals white or pinkish to yellow, broadly wedge shaped, 3–4 mm long, often with inrolled margins. Stamen filaments stout, white, 3–5 mm long. Styles 2, joined to above midlength. Berry reddish purple, covered with stiff, gland-tipped hairs, not palatable. *Flowering:* late March–early May. *Fruiting:* May–July.

Found in canyons and on flats, increasing in moist sites following partial timber harvest. From San Luis Obispo County, California, north to Lane County, Oregon, below 300 m elevation.

090 RIBES SANGUINEUM Pursh.
Red Flowering Currant, Blood Currant

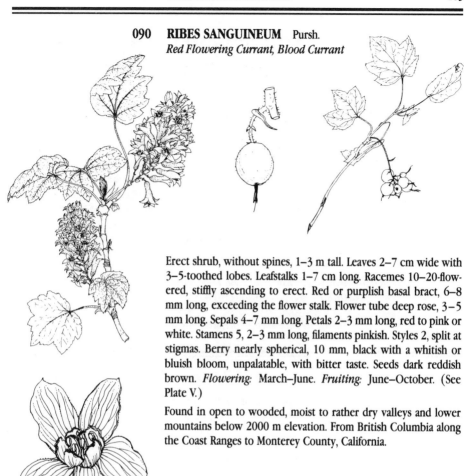

Erect shrub, without spines, 1–3 m tall. Leaves 2–7 cm wide with 3–5-toothed lobes. Leafstalks 1–7 cm long. Racemes 10–20-flowered, stiffly ascending to erect. Red or purplish basal bract, 6–8 mm long, exceeding the flower stalk. Flower tube deep rose, 3–5 mm long. Sepals 4–7 mm long. Petals 2–3 mm long, red to pink or white. Stamens 5, 2–3 mm long, filaments pinkish. Styles 2, split at stigmas. Berry nearly spherical, 10 mm, black with a whitish or bluish bloom, unpalatable, with bitter taste. Seeds dark reddish brown. *Flowering:* March–June. *Fruiting:* June–October. (See Plate V.)

Found in open to wooded, moist to rather dry valleys and lower mountains below 2000 m elevation. From British Columbia along the Coast Ranges to Monterey County, California.

HELLEBORACEAE
Hellebore (Baneberry) Family

Habit	Perennial herbs with compound leaves.
Life Form	Geophyte.
Roots	Short and branching rootstocks.
Leaves	Basal or along the stem and opposite. Divided into 3 leaflets with sawtoothed or rounded teeth.
Inflorescence	Dense, erect racemes, or terminal, solitary flowers.
Flowers	Regular and bisexual. Sepals 3–5, small and whitish purplish, or larger and red. Petals usually 5(4–10), sometimes absent, white, narrow and scarcely larger than the sepals, or yellow, large and showy, each with a red, elongate pouch or spur for nectar storage. Stamens many, exceeding the petals in length. Pistils 1 with a 2-lobed stigma, or 5 and free with unbranched styles.
Fruit	Fleshy, dark red (or rarely, white) berry, or 5 separate follicles.
Distribution	North Temperate Zone, in 2 genera and 71 species.
Ecology	Rich, moist, shaded woods or moist, open woods and rocky canyons.
Uses	Some species of horticultural value.

Key to HELLEBORACEAE

1   Sepals whitish or purplish tinged, 2–3 mm long. Petals white, 3–4 mm long. Flowers in dense racemes. Basal leaves smaller than the terminal leaves; leaflets 3, sawtoothed on the margin, 2.5–6 cm long. Fruit a shiny, fleshy, dark red (rarely, white) berry, 5–11 mm long.   **ACTAEA**

Perennial herb with 1–several, sparsely hairy stems, branching above. Racemes dense and erect in flower. Found in rich, moist woods.   **ACTAEA RUBRA ssp. ARGUTA**

1   Sepals red, 15–25 mm long. Petals yellow, 3–5 mm long, each with a red spur projecting backward, 10–20 mm long. Flowers solitary and terminal. Basal leaves larger than the terminal leaves; leaflets 3, cleft, lobed on the margin, 2–4 cm long. Fruit a glandular-hairy follicle, 15–30 mm long, beaked with a persistent style, 15–25 mm long.   **AQUILEGIA**

Perennial herb, stem branched above and glandular-hairy, covered with a bloom. Flowers large and showy. Found in moist, open woods and moist, rocky canyons and on rock outcrops.   **AQUI-LEGIA FORMOSA**

091 ACTAEA RUBRA (Ait.) Willd.
ssp. ARGUTA (Nutt.) Hult.
Baneberry

Perennial herb bearing several stems (20–100 cm) with odd-pinnately compound leaves, the lower leaves 10–20 cm wide, upper leaves larger. Leaflets ovate, incised, sawtoothed, 25–60 mm long. Leafstalks to about 10 cm. Inflorescence 1–5 erect racemes (6–10 cm long) bearing white flowers (1 cm across). Fruit a round, fleshy, dark red (rarely, white) berry (5–11 mm). Seed a nutlet, dark brown, flattened with pitted shell, 3 mm. *Flowering:* May–July. *Fruiting:* June–September.

Found in rich, moist woods from Alaska south to the Sierra Nevada and the San Bernardino Mountains of California, to San Luis Obispo County, California, in the Coast Ranges; extends eastward to the Rocky Mountains of New Mexico and Arizona, on to the Atlantic. Below 3300 m elevation.

092 AQUILEGIA FORMOSA Fisch. in DC.
Northwest Crimson, Columbine

Perennial, erect herb with leafy, branched stem, terminating in a loose, leafy raceme of showy, drooping flowers. Leaves basal, compound, with 2 or 3 obovate leaflets (2–4 cm), cleft, lobed, and with rounded teeth. Flowers solitary, hanging, terminal, hairy. Sepals red, ovate-lance shaped, wide spreading to reflexed, 15–25 mm long, pointed. Petals platelike, yellow, rounded to squared or with frayed margin, 3–5 mm long. Spurs red, 10–20 mm long, straight rather than incurved. Stamens distinctly exerted. Fruit a follicle, glandular-hairy, 15–30 mm long. Seeds 2 mm long. *Flowering:* May–August. *Fruiting:* August–September.

Found in moist, open woods, and moist, rocky canyons and on rock outcrops. Mono and Fresno counties to Modoc, Siskiyou, and Del Norte counties, California, to Alaska, Montana, and Utah, 1300–3000 m elevation.

HIPPOCASTANACEAE
Buckeye Family

Habit   Trees or shrubs, deciduous.

Leaves   Palmate, without stipules.

Inflorescence   Terminal, open panicle or compact, ovate panicle. Flowers borne on jointed stalks.

Flowers   Flowers unisexual and bisexual within the same panicle, irregular, showy, sepals united, tubular or bell shaped, 5-parted, the segments unequal. Petals 4 or 5, clawed, unequal. Stamens 5–8, filaments long, slender. Ovary 3-celled, ovules 2 in each cell. Style slender.

Fruit   Capsule, spherical or slightly 3-lobed, smooth or spiny, leathery, 3-celled or by abortion 1- or 2-celled and seeded.

Seeds   Large with shiny or polished seed coat. Endosperm absent. Cotyledons large and thick.

Distribution   Northern Hemisphere, 3 genera and about 18 species.

Uses   Trees principally understory forest trees; wood soft, light, not very durable, cross-grained, and hard to work. A number of species highly esteemed for their ornamental value because of their showy flowers and handsome foliage.

093   AESCULUS CALIFORNICA (Spach) Nutt.
California Buckeye

Large bush or tree up to 12 m tall. Bole branched, gnarled. Leaves palmately compound, leaflets 5–7, oblong–lance shaped, pointed, 5–15 cm long, deciduous, turning yellow in fall. Inflorescence a compact, erect, ovate panicle, 10–20 cm long. Perianth white to light rose. Sepals united, 7–8 mm long. Petals 13–15 mm long. Stamens 5–8, anthers orange. Fruit pear shaped, smooth. Seeds mostly 1, glossy brown, 2–3 cm diameter. *Flowering:* May–June. *Fruiting:* June–October.

Common on dry, gravelly slopes in the Coast Ranges and the Sierra Nevada from Del Norte and Shasta counties south to northern Los Angeles and Kern counties, California, below 1350 m elevation.

HYDROPHYLLACEAE
Waterleaf Family

Habit   Annual, perennial, or biennial herbs or shrubs, with alternate or sometimes partly or wholly opposite entire to cleft or compound leaves.

Inflorescence   Flowers solitary or in variously modified, often curled-up racemes.

Flowers   Bisexual, regular or nearly so. Sepals usually 5, united, deeply lobed, the divisions alike or unalike. Corolla consisting of 5 united petals, usually with a pair of scales at the base of each filament. Stamens 5, alternate with the petals. Ovary superior, ordinarily of 2 carpels. Placentae 2, usually on the ovary walls. Styles separate or partly united. Stigmas 2, densely clustered.

Fruit   Capsule 1-celled or partially 2-celled by the intrusion of the placentae, splitting by 2 or 4 valves or irregularly, 1–many-seeded.

Seeds   Endosperm present. Embryo straight. Cotyledons 2, entire.

Distribution   About 25 genera and 250–300 species of wide distribution, best developed in the western United States.

Key to HYDROPHYLLACEAE

1   Flowers numerous in congested cymes. Stamens and styles conspicuously protruding from the corolla. Sepals without appendages between the lobes. Leaves mainly basal, stem leaves alternate. Perennial herb with rootstock. **HYDROPHYLLUM**

Leaves semicircular in outline, 8–20 cm in diameter, pinnately divided into 5(7–9) principal divisions. Corolla creamy, greenish, purple, or blue, 5–7 mm long. Capsule 3–5 mm in diameter. **HYDROPHYLLUM TENUIPES**

1   Flowers few, solitary in the leaf axils or opposite the leaves. Stamens and styles not protruding from the corolla. Sepals with appendages in the corners between the lobes. Leaves mainly along the stem, opposite, at least below. Annual herb with taproot. **NEMOPHILA**

Leaves 10–40 mm long, 8–25 mm broad, pinnately parted into usually 5 lobes. Corolla white to blue, bell shaped, 2–4 mm broad. Capsule spherical, 3–5 mm in diameter. **NEMOPHILA PARVIFLORA**

094   HYDROPHYLLUM TENUIPES   Heller
Pacific Waterleaf

Perennial herb 20–80 cm tall, from a rootstock. Stem rough with stiff or bristlelike hairs. Leaves alternate, basal or along the stem or both, with sharp, stiff, straight hairs, pinnately divided, 8–20 cm in diameter. Flowers coarsely hairy on stalks, 5–12 mm long in open cymes. Sepals 5, united at the base, 4–7 mm long, bristly-hairy on the margins. Corolla of 5 fused, creamy, greenish, purple, or blue petals, 5–7 mm long. Stamens 5, protruding from the corolla along with the style. Capsule fruit 3–5 mm in diameter, seed. 2–4 mm in diameter, solitary. *Flowering:* April–July. *Fruiting:* July–August. (See Plate V.)

Moist, shaded, mixed evergreen forests and on river flats. Below 1700 m elevation on the western flank of the Cascades to the coast, from Vancouver Island, British Columbia, and northern Washington to Mendocino County, California.

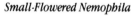

095   NEMOPHILA PARVIFLORA   Dougl. *ex* Benth.
Small-Flowered Nemophila

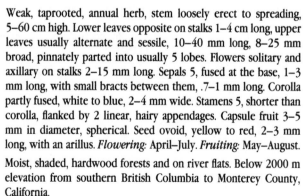

Weak, taprooted, annual herb, stem loosely erect to spreading, 5–60 cm high. Lower leaves opposite on stalks 1–4 cm long, upper leaves usually alternate and sessile, 10–40 mm long, 8–25 mm broad, pinnately parted into usually 5 lobes. Flowers solitary and axillary on stalks 2–15 mm long. Sepals 5, fused at the base, 1–3 mm long, with small bracts between them, .7–1 mm long. Corolla partly fused, white to blue, 2–4 mm wide. Stamens 5, shorter than corolla, flanked by 2 linear, hairy appendages. Capsule fruit 3–5 mm in diameter, spherical. Seed ovoid, yellow to red, 2–3 mm long, with an arillus. *Flowering:* April–July. *Fruiting:* May–August.

Moist, shaded, hardwood forests and on river flats. Below 2000 m elevation from southern British Columbia to Monterey County, California.

IRIDACEAE
Iris Family

Habit	Perennial herbs, mostly low with simple or branching stems. Arising from bulbs or rootstocks.
Life Form	Geophyte.
Leaves	Mostly basal and vertically flattened around stem, parallel veined, linear or sword shaped, 2-ranked.
Inflorescence	Umbel, raceme, or panicle.
Flowers	Perfect, regular or irregular, subtended by large bracts. Perianth of 6 clawed segments in 2 series of 3 segments each, the 3 outer segments sometimes sepallike. Stamens 3, inserted at the base of the outer segments, facing outward from the axis. Filaments threadlike, separate or united, 2-celled. Pistil 1, ovary inferior, mostly 3-celled with ovules attached centrally. Style 3-parted or simple, sometimes petallike. Upper portion of petallike styles forming the so-called style crest. Stigmas 3, sometimes expanded or divided.
Fruit	Capsule, few to many-seeded, splitting lengthwise through the middle vein of the carpel on ripening, 3-celled, 3-angled or 3-lobed (sometimes 6-lobed).
Seeds	Numerous in 1 or 2 rows in each cell of the capsule. Endosperm fleshy or hardened. Embryo straight, small.
Distribution	Approximately 57 genera and 1000 species, widely distributed in temperate to tropical regions of both hemispheres.
Uses	Ornamentals for gardens because of their colorful and attractive flowers.

Key to IRIDACEAE

Only 1 genus, *Iris,* is represented.

1   Leaves under 8 mm wide. Perianth tube 30–90 mm long. Flowering stalk unbranched, usually 2-flowered.   **IRIS CHRYSOPHYLLA**

1   Leaves 8–20 mm wide. Perianth tube 15–30 mm long. Flowering stalk usually with 1–4 side branches, each usually 3-flowered. **IRIS DOUGLASIANA**

096   IRIS CHRYSOPHYLLA Howell
Slender Yellow Iris

Herbaceous perennial, 7–20 cm tall. Leaves much exceeding stems, light green, the bases pink to red, 3–7 mm wide, 20–40 cm long. Flowering stems 7–20 cm tall with 1–3 reduced leaves. Spathe bracts reddish or purplish, opposite, lance shaped to narrower. Perianth tube very slender, pale creamy yellow to almost white, usually dark veined and sometimes with faint bluish tinge, 4–10 cm long. Fruit an oblong, beaked capsule, 2–3 cm long. *Flowering:* May–July. *Fruiting:* August–October.

Found on dry, open slopes in the redwood forest, occasionally in dry, open, rocky prairies, especially on serpentine soils. Willamette valley from Marion County, Oregon, to Humboldt County, California.

097   IRIS DOUGLASIANA Herb.
Douglas's Iris

Herbaceous perennial, densely matted from thick rootstocks 25–50 cm tall. Stems flattened with 2 or 3 leaves. Stem leaves distinctly ribbed, 30–100 cm long, 9–20 mm wide. Basal leaves equaling or slightly exceeding the stem, 7–15 cm long. Inflorescence stalk 15–80 cm long, usually with 1–4 side branches, each usually 2- or 3-flowered. Flower stalk 20–53 mm long. Perianth tube 15–28 mm long. Perianth varying from pale cream through light and dark lavender to deep purple. Fruit a brown capsule. *Flowering:* March–June. *Fruiting:* July–October. (See Plate V.)

Abundant on grassy places, open slopes, and along deer trails in forests. From Santa Barbara County, California, to Curry County, Oregon.

LAMIACEAE
Mint Family

Habit	Herbs or shrubs, rarely trees, usually with aromatic foliage.
Stems	Mostly distinctly 4-angled or distinctly 4-ribbed.
Leaves	Opposite or whorled, simple, often hairy with epidermal glands secreting various volatile oils. Stipules absent.
Inflorescence	Flowers solitary or variously clustered in corymbs and with secondary bracts.
Flowers	Bisexual, usually irregular, 2-lipped. Sepals 5(10), united, sometimes 2-lipped. Petals 5, united, 2-lipped with 2 fused upper petals and 3 fused lower petals. Stamens on the tube formed by the petals, mostly 4 and paired or 1 pair abortive. Anthers 2-celled or sometimes 1 of the cells abortive. Ovary superior 4-lobed or parted, 2-celled, often appearing as 4-celled by secondary constriction of ovary wall. Style single, arising between the lobes, mostly with 2(4)-pointed unequal stigmas.
Fruit	Individual 1-seeded nutlets, clustered in 4s, rarely fleshy, included in the persistent calyx.
Seeds	Nutlets 1-seeded, endosperm none or scanty, embryo mostly upright with a short, inferior rootlet.
Distribution	Widely distributed in temperate and tropical regions, 180 genera and 3500 species.
Uses	Of considerable economic importance as a source of numerous ornamentals and aromatic oils used as flavoring.

Key to LAMIACEAE

1   Corolla noticeably 2-lipped, the lobes unequal. Stamens not exceeding the petals. **2**

1   Corolla united into a floral tube, regular or nearly so, all the lobes nearly equal. Stamens usually exceeding the petals. **MENTHA**

Flower whorls crowded densely in terminal spikes or some of the lower whorls more scattered along the leafy stems. Corolla pink lavender to white. Leaves lance-ovate to somewhat elliptic, often shaggy haired along the main veins beneath, 3–6 cm long. **MENTHA PIPERITA**

2   Flowers in a spike or in whorls of spikes interrupted by leaves, upper lip of corolla concave. **3**

2   Flowers solitary in axils, upper lip of corolla not curved. **SATUREJA**

Herb with low-spreading stems that frequently root. Leaves round-ovate, shallowly scalloped or sawtoothed, 15–25 mm long. Corolla

Lamiaceae = Labiatae.

externally hairy with short lips, white or tinged with purple.
SATUREJA DOUGLASII

3   Calyx 2-lipped, closed in fruit, the upper lip squarely cut off and with 3 teeth. Flowers bluish, violet, or lavender. Leaves short, 1–5 cm long. Low, spreading herb.   **PRUNELLA**

Stems mostly tufted or loosely ascending, 10–50 cm high, simple or branched.   **PRUNELLA VULGARIS**

3   Calyx 5-toothed, not closed in fruit. Flowers red purple to pink purple. Leaves longer, usually 5–18 cm. Rather tall herbs. **STACHYS**   4

4   Corolla tube 18–20 mm long. Flowers in a dense, terminal, continuous spike. Stamens exserted 4–5 mm past the corolla tube. **STACHYS CHAMISSONIS**

4   Corolla tube usually less than 16 mm long. Flowers in whorls of spikes interrupted by leaves, at least in age. Stamens usually not exserted more than 2–3 mm beyond the corolla tube.   **5**

5   Leaves ovate to lance shaped, or oblong-ovate, 6–18 cm long. Flowers 6–20 per whorl.   **6**

5   Leaves triangular-oblong to lance-oblong, 5–9 cm long. Flowers 1–3 in the axils of each bract. Petals rose purple or purple veined. **STACHYS RIGIDA**

6   Flowers 6 per whorl. Corolla tube purple, upper lip small, 3.5–5.5 mm long, lower lip 6–10 mm long, not with white spots, with a ring of hairs inside the tube near the base.   **STACHYS BULLATA**

6   Flowers 6–20 per whorl. Corolla tube red purple, upper lip large, 8–11 mm long, lower lip 6–8 mm long with white spots, with a ring of hairs inside the tube near the middle.   **STACHYS MEXI-CANA**

098 MENTHA PIPERITA L.
Peppermint

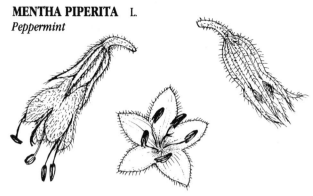

Perennial herb with rootstalks and densely branched, erect, flowering stems, 30–120 cm tall. Leaves sharply sawtoothed, ovate to lance shaped to elliptic, 3–6 cm × 1.5–3 cm. Flowers in whorls without subtending leaves, crowded into dense, terminal, 2–7 cm long spikes. Corolla pink lavender to white, funnel shaped, 3.5–5 mm long. Calyx green, 2.5–3 mm long. Fruit 4 free nutlets. Seeds smooth, gray black. *Flowering:* July–October. *Fruiting:* October–November.

Common to moist areas from Washington to southern California and eastward across the continent.

099 PRUNELLA VULGARIS L.
Heal-All, Self-Heal

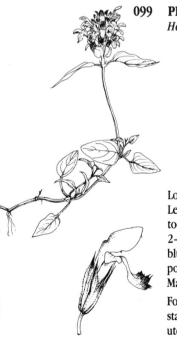

Low, perennial herb with tufted or ascending stems, 10–50 cm tall. Leaves ovate to ovate-oblong, entire or irregularly and remotely toothed, 1–5 cm long, stalked. Inflorescence of terminal spikes, 2–5 cm long. Calyx tube 4–5(10) mm long, purplish. Corolla tube bluish, violet, or lavender, 8–10(20) mm long. Stamens bluish, pollen white. Nutlets 4, light brown with black lines. *Flowering:* May–September. *Fruiting:* September–October.

Found in moist, open woods or as a weed in lawns. In the Pacific states from Washington to southern California but widely distributed in North America and variable in habitat and flower size.

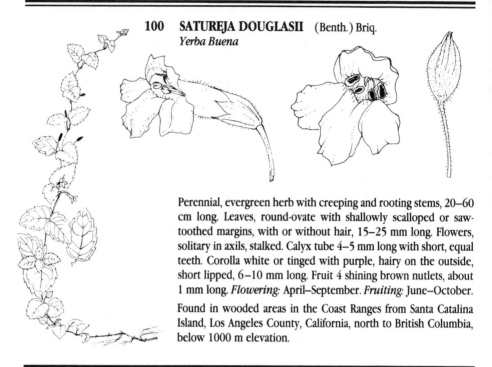

100   SATUREJA DOUGLASII   (Benth.) Briq.
Yerba Buena

Perennial, evergreen herb with creeping and rooting stems, 20–60 cm long. Leaves, round-ovate with shallowly scalloped or saw-toothed margins, with or without hair, 15–25 mm long. Flowers, solitary in axils, stalked. Calyx tube 4–5 mm long with short, equal teeth. Corolla white or tinged with purple, hairy on the outside, short lipped, 6–10 mm long. Fruit 4 shining brown nutlets, about 1 mm long. *Flowering:* April–September. *Fruiting:* June–October.

Found in wooded areas in the Coast Ranges from Santa Catalina Island, Los Angeles County, California, north to British Columbia, below 1000 m elevation.

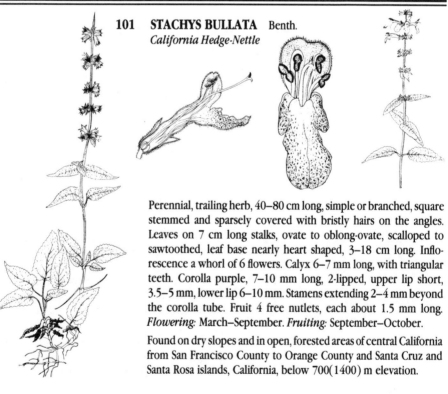

101   STACHYS BULLATA Benth.
California Hedge-Nettle

Perennial, trailing herb, 40–80 cm long, simple or branched, square stemmed and sparsely covered with bristly hairs on the angles. Leaves on 7 cm long stalks, ovate to oblong-ovate, scalloped to sawtoothed, leaf base nearly heart shaped, 3–18 cm long. Inflo-rescence a whorl of 6 flowers. Calyx 6–7 mm long, with triangular teeth. Corolla purple, 7–10 mm long, 2-lipped, upper lip short, 3.5–5 mm, lower lip 6–10 mm. Stamens extending 2–4 mm beyond the corolla tube. Fruit 4 free nutlets, each about 1.5 mm long. *Flowering:* March–September. *Fruiting:* September–October.

Found on dry slopes and in open, forested areas of central California from San Francisco County to Orange County and Santa Cruz and Santa Rosa islands, California, below 700(1400) m elevation.

102 STACHYS CHAMISSONIS Benth.
Coast Hedge-Nettle

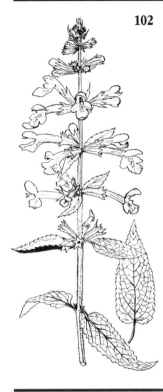

Perennial, erect herb, 60–100 cm high, simple or branched stout stems, covered with bristlelike hairs. Leaves on 5 cm long stalks, narrow-ovate, coarsely scalloped to sawtoothed, sharp pointed, heart shaped at base, 6–18 cm long. Inflorescence a whorl of usually 2–5 flowers. Calyx 11–15 mm long, densely shaggy haired with triangular teeth. Corolla rose purple, 18–20 mm long, 2-lipped, upper lip 7–9 mm long, lower lip 12–13 mm. Stamens extending 4–5 mm beyond the corolla. Fruit 4 free nutlets, each about 2.5–3 mm long. *Flowering:* June–October. *Fruiting:* October–November.

Found in moist areas near the Pacific coast from Humboldt County to San Mateo County, San Luis Obispo County, California.

103 STACHYS MEXICANA Benth.
Emerson's Hedge-Nettle

Perennial herb, 40–120 cm tall with unbranched stems. Stems rough with shaggy hairs. Leaves ovate to lance-shaped 6–12 cm long, coarsely scalloped to sawtoothed on 2–4 cm long stalks. Flowers, 6–20 per whorl in interrupted spikes. Calyx 5–7 mm long, lobes triangular, short spined. Corolla red purple, 8–11 mm long, upper lip 5–8 mm, lower lip 6–8 mm. Nutlets 4, black with wrinkled seed coat. *Flowering:* June–August. *Fruiting:* August–September.

Found in moist places in Mendocino and Del Norte counties, California, to British Columbia.

104 STACHYS RIGIDA Nutt. *ex* Benth.
Rigid Hedge-Nettle

Low, perennial herb, erect or spreading, simple or branched, 60–100 cm tall, shaggy-coarse haired on stems. Leaves triangular oblong to lance-oblong, scalloped to sawtoothed, 5–9 cm long. Flowers in 10–20 cm long, interrupted spikes, 1–3 per whorl in axil of each bract. Calyx 5–8 mm long with narrow triangular teeth, shaggy haired. Corolla rose purple or purple veined, 12–16 mm long, 2-lipped, upper lip 3–5.5 mm, lower lip 7–9 mm. Stamens extending 2–3 mm beyond corolla. Fruit, 4 free nutlets, seed coat slightly rough. *Flowering:* July–August. *Fruiting:* August–September.

Found on moist lands and forest edges from Plumas, Butte, Humboldt, and Trinity counties north, also in mountains of Riverside, Orange, and San Diego counties, California, to Washington, below 2600 m elevation.

LAURACEAE
Laurel Family

Habit	Trees and shrubs with aromatic foliage and wood, usually evergreen.
Leaves	Alternate, rarely opposite, simple, mostly leathery, leaf blade dotted with translucent glands, without stipules.
Inflorescence	Panicles, racemes, or umbels.
Flowers	Bisexual or unisexual, calyx 4–6-parted, in 2 whorls, 2 or 3 segments per whorl. No petals. Stamens in 3 or 4 whorls of 3 each, some stamens frequently lacking the anther. Anthers 2–4-celled, opening by 4 uplifting valves. Ovary usually superior and free, 1-celled, with 1 ovule. Style single, 3-lobed.
Fruit	Berry or a fleshy, nonopening drupe.
Seeds	Seed coat smooth, hard.
Distribution	About 40 genera and 1000 species widely distributed in tropical and subtropical regions, less widely distributed in temperate regions.
Uses	Some species grown for ornamental purposes; some such as avocado, cinnamon, and camphor of great economic importance.

105 UMBELLULARIA CALIFORNICA Nutt.
California Bay, California Laurel, Myrtle-Wood, Oregon Myrtle

Tree up to 30–45 m tall, or an erect shrub in dry areas. Bark greenish to reddish brown to dark brown. Leaves oblong to lance shaped, 3–8 cm long, without hairs, somewhat glossy, aromatic, yellowish green. Inflorescence an umbel or short panicle with 6–10 flowers. Sepals, 6–8 mm, oblong-ovate, no petals. Stamens 9, 6 basal, much reduced and sterile, 3 larger and fertile. Stigma 3-lobed. Fruit a fleshy drupe, 20–25 mm, green to purplish. *Flowering:* December–May. *Fruiting:* May–October.

Found in canyons and river valleys and on river flats in the Coast Ranges and the Sierra Nevada and in San Diego County, California, to northwestern California and southwestern Oregon, below 1700 m elevation.

LILIACEAE
Lily Family

Habit	Perennial herbs, sometimes woody stems or climbing, with bulbs or rootstocks and mostly showy flowers.
Life Form	Predominantly geophytic.
Underground Parts	Bulbs or with thickened to slender rootstock.
Stems	Erect, sometimes woody, climbing, trailing, or creeping.
Leaves	Broad or grasslike, parallel veined, alternate, never all whorled at top of the stem, sometimes all basal leaves or all stem leaves.
Inflorescence	Racemes, panicles, or solitary.
Flowers	Bisexual or rarely unisexual, regular or slightly irregular. Perianth usually 2 distinct rows of 3, rarely of 2 (*Maianthemum*). Sepals often greenish but also colored. Petals highly colored or white, showy. Stamens 6, but sometimes 3 fertile and 3 infertile, mostly 3-celled. Styles fully fused to rarely free, stigma entire to 3-cleft.
Fruit	Capsule or berry.
Seeds	With a hard seedcoat and abundant endosperm.
Distribution	About 200 genera and 6500 species. Distributed worldwide but especially abundant and diverse in drier temperate regions.
Uses	Many species with showy flowers used as ornamentals; other species with edible bulbs or rootstocks.

Key to LILIACEAE

1   Plants with a scaly, membrane-coated bulb (onionlike), or a fiber-coated bulb, or a solid, swollen, bulblike underground stem, giving rise to a single flowering stem from the same bulb.   **2**

1   Plants with a rootstock, slender or swollen, thickened and much-branched, several bunched, leafy, and flowering stems sometimes arising from the same rootstock.   **6**

2   Stem leafy, sometimes forked above. Leaves basal but also with numerous, often reduced stem leaves. Style 1. Perianth segments alike.   **3**

     Perianth open bell shaped. Perianth segments showy, large, orange or white, strongly recurved backward, exposing fully pistil and anthers. Perianth segments deciduous with a nectar gland at the base. Filament attached to the middle of the back of the anther. Bulbs ovoid with numerous, loose, fleshy scales.   **LILIUM**   **4**

2   Stem usually leafless, sometimes forked. Stem leaves reduced to short, pointed bracts. Inflorescence a widely branching, spreading panicle. Perianth segments lance shaped, lined, white, strongly recurved, opening in the evening, closed during the day.   **CHLO-ROGALUM**

     Bulb, deep seated, oblong to obovate, large, 8–12 cm long, densely coated with coarse, black fibers. Stems 40–160 cm tall. Basal leaves with strongly wavy margins, 15–75 cm long, 8–20 mm wide. Flower stalks 10–35 mm long. Perianth 15–20 mm long.   **CHLO-ROGALUM POMERIDIANUM**

3   Perianth segments white to pink or purplish or red, finely dotted. Flowers fragrant.   **LILIUM**   4

3   Perianth segments yellow to orange or red, very conspicuously dotted. Flowers usually not fragrant.   **LILIUM**   5

4   Flowers erect to ascending, trumpet shaped. Perianth segments nearly white, aging to rose purple, finely dotted with brown, the upper third recurved. Anthers 5–6 mm long. Capsule 25–35 mm long, narrowed at base.   **LILIUM RUBESCENS**

4   Flowers nodding. Perianth segments strongly recurved to the base, pinkish with a central yellow band, aging to rose purple, finely and densely dotted with purple. Anthers 8–9 mm long. Capsule 40–50 mm long, cylindrical.   **LILIUM KELLOGGII**

5   Bulbs over 25 mm long, pointed, with numerous loose, fleshy scales, scales not fused. Leaves in whorls of 5–9. Anthers 4–6 mm long. Perianth orange with dark purple spots, 35–60 mm long, recurved for half its length. Drier sites, roadsides.   **LILIUM COLUMBIANUM**

5   Bulbs numerous, mostly less than 25 mm long, fused into a branching rootstock. Scales fused, fleshy. Leaves in whorls of 9–15. Anthers 10–15 mm long. Perianth orange with maroon spots and dark red center, 50–80 mm long, recurving to below the middle of its length. Exclusively along stream banks and in springy places.   **LILIUM PARDALINUM**

6   Stamens 4. Perianth with 4 segments. Ovary 2-celled, 1–4-seeded.   **MAIANTHEMUM**

Leaves 1–3, on short, erect stalks, heart shaped with numerous parallel veins. Raceme terminal. Perianth white. Berry light tan brown with darker gray marbling, discoloring in late winter to deep red and becoming soft, juicy, spherical, 6 mm long.   **MAIANTHEMUM DILATATUM**

6   Stamens 6. Stem distinct and evident above the ground. Basal and stem leaves generally more than 2.   7

7   Leaves all basal or the basal leaves much larger than the reduced stem leaves. Rootstock not thickened.   8

7   Leaves not all basal but well distributed on the stem. Rootstock heavily rooted, thickened.   9

8   Basal leaves 2–6, not grasslike, large, broadly oblong, glossy-waxy, 15–60 cm long, no stem leaves.

Flowers nodding, stalked, many in terminal umbel with lateral umbels, or solitary. Basal leaves 4–6, broad oblong, glossy-waxy, with only a pronounced midvein. Perianth segments erect, spreading. **CLINTONIA**

Stem stout, 25–50 cm tall. Leaves large, 15–25 cm long. Perianth deep rose purple. Berry metallic dark blue, ovoid, 8–10 seeded. **CLINTONIA ANDREWSIANA**

8   Basal leaves and reduced stem leaves wiry, grasslike, 50–100 cm long, 3–6 mm wide, dry with rough margins, leafstalks 2–5 cm long. **XEROPHYLLUM**

Perianth yellowish white, fragrant flowers and fruits ascending. **XEROPHYLLUM TENAX**

9   Flowers solitary or in small 2–7-flowered umbels, drooping in the axils of leaves near the tip of the stalk. Stem variously branched.   **10**

9   Flowers in terminal panicles or racemes. Stem not branched. **SMILACINA**   **12**

10   Flowers solitary, rarely 2, in the axils of leaves, well distributed along the entire stalk. Flower stalks typically kinked or bent at about one-half their length, then drooping. Stems green. Leaves ovate. **STREPTOPUS**

Stems stout, 50–120 cm tall. Stems thickened at base, soft green, pricklelike hairs with swollen bases. Outer 3 segments 9–12 mm long, much longer than inner segments, strongly recurved, greenish to deep purple black. Stamens short, hidden. Style long, white. Berry elliptical, yellow to red, 10–18 mm in diameter. **STREP-TOPUS AMPLEXIFOLIUS**

10   Flowers solitary or in 2–7-flowered umbels. Flower stalks not kinked or bent. Stems brownish, soft-hairy. Leaves ovate to lance shaped. Leaf blade asymmetrical along midvein. **DISPORUM**   **11**

11   Leaves and stems with short, stiff or rough hairs. Perianth bell shaped, recurved and spreading, creamy white, 9–16 mm long. Stamens and pistil extending beyond perianth. Berry roundish, red orange, 6–9 mm long. **DISPORUM HOOKERI**

11   Leaves and stems with soft, fine hairs, leaf blade waxy, shiny. Perianth long, cylindrical, adpressed, and hiding the stamens and pistil, 15–28 mm long, segments only slightly flaring at the tip. Berry pear shaped, orange yellow, 12–16 mm long. **DISPORUM SMITHII**

12   Inflorescence a dense panicle, many-flowered. Perianth white, shorter than stamens. Berry bright red, 1–3-seeded, 4–7 mm in diameter. Stem 30–100 cm tall. Rootstock stout, fleshy. **SMILA-CINA RACEMOSA**

12   Inflorescence an open raceme, 3–10-flowered. Perianth white, longer than stamens. Berry greenish yellow with dark purple, longitudinal markings, 6–10 mm in diameter. Filaments slender. Stems 30–60 cm tall. Rootstock slender, fleshy. **SMILACINA STEL-LATA**

106   CHLOROGALUM POMERIDIANUM   Kunth
Common Soap Plant, Amole

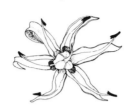

Perennial herb with black brown, densely fiber-coated bulbs 7–15 cm long. Basal leaves linear, 20–70 cm × 8–20 mm, strongly ridged at midrib, with distinctly wavy margins. Inflorescence a tall, open panicle 70 cm long. Flower stalks ascending or widely spreading. Sepals 3, whitish, broader than the petals. Petals 3, more pinkish white. Stamens 6, with hairy, swollen base. Stigma minutely 3-pointed. Fruit a capsule, ovate, compressed, 5–7 mm long. Flowers opening from base of panicle toward tip after 4:00 P.M. for one evening. *Flowering:* May–August. *Fruiting:* July–September.

Found from southern Oregon to San Diego County, California, below 1600 m elevation.

107   CLINTONIA ANDREWSIANA   Torr.
Red Clintonia

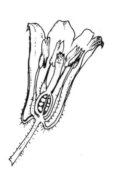

Perennial herb with stout, light brown, hollow, mainly underground stem, 25–50 cm long. Leaves oval to oblanceolate, glossy green, pointed at tip, hairy on margins and on midrib near base, 15–25 cm long. Inflorescence a terminal umbel with 1 or more side umbels and hairy stems. Flower stalks 10–30 mm long. Perianth deep rose purple. Filaments hairy, anthers oblong. Fruit an ovoid, deep metallic blue berry, 8–12 mm long, with 8–10 seeds. *Flowering:* May–July. *Fruiting:* July–September.

Shaded damp woods, redwood forest in Coast Ranges from Monterey County, California, north to southwestern Oregon.

108   DISPORUM HOOKERI   (Torr.) Nichols.
Hairy Fairy Bell

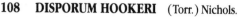

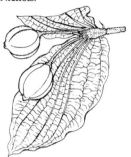

Perennial herbs, sparingly branched, 30–80 cm tall. Stem brown with short, stiff, rough hairs. Leaves distinctly heart shaped and unequal sided at base, pointed at tip, distinctly roughly hairy and on touch not waxy, 3–10 cm long. Perianth bell shaped, curved backward, creamy to greenish white, 9–18 mm. Stamens exceeding the perianth, style smooth, slightly 3-lobed at tip. Ovary elliptical, often hairy. Fruit a roundish, red orange berry, 6–9 mm long. *Flowering:* March–July. *Fruiting:* July–September.

Common in moist, shaded woods more inland and away from the coast from British Columbia, Alberta, northern Idaho, western Montana, Washington, and Oregon south to Monterey County, California.

109   DISPORUM SMITHII   (Hook.) Piper
Large-Flowered Fairy Bell

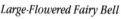

Perennial herbs, rather freely branched with short, fine-woolly hairs or almost hairless, 20–90 cm tall. Leaves rounded or slightly heart shaped at base, pointed at tip, on touch waxy, glossy above, 4–14 cm long. Flower stalks hairy, segments appressed. Perianth tubelike but flared at tip, pointed, 12–28 mm long. Stamens and style short, enclosed within the perianth; style distinctly hairy, 3-lobed. Fruit a pear-shaped berry, bright, salmon red to deep orange, 12–15 mm long. *Flowering:* March–June. *Fruiting:* July–September.

Found on moist, shaded banks on concave slopes and alluvial flats. In the Coast Ranges from British Columbia to Santa Cruz County, California, always close to the Pacific Ocean.

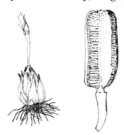

110 **LILIUM COLUMBIANUM** Hanson
Tiger Lily, Columbia Lily, Oregon Lily

Perennial herb with sturdy, hairless stems, (20)60–120(200) cm tall. Bulb ovoid with white, thick, loose, fleshy scales, 2–5 cm long. Leaves lance shaped to elliptic, pointed at tip, from all whorled to nearly all scattered (20)40–100 mm × 12–30(35) mm. Inflorescence a 1–20-flowered raceme or whorled below. Perianth segments strongly recurved for one-half their length, yellow red to red orange, spotted with deep red or purple, 35–70 mm × 6–12 mm. Filaments sticking far out of the petals, usually longer than the style. Fruit a capsule, greenish brown, 6-angled, 3–6 cm long. *Flowering:* May–August. *Fruiting:* July–October.

Found in prairies, thickets, and at the edge of coniferous forests in drier areas, from British Columbia south on both sides of the Cascades to northern California and east to northern Idaho and Nevada. Up to 2000 m elevation.

111 **LILIUM KELLOGGII** Purdy
Kellogg's Tiger Lily

Perennial herb, 60–90(300) cm high. Bulbs broadly ovoid-conical, 4–6 cm long, scales free and separate, lance-ovate, dark green above, paler beneath, 60–100 mm × 10–20 mm. Flowers 1–many, nodding, fragrant. Perianth segments pale pink aging to rose purple, with a central yellow band, finely but densely dotted with purple, strongly recurved to base, 3–5 cm long. Anthers dark orange. Fruit a light brown, cylindrical capsule, 4–5 cm long. *Flowering:* June–July. *Fruiting:* July–September.

Found in dry, rocky places or shaded, deeper soils in the redwood and mixed evergreen forest of Humboldt and Del Norte counties, California. Rare and known in a few localities only.

112   LILIUM PARDALINUM   Kell.
Leopard Lily

Perennial herb with stout, hairless stem, 100–250 cm high. Bulbs numerous, fused into a branching rootstock, 6–10 cm long. Scales fleshy, jointed once near the base, less than 30 mm long. Leaves linear to lance shaped, pointed at tips, usually in 3 or 4 whorls of 9–15, scattered above or below, or all scattered, 80–200 mm × 6–25 mm. Flowers nodding, usually not fragrant. Perianth segments recurving to below the middle of their length, orange to red orange at center, light orange at base, spotted with maroon, 50–80 mm × 12–18 mm. Stamens and style shorter than perianth segments. Fruit a narrowly oblong, sharply 6-angled capsule, 3 cm × 1 cm. *Flowering:* May–July. *Fruiting:* July–October.

Riparian habitats in Coast Ranges from southern Oregon to Santa Barbara County, California, from the Sierra Nevada south to Kern County, California, and in the mountains of east San Diego County, California. Up to 2000 m elevation.

113   LILIUM RUBESCENS   Wats.
Lilac

Perennial herb with stout stem, 50–200(300) cm tall. Bulbs ovoid, somewhat asymmetrical with an indistinct rootstock, 3.5–5 cm long. Scales thick, broadly lance shaped, not jointed, 25–35 mm long. Leaves inversely lance shaped, pointed at tip, whitish beneath, 4–8 cm × 12–25 mm. Upper leaves in 2–7 whorls of 5–10 leaves each, the lower ones scattered. Flowers 3–8, erect or ascending, trumpet shaped, fragrant. Perianth segments recurved only for the upper one-third of their length, white to purplish white, deepening to red wine color with age, spotted with purple, 35–50(60) mm × 10 mm. Fruit a light brown, papery, 3-valved capsule, narrowed at base, 25–35 mm long. *Flowering:* June–July. *Fruiting:* July–October.

Wooded slopes and ridges from southern Oregon to Santa Cruz County, California; below 1700 m elevation.

114 MAIANTHEMUM DILATATUM (Wood) Nels. & Macbr.
Two-Leaved Solomon's Seal

Perennial herb with creeping rootstock and 2–4-leaved, erect stem, 15–45 cm. Leaves distinctly parallel veined, flaring outward at the heart-shaped base and converging at the tip, 5–20 cm long × 5–10 cm wide. Leafstalks 2–9 cm long. Inflorescence a many-flowered terminal raceme, 3–6 cm long. Stalk with dry bract. Flowers white, 4 petals, 2–3 mm long. Fruit light tan brown to deep red berry, 6 mm in diameter. Seed 3 mm long. *Flowering:* May–July. *Fruiting:* August–January.

Found in riparian locations, moist woods and seepage slopes. From Alaska south to Marin County, California, east to central British Columbia and northern Idaho; up to 1100 m elevation.

115 SMILACINA RACEMOSA (L.) Desf.
False Solomon's Seal

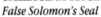

Geophyte (30–100 cm tall), with stout, fleshy rootstock. Leaves finely short-hairy, ovate to oblong lance shaped, mostly pointed at tip, nearly sessile or sessile with a more or less clasping base, 7–20 cm long, 3–10 cm wide. Inflorescence a dense panicle, freely branching with numerous flowers, 3–18 cm long. Flower stalks white, .5–2 mm long. Perianth segments, ovate to lance shaped, white, 1–2 mm long. Filaments distinctly swollen. Stamens 1.5–3 mm long, much broader and longer than perianth segments. Fruit a bright red berry with small, purple spots, 1–3-seeded, 4–7 mm in diameter. *Flowering:* April–July. *Fruiting:* August–October.

Occurs in moist woods and stream banks to open forests from Alaska to California, east to Nova Scotia and south to Georgia, Mississippi, Missouri, Colorado, and Arizona. Below 2000 m elevation.

116   SMILACINA STELLATA   (L.) Desf.
Star Solomon's Seal

Geophyte (30–60 cm tall), with slender, fleshy rootstock (2–4 mm thick). Leaves alternate, in 2 vertical rows or spiral, many-veined or with 3 or 5 veins more prominent, lance shaped to oblong lance shaped, sessile or somewhat clasping, 5–17 cm long, 15–50 mm wide. Terminal raceme 3–10 cm long, of 3–10(20) flowers, usually with a zigzagging, finely hairy, main stalk. Perianth segments creamy white with a light purple central vein, narrowly oblong, 3–7 mm long. Filaments white, slender, twisted. Anthers light yellow. Fruit a greenish yellow berry with dark purple, lengthwise markings, becoming blackish, 6–10 mm in diameter. *Flowering:* April–July. *Fruiting:* August–October.

Found in moist woods, along streams, on rocky well-drained hillsides, often dominating in alluvial flats in half shade. From Alaska to California east to the Atlantic coast.

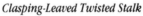

117   STREPTOPUS AMPLEXIFOLIUS   (L.) DC.
Clasping-Leaved Twisted Stalk

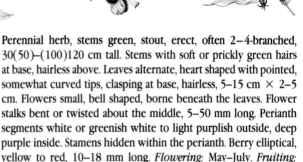

Perennial herb, stems green, stout, erect, often 2–4-branched, 30(50)–(100)120 cm tall. Stems with soft or prickly green hairs at base, hairless above. Leaves alternate, heart shaped with pointed, somewhat curved tips, clasping at base, hairless, 5–15 cm × 2–5 cm. Flowers small, bell shaped, borne beneath the leaves. Flower stalks bent or twisted about the middle, 5–50 mm long. Perianth segments white or greenish white to light purplish outside, deep purple inside. Stamens hidden within the perianth. Berry elliptical, yellow to red, 10–18 mm long. *Flowering:* May–July. *Fruiting:* July–September.

Found in moist forests and on stream banks. From Alaska to California, east through most of Canada and the United States, 300–1800 m elevation.

118 XEROPHYLLUM TENAX (Pursh.) Nutt.
Indian Basket-Grass

Perennial herb, slender, 20–150(180) cm tall. Leaves pale green, ascending, wirelike. Basal leaves densely clumped, narrowly linear, 50–100 cm long, 6 mm wide. Stem leaves abundant, much reduced. Raceme at first flattopped and compact, but elongating and becoming 10–60 cm long. Flowers fragrant, yellowish white. Capsule light brown, 3-valved, 5–7 mm long. *Flowering:* May–August. *Fruiting:* August–October.

Found on open, dry slopes and exposed ridges in the Coast Ranges from British Columbia to Monterey County, California, from the western slope of the Sierra Nevada south to Placer County, California, and in the Rocky Mountains. Below 2000 m elevation. Becoming locally dominant after light forest fires.

LYCOPODIACEAE
Club Moss Family

Habit Perennial herbs with 2 alternating generations, both generations physiologically independent at maturity.

Gametophyte Sexual generation, very minute, not clearly differentiated into roots, stems, and leaves, photosynthetic (green) or mycorrhizal (whitish).

Sporophyte Nonsexual generation, well differentiated into roots, stems, and leaves. It is the most conspicuous generation. Sporangia present in a cone structure or in leaf axils.

Stems Branched, forking always into 2 branches, or arising from a simple axis but never from axillary buds.

Leaves Mostly alternate or opposite, simple, 1-nerved, often overlapping.

Cones Terminal with numerous, crowded, modified leaves subtending sporangia. Sporangia solitary, axillary, and ventral to the modified leaves or grown together with the base of these leaves. Spores numerous, small, spherical, yellow, without elongated bands.

Distribution Only 2 genera, *Lycopodium* and *Phylloglossum*, the latter a single species of Australia, New Zealand, and Tasmania.

119   LYCOPODIUM CLAVATUM L.
Club Moss

Perennial herb. Sporophyte: main stem prostrate or arching, giving rise to scattered, simple or few-branched stems up to 25 cm tall. Leaves crowded in 10 vertical rows, linear to inversely lance shaped, mostly 3–8 mm long and up to 1 mm wide. Erect stems (or some of them) terminating in a well-defined stalk 3–15 cm long, bracts of stalk fewer, paler, thinner but not smaller than leaves of vegetative branches. Cones 1 to several per stalk, 15–70 mm long. Modified leaves bearing sporangia, well differentiated from the foliage leaves, 2–3 mm long and up to 2.5 mm wide, with thin, irregularly toothed or torn margins.

Forming dense masses on soil in moist, coniferous woods and swamps. From Humboldt County, California, to Alaska; Atlantic coast; Eurasia; below 170 m elevation.

MONOTROPACEAE
Indian Pipe Family

Habit   Saprophytes or root parasites, from white to bright red.
Stems   Thick and fleshy or slender and always without leaves except bract-like scales.
Leaves   Reduced to bractlike scales, without chlorophyll, white to bright red.
Inflorescence Solitary or in drooping or flattopped racemes.
Flowers   Bisexual, regular or nearly regular, with bracts. Sepals 2–6, free from the ovary, usually united at least at the base. Petals 3–6 or lacking. Stamens 6–12. Filaments free or united at the base. Anthers attached to filaments by their backs or bases, with 1 or 2 hornlike appendages. Ovary superior, 1–6-celled, 4–6-lobed. Ovules many, inverted and straight.
Fruit   Capsule splitting into 4–6 valves along the midveins of the carpels.
Seeds   Numerous, minute, smooth, often sticky seed coats.
Distribution Mostly in western North America, 12 genera and about 15 species.

Key to MONOTROPACEAE

1 Petals united into a tube. **HEMITOMES**

Stem swollen, fleshy, 3–20 cm. Flowers in a short, terminal, dense spike or corymbiform head, with broad bracts. Corolla tubular to bell shaped, hairy within, white to pink when flowering, dark brown in fruit. Filaments hairy. **HEMITOMES CONGESTUM**

1 Petals separate, not united into a tube. 2

2 Flowers solitary and terminal on unbranched stalks. **MONOTROPA**

Stems usually many, unbranched, clustered, 5–30 cm. Flowers solitary and terminal, nodding when flowering, erect in fruit, waxy white to reddish, aging to black. Filaments hairy. **MONOTROPA UNIFLORA**

2 Flowers in a raceme or dense, headlike raceme. 3

3 Flowers in a raceme. Ovary 3–5-celled below, the ovules attached on a central axis; ovary 1-celled above, the ovules attached on the walls. **HYPOPITYS**

Plants white to yellow to pink, 5–25 cm. Flowers in a raceme, drooping when young, later erect. Petals usually hairy on both surfaces. Filaments and style hairy, stigma with downward-pointing hairs on the margin. **HYPOPITYS MONOTROPA**

This family Monotropaceae is often considered as part of the family Pyrolaceae (Munz) or of the family Ericaceae (Hitchcock), not as a separate family. Following Hutchinson, I consider it a separate family.

3   Flowers in a dense, clustered, spikelike raceme. Ovary 1-celled with the ovules attached on the walls.   **PLEURICOSPORA**

Plants white to yellow to brown, 3–12(25) cm. Flowers crowded in a terminal, spikelike raceme. Petals and filaments not noticeably hairy.   **PLEURICOSPORA FIMBRIOLATA**

120   HEMITOMES CONGESTUM   Gray
Hemitomes, Gnome Plant, Coneflower

Saprophytic, pinkish to white herb, fleshy, swollen stem generally densely clustered, 3–20 cm tall. Leaves ovate, rounded at the tip, irregular at the margins. Flowers in short, terminal, dense spike or corymbose head, with broad bracts. Bracts brown tipped in full bloom. Calyx and corolla similar, pinkish, often with a violet hue. Petals united into a tube. Corolla often unequally lobed, 10–20 mm long. Fruit whitish, shiny, juicy, amidst dried bracts and persistent sepals. *Flowering:* May–August. *Fruiting:* September–November.

Found in deep humus in dense conifer forests; rather infrequent; from the Olympic Peninsula, Washington, south to Monterey County, California. Below 800 m elevation.

121   HYPOPITYS MONOTROPA   L.
American Pinesap

Herb, yellowish to pinkish, finely hairy, 5–30 cm tall. Stems single or clustered, 10–30 cm long. Leaves scalelike, oblong-ovate, 5–8 mm long. Flower stalks 3–6 mm long. Flowers in a raceme drooping when young, later erect. Sepals yellowish white, raggedly fringed, 5–10 mm long. Petals yellowish to reddish white, erect, overlapping, oblong to wedge shaped, raggedly fringed, 10–18 mm long. Anthers purple brown, oval, about 1 mm long. Ovary 3–5-celled below, the ovules attached to a central axis, ovary 1-celled above, the ovules attached on the walls. Fruit a capsule, 4–8 mm in diameter. *Flowering:* May–August. *Fruiting:* July–September.

Found in moist woods in deep humus, especially in dense coniferous forests. British Columbia south to Mendocino County, California; east to Atlantic coast; Europe; at 200–2400 m elevation.

Plate I

002 ACER MACROPHYLLUM
Big-Leaf Maple

003 ADIANTUM PEDATUM
Maidenhair Fern, Five-Finger Fern

013 ARALIA CALIFORNICA
California Spikenard

Plate II

014   ASARUM CAUDATUM
Wild Ginger

022   ACHILLEA BOREALIS var. CALIFORNICA
Yarrow

048   BLECHNUM SPICANT
Deer Fern

053   LONICERA INVOLUCRATA
Black Twinberry

Plate III

054 SAMBUCUS CALLICARPA
Coast Red Elderberry

059 MARAH OREGANUS
Coastal Manroot, Western Wild Cucumber

063 PTERIDIUM AQUILINUM
Western Bracken Fern

065 EQUISETUM TELMATEIA
Giant Horsetail

Plate IV

066 ARBUTUS MENZIESII
Madrone

068 GAULTHERIA SHALLON
Salal

072 LATHYRUS VESTITUS
Common Pacific Pea

082 LITHOCARPUS DENSIFLORA
Tan Oak, Tanbark Oak

Plate V

090 **RIBES SANGUINEUM**
Red Flowering Currant, Blood Currant

094 **HYDROPHYLLUM TENUIPES**
Pacific Waterleaf

097 **IRIS DOUGLASIANA**
Douglas's Iris

Plate VI

150 VANCOUVERIA HEXANDRA
Inside-Out Flower

152 POLYGALA CALIFORNICA
California Milkwort, Polygala

155 POLYPODIUM SCOULERI
Leather Fern

168 FRAGARIA CALIFORNICA
California Strawberry

Plate VII

170   OSMARONIA CERASIFORMIS
Oso Berry, Indian Plum

178   RUBUS URSINUS
Pacific Blackberry

187   MITELLA CAULESCENS
Star-Shaped Miterwort

191   TOLMIEA MENZIESII   *Thousand Mothers,*
Youth-on-Age, Pig-a-Back Plant

Plate VIII

199 SYNTHYRIS RENIFORMIS
Round-Leaved Synthyris, Snow-Queen

202 TAXUS BREVIFOLIA
Western Yew

209 VACCINIUM OVATUM
Huckleberry

122 MONOTROPA UNIFLORA L.
Indian Pipe

Plant with a cluster of flowering stems, 5–30 cm tall, waxy white to reddish, blackening with age. Leaves scalelike, 5–12 mm long. Flower narrowly bell shaped. Sepals 2–4, oblong, more or less fringed with hairs near base. Petals 5 or 6, 15–20 mm long, more or less hairy within. Stamens white. Pistil light yellow. Fruit a capsule, 10–15 mm long. *Flowering:* June–August. *Fruiting:* August–October.

Found in deep, shaded, damp conifer woods from Alaska to Humboldt County, California, east to the Atlantic coast; Asia. Below 800 m elevation.

123 PLEURICOSPORA FIMBRIOLATA Gray
Fringed Pinesap

Saprophyte, pinkish to white, stout, 3–12(25) cm, tall, usually barely emerging above the duff. Leaves ovate or lance-ovate, entire to ragged or fringed at the margins, 8–12 mm long. Flowers subtended by slightly shorter bracts. Sepals oblong-ovate, 5–10 mm long. Petals oblong, entire to fringed at the margins but without hairs on the inside, 8–12 mm long. Ovary 1-celled. Fruit a white berry, drying to blackish. *Flowering:* June–August. *Fruiting:* July–September.

Found in dry, deep humus in dense coniferous forests from the Sierra Nevada to northwestern California and from the western side of the Cascades to the Olympic Mountains of Washington; 100–2800 m elevation.

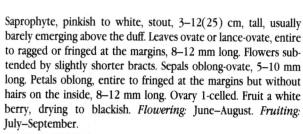

MYRICACEAE
Sweet Gale (Wax Myrtle) Family

Habit	Trees or shrubs, small, with deciduous or evergreen foliage.
Leaves	Deciduous or evergreen, resin dotted, often fragrant, without stipules, alternate, simple.
Inflorescence	Both male and female flowers in short, scaly catkins, each borne either on different branches of the same tree or on different trees.
Flowers	Male flowers, stamens 2–16 but usually 4–8, filaments short, distinct or united, anthers 2-celled, ovate, opening spontaneously by a longitudinal slit when ripe. Female flowers with a solitary, 1-celled ovary, subtended by 2–8 bractlets, ovule 1, erect, styles 2, linear.
Fruit	Drupe, small, oblong, surrounded by a fleshy, often waxy coating.
Seeds	Erect without endosperm.
Distribution	Widely distributed through the temperate and tropical regions, 2 genera and about 40 species.
Uses	Economically important as handsome ornamentals, food plants, and wood; dried leaves used as spice for food.

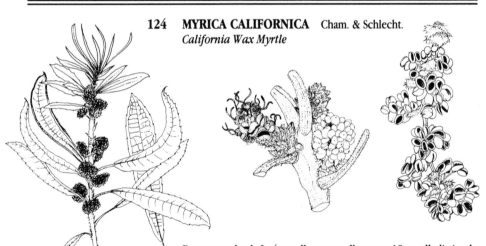

124   MYRICA CALIFORNICA   Cham. & Schlecht.
California Wax Myrtle

Evergreen shrub 2–4 m tall, or a small tree to 18 m tall, distinctly aromatic. Bark smooth, thin, gray or light brown. Leaves persistent, 5–10 cm long, without hairs, thick, oblong, margins remotely sawtoothed or nearly entire. Male and female catkins clustered and borne on different branches of the same tree. Male bracts light brown, papery, with irregularly frizzled margins. Female bracts greenish. Drupe brownish purple, 6–8 mm in diameter, covered with a whitish wax. *Flowering:* March–April. *Fruiting:* June–August.

In canyons and on moist slopes from the Santa Monica Mountains, California, to Washington, always near the Pacific Ocean, elevation below 170 m. California wax myrtle is an important species in the fixation of sand dunes; it has a symbiotic relationship with nitrogen-fixing bacteria by way of root nodules.

ONAGRACEAE
Evening Primrose Family

Habit — Herbs, shrubs, or trees.

Roots — Generally with well-developed taproots.

Leaves — Simple, alternate or opposite. Stipules absent or glandular.

Inflorescence — Flowers axillary or in terminal racemes or bracteate spikes.

Flowers — Bisexual, mostly symmetrical, inferior. Sepals and petals free (*Circaea*) or united (*Epilobium, Oenothera*). Petals united, floral tube fused to ovary and usually prolonged beyond the ovary. Sepals 4, sometimes 2, 5, 6. Petals 4, sometimes 2, 5, 6, inserted at summit of floral tube. Stamens as many or twice as many as petals, borne at summit of floral tube. Style 1, slender, stigma 2–4-lobed or disk shaped, club shaped, or round. Ovary 2–4-celled. Pollen grains often connected by cobwebby threads.

Fruit — Capsule splitting open longitudinally, or berry, or nutlike and non-splitting.

Seeds — Without endosperm, 1–many.

Distribution — About 20 genera, 650 species primarily in temperate and subtropical regions.

Key to ONAGRACEAE

1   Sepals, petals, and anthers 2. Fruit nutlike and nonsplitting. Leaves ovate to roundish, sometimes more or less heart shaped at the base. **CIRCAEA ALPINA var. PACIFICA**

1   Sepals and petals 4. Anthers 8. Fruit a capsule splitting open lengthwise. Leaves lance shaped or elliptic to inversely lance shaped, rounded, or tapered at base.   **2**

2   Petals white to yellow, or rose, aging to reddish or purplish. Sepals reflexed when in bloom. Floral tube greatly prolonged beyond the ovary. Seed not tufted by hairs at one end.   **OENOTHERA**

Flowers yellow to orange. Leaf margins wavy to toothed, lance shaped on stalks 5–10 cm long. Stem leaves nearly sessile, alternate. **OENOTHERA HOOKERI ssp. WOLFII**

2   Petals pink purple, white, or sometimes yellow, but not red. Sepals not reflexed when in bloom. Floral tube short or only slightly prolonged beyond the ovary. Seed tufted with hairs at one end. **EPILOBIUM**   **3**

3   Leaves alternate, lance shaped, sessile or nearly so. Stem mostly simple. Sepals 8–12 mm long. Petals lilac purple, rose, rarely white, 8–18 mm long.   **EPILOBIUM ANGUSTIFOLIUM**

3   Leaves ovate to elliptic-lance shaped, minutely sawtoothed, on very short, flat stalks. Upper stem freely branched. Sepals 2 mm long. Petals white or pale to more or less reddish, 3–4 mm long. **EPILOBIUM ADENOCAULON**

125   CIRCAEA ALPINA L. var. PACIFICA
(Asch. & Magnus) Jones
Small Pacific Enchanter's Nightshade

Perennial herb with tuberous rootstock. Stem simple, 20–40 cm tall, generally with tiny, sharp hairs. Leaves ovate to heart shaped, margin entire, minutely toothed or wavy. Racemes with tiny white to pink flowers. Petals 2, notched. Sepals 2, reflexed. Stamens 2. Ovary 1- or 2-celled. Fruit a capsule, obovoid, nutlike, nonsplitting, 1–2 mm long. Seed soft, white. *Flowering:* May–August. *Fruiting:* July–September.

In the San Bernardino Mountains and the Sierra Nevada and in the Coast Ranges from Marin County, California, north to British Columbia and the Rocky Mountains. Below 2700 m elevation.

126   EPILOBIUM ADENOCAULON   Hausskn.
Northern Willow Herb

Perennial herb overwintering as leaf rosettes. Stem erect, 30–100 cm tall. Simple below, branched above. Leaves ovate to lance shaped, minutely sawtoothed. Flowers axillary and solitary, 3–4 mm long. Petals 4, white to red with purple veins. Sepals 4, silvery green, curly, 2 mm. Petals white to pale red, 3–4 mm. Stamens 8, alternately long and short, white. Capsule reddish, slender, 4–6 cm long. Seeds many, obovoid, with whitish tuft of hairs, ribbed. *Flowering:* July–September. *Fruiting:* July–October.

In moist places, common in cutover forest areas. Throughout mountains of California to Alaska and in Atlantic states; below 3700 m elevation.

127 EPILOBIUM ANGUSTIFOLIUM L.
Common Fireweed

Perennial herb with creeping rootstock, 1–3 m tall. Stem hairy but hairless at base. Leaves lance shaped, nearly sessile, alternate with entire margin paler beneath. Long, terminal raceme with many flowers and small bracts. Perianth rose to purple, rarely white, petals with claws. Stamens 8, shorter than petals. Style hairy at base, stigma lobes long and slender. Seed 1–1.5 mm long with hairy tuft. *Flowering:* July–September. *Fruiting:* September–October.

Following disturbances, burns, and clearings in moist sites, often locally dominant. From San Diego County, California, north in coastal zones to Alaska, east to the Atlantic coast; Eurasia; at elevations below 3000 m.

128 OENOTHERA HOOKERI Torr. & Gray
ssp. WOLFII Munz
Hooker's Evening-Primrose

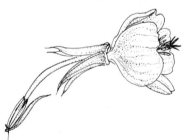

Annual or biennial herb with rosette leaves at base. Stem ascending, stout, hairy, often red. Leaves inversely lance shaped, hairy with wavy to toothed margin. Inflorescence stalk bearing axillary flowers subtended by bracts. Petals 4, yellow to orange red, 25–40 mm long, notched. Sepals 4, red, reflexed. Stigma 4- or 5-lobed. Stamens 8. Capsule long, slender, hairy, naked at maturity. Seed angled. *Flowering:* June–September. *Fruiting:* August–October.

In moist, open places and along roadsides. In the Coast Ranges from Del Norte and Trinity counties to San Luis Obispo County, California.

ORCHIDACEAE
Orchid Family

Habit	Perennial herbs or vines to semishrubs, epiphytic, sometimes saprophytic and without green leaves.
Roots	Rhizomes corallike, roots fibrous to fleshy or bulbous.
Leaves	Alternate and often arranged in 2 vertical rows, simple, sheathing, sometimes reduced to scales.
Inflorescence	Flowers in racemes, spikes, or panicles, sometimes solitary.
Flowers	Bisexual, very rarely unisexual, inverted, irregular, inferior, with bracts, 3-parted. Calyx of 3 sepals, either green or brightly colored and petallike. Corolla of 3 petals usually highly colored, the upper 1 appearing as the lower because of a 180 degree twist in the ovary. Lower petal is often elaborately modified into a lip. It may be a rather simple structure or heavily modified into a sac or spur. The 2 upper petals are sometimes more or less united to the upper sepal, forming a slight to prominent hood. Stamens more or less completely fused with the style and stigmas to form a short to very prominent structure, the column. Fertile anthers usually 1, but occasionally 2, very rarely 3, the third sometimes sterile and reduced to a staminode. Pollen mostly in 2s or 4s, the masses waxy or powdery, attached at the base to a sticky gland. May have a sterile taillike portion, the caudicle. Ovary inferior, usually long and sometimes twisted, 1- or 3-celled. Ovules numerous, on 3 parietal placentae. Stigma often appears as a shallow depression on the inner side of the column. All 3 stigmas may be fertile, but more commonly the 2 lateral ones are fertile and the third modified into a small sterile outgrowth or beak. A portion of this beak may be further modified into a sticky disk to which the pollinia are attached.
Fruit	Capsule, 3-valved, usually dry, opening with longitudinal slits.
Seeds	Numerous minute, dry and winged, embryo minute, undifferentiated. Endosperm lacking. Embryo fleshy.
Distribution	About 450 genera and over 15,000 species. Widespread and abundant in the tropics, becoming increasingly less common in cool temperate and subarctic regions.
Uses	Source of numerous outstanding ornamentals; hybrids common in cultivation; fruit of a genus in this family source of vanilla.

Key to ORCHIDACEAE

1　Plants lacking green foliage, saprophytic. Leaves reduced, scalelike along stem. Rootstocks much thickened, branched, shortened, corallike, not bulblike.　　　　**2**

1　Plants with green foliage, not saprophytic. Leaves not reduced, scalelike. Rootstocks fleshy, slender or thickened, or swollen to bulblike.　　　　**4**

2 Stems and flowers reddish, brownish, purplish, or yellowish. Capsule drooping, 10–25 mm long.   **CORALLORHIZA**   **3**

2 Stems and flowers ghostly white, aging to brown. Capsule erect, 10–15 mm long.   **EBUROPHYTON**

Raceme 5–20-flowered. Sepals and petals similar, mostly elliptic-lance shaped, 10–20 mm long. Lip somewhat shorter, bent abruptly downward. Column with a single, 2-celled anther.   **EBUROPHYTON AUSTINAE**

3 Perianth showy, yellowish with distinct purple stripes. Lip similar, slightly larger, entire, purple striped, spur absent.   **CORALLORHIZA STRIATA**

3 Perianth smaller, not striped. Lip much larger than other perianth, parts prominently 3-lobed, white, often with dark purple spots. Spur prominent, yellow.   **CORALLORHIZA MACULATA**

4 Flowers 1 to occasionally 2 or 3 per plant. Leaf 1, basal, with elongated stalk. Rootstock often swollen, bulblike, solid, roots slender and long or short and corallike.   **CALYPSO**

Flower 1, terminal. Leaf 1, rounded or nearly heart shaped at base, 25–35 mm long. Leafstalk 15–50 mm long. Sepals and petals erect or spreading, magenta crimson, rarely white. Lip spotted red purple with a whitish pouch and marked with purple.   **CALYPSO BULBOSA**

4 Flowers many, always more than 1, in a spike or raceme. Leaves 2 or more, basal or along the stem, sessile or nearly so. Rootstock fibrous or fleshy, long, slender or tuberous, not corallike.   **5**

5 Flowers without an elongated spur at base of lip, not fragrant. Mature basal leaves withering at time of flowering. Stem arising from large, elongated, naked tuber, shriveling at time of flowering. Column with 2 anthers.   **PIPERIA**   **6**

5 Flowers without an elongated spur at base of lip, not fragrant. Mature leaves not withering at time of flowering. Stem not arising from tubers. Column with 1 anther.   **7**

6 Raceme slender. Spurs of most flowers perpendicular to and crossing the main axis of the inflorescence. Flower yellowish green to whitish green or white. Capsule ellipsoid 4.5–6.5 mm long.   **PIPERIA TRANSVERSA**

6 Raceme tall and robust to short and stout. Spurs extending downward along the main axis and not horizontal. Flower white except the dark green midnerve of the sepals and lateral petals. Capsule narrowly cylindrical, 5–10 mm long.   **PIPERIA ELEGANS**

7 Raceme short stalked. Leaves 2, opposite, about at the middle of the slender stem.   **LISTERA**

Flower pale green to purplish green, the lower lip elongated and cleft one-half to three-fifths its length into linear-lance-shaped, long-

pointed lobes. Capsule nearly spherical-ovoid.   **LISTERA COR-
DATA**

7   Raceme spikelike, sessile or nearly so. Leaves more than 2, basal,
     alternate, or along the stem.   **8**

8   Leaves basal, oblong-ovate, margin undulating, stalks winged and
     broad. Raceme closely many-flowered, densely clustered with flow-
     ers.   **GOODYERA**

     Flower pale greenish white, hairy. Capsule roundish-elliptic.
     GOODYERA OBLONGIFOLIA

8   Leaves along the stem, not basal, the lower ovate, upper lance
     shaped, gradually becoming reduced, sessile. Raceme loosely sev-
     eral-flowered.   **EPIPACTIS**

     Flowers coppery green, lightly brownish parallel veined. Capsule
     ellipsoid to cylindrical.   **EPIPACTIS GIGANTEA**

129   **CALYPSO BULBOSA**   (L.) Oakes
      Calypso

Perennial herb with a single, basal leaf 25–35 mm long and a single
terminal flower. Stem arising from a bulblike rootstock, smooth,
5–25 cm long. Flower solitary, 15–50 mm. Sepals 10–25 mm, dark
rose, erect and spreading, upper 2 petals same as sepals. Lower
petal a pouchlike lip 10 mm wide, spotted purple with whitish
mottled sac, hairs yellowish. Fruit erect, purple, cylindrical capsule,
1 cm. *Flowering:* March–July. *Fruiting:* July–August.

Distributed from Marin County to Del Norte and Siskiyou counties,
California, to Alaska; northern Midwest across Michigan to Atlantic
coast; Eurasia; preferring bogs or leaf mold in rich woods. In dense,
conifer forests of Pacific coast. Rarely, almost-white flowers are
found.

130 CORALLORHIZA MACULATA Raf.
Spotted Coral Root

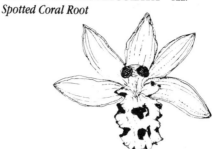

Perennial saprophyte, with short, erect stem 20–70 cm high, usually purplish but often yellow, ending in a raceme. Whitish scalelike leaves, bracts minute. Sepals linear-lance shaped, reddish purple (pale yellow). Petals converging at base, lance-oblong to oblong-elliptic. Lip white, spotted and lined with crimson, spur prominent, yellowish. Seed 2-winged, minute. *Flowering:* June–July. *Fruiting:* July–August.

Found in mountains from San Diego County north through the Sierra Nevada and Coastal Ranges to British Columbia; Newfoundland; North Carolina; Guatemala. Below 3000 m elevation, in dense mesic to dry redwood forests.

131 CORALLORHIZA STRIATA Lindl.
Striped Coral Root

Perennial saprophyte, 15–50 cm tall with an erect stem and sheathing leaves, white to purple leading to terminal raceme 5–15 cm; 7–30 flowers pinkish yellow to white, distinctly tinged and striped with purple. Sepals oblong-elliptic to linear-lance shaped, 6–17 mm, swollen at base. Petals linear-oblong to obovate-elliptic, 6–15 mm long. Lip 6–12 mm long, white with purple veins, broadly elliptic. Fruit a capsule, 6-ribbed, purple, elliptical, 12–15 mm. Seed oval with ends winged. *Flowering:* April–July. *Fruiting:* July–August.

Prefers rich, shaded woods, such as coniferous, mixed, deciduous or redwood forests. Common in Coast Ranges from Santa Cruz Mountains north, Sierras north from Sierra County, California, to Washington; east to Quebec, Wyoming, Michigan, Utah, Nuevo León, Mexico, and Texas. Below 2500 m elevation.

132   EBUROPHYTON AUSTINAE   (Gray) Heller
Phantom Orchid

Saprophyte with white to beige stout stem 20–50 cm tall, 2–5 bractlike leaves, sheathed except upper 1 or 2, 2–4 cm. Raceme 5–15 cm with 5–20 cream-colored flowers, sepals and petals mostly elliptic-lance shaped, 10–20 mm, lower lip shorter with terminal lobe 5 mm, bent downward, bright yellow on upper margin. Fruit an erect, oblong capsule, 10–15 mm. Seed ovate winged at both ends. *Flowering:* May–July. *Fruiting:* July–August.

Prefers dry to moist, densely forested slopes of montane and coniferous forests. Rare in the redwood forests. Ranges from Fresno County, California, north to the western Sierra Nevada; Monterey County, California, north in the Coast Ranges to Washington and Idaho. Also in the San Bernardino Mountains below 2000 m elevation.

133   EPIPACTIS GIGANTEA   Dougl.
False Lady's-Slipper

Perennial with spreading rootstock and many clumped, erect, leafy stems and showy flowers. Stem leaves ovate, upper lance shaped, gradually reduced. Flowers usually arranged as a 1-sided raceme. Sepals coppery green and lightly brownish veined. Petals similar to sepals, but thinner, venation more brownish purple, the sac with prominent, raised, purplish ridges leading to the base. *Flowering:* April–August. *Fruiting:* August–September.

Found on rocky stream banks, lake margins, and around springs and spring areas, always at water's edge. From lower California to British Columbia, South Dakota, Montana, Texas, below 2500 m elevation.

134 GOODYERA OBLONGIFOLIA Raf.
Green-Leaved Rattlesnake Orchid

Low, perennial herb with prominent, white-veined, mottled, fleshy, basal leaves. Leaves oblong-ovate, thickish, dark green, usually somewhat whitish, mottled or striped, white along midrib. Roots short, fleshy, whitish. Stem stout, with 2–4 small, membranous, whitish, sheathing bracts, glandular-soft, straight haired. Spikelike raceme with many, often spiraled, nearly sessile flowers. Flower usually pale greenish white, hairy. Upper sepal converging with fused lateral petals, forming a forward-pointed hood. *Flowering:* July–August. *Fruiting:* August–September.

From Alaska to Nova Scotia, south in Coast Ranges to Marin County, California, and the Sierra Nevada to Mariposa County, California, below 1700 m elevation.

135 LISTERA CORDATA R. Br.
Heart-Leaved Twayblade

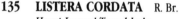
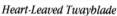

Perennial herb 10–25 cm tall with slender, annual stem without hairs except hairy just above the leaves. Leaves opposite, broadly oval-heart shaped to triangular-rounded but short tipped, 1–4 cm long, nearly as broad. Raceme 3–20-flowered with bracts 1.5 cm, flowers borne on stalks 1–4 cm long, pale green to purplish green. Sepals spreading, upper ovate-triangular, 2.5–4 mm, arched forward; lower pair narrower, slightly oblique. Petals 2–4.5 mm long, oblong to linear-elliptic, lower one 8–11 mm, linear-lance shaped, undivided portion with hard knobs extending to prominent, linear-awl shaped teeth. Fruit an oval, hairless capsule 4 mm. Seed oval-ovate winged. *Flowering:* June–August. *Fruiting:* August–September.

Prefers damp, mossy places along streams and bogs, sometimes on dry, open slopes. Ranges from Humboldt County, California, to Alaska; Atlantic coast; and Eurasia.

136   PIPERIA ELEGANS   (Lindl.) Rydb.
Wood Rein Orchid

Perennial herb, 13–70 cm high with 2–5 basal leaves. Leaves often shiny, rounded to pointed, 5–15(20) cm long. Stem leaves reduced to 4–17 bracts, on upper one-half to one-third of stem. Raceme 10–30 cm long, moderately to densely flowered, sometimes thick and congested. Flowers white except for a dark green midnerve, fragrant. Upper sepals oval-blunt to point erect, lateral oval-elliptic to oblong-lance shaped, 3–6 mm × 2–3 mm. Petals fleshy, erect, spreading, obtuse, oval-lance to oblong-lance shaped, 3–6 mm long. Lip lance shaped, earlike appendages at base. Capsule light brown with darker ribs. *Flowering:* May–early October. *Fruiting:* October–November.

Prefers dry, inland, open woods with raw humus layers. From southwestern British Columbia to San Diego County, California; from the Sierras to the coast.

137   PIPERIA TRANSVERSA   Suksd.
Rein Orchid

Perennial herb, 16–31 cm high with basal leaves, and a grayish brown tuber. Leaves lance shaped to inversely lance shaped. Bracts 4–6, evenly distributed or concentrated on upper half of stem. Flower yellowish green to whitish green or white, developing distinct, sweetish, musk fragrance at dusk and evening. Upper sepals lance shaped to ovate, pointed to obtuse, lateral sepals oblong-lance shaped, slightly oblique, reflexed spreading nerve obvious. Petals fleshy, oblong to oblong-lance shaped to ovate-elliptic. Capsule brown, 4–7 mm long. *Flowering:* late May–mid-August. *Fruiting:* August–September.

Found mostly in dry, open woods. From Vancouver Island and British Columbia south to Santa Cruz County, California, along the Coast Ranges.

OROBANCHACEAE
Broomrape Family

Habit	Fleshy herbs, annual or perennial, root parasites without green foliage.
Roots	Root parasites, often causing the host root to swell in the point of attachment and the host root to die off beyond the swelling.
Stems	Erect, simple or branched, usually yellowish or purple.
Leaves	Reduced to scales, alternate, appressed to the main stem.
Inflorescence	Flowers solitary, stalked or sessile, in terminal racemes or spikes with bracts.
Flowers	Bisexual, usually irregular. Sepals 4 or 5, united but deeply cleft or split to the base on 1 or both sides, free from the ovary. Petals united into tube, more or less irregular, the floral tube more or less 2-lipped and 4 or 5 lobed, usually with a pair of small, basal bracts. Stamens 4 in 2 pairs of unequal length, slender, inserted on the tube formed by the petals, a rudimentary fifth stamen sometimes present, filaments slender, anthers 2-celled, the pollen sacs parallel and equal. Ovary superior, 1-celled, with 4 placentae attached to the wall, ovules numerous, style slender, stigma disk shaped or broadly 2–4 lobed.
Fruit	Capsule 1-celled, 2- or 4-valved, splitting open from the top downward.
Seeds	Numerous, with a network of wrinkles or stripes on seed coat.
Distribution	Wide geographical distribution, 14 genera and over 200 species.

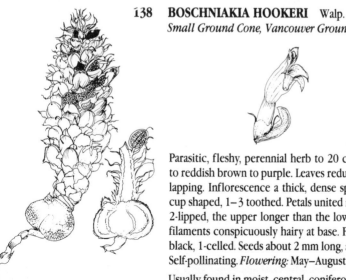

138 BOSCHNIAKIA HOOKERI Walp.
Small Ground Cone, Vancouver Ground Cone

Parasitic, fleshy, perennial herb to 20 cm tall. Entire plant yellow to reddish brown to purple. Leaves reduced to scales, closely overlapping. Inflorescence a thick, dense spike, 7–15 cm long. Calyx cup shaped, 1–3 toothed. Petals united into tube, 10–15 mm long, 2-lipped, the upper longer than the lower. Anthers sparsely hairy, filaments conspicuously hairy at base. Fruit a capsule, dark purple black, 1-celled. Seeds about 2 mm long, angled, dark yellow brown. Self-pollinating. *Flowering:* May–August. *Fruiting:* July–September.

Usually found in moist, central, coniferous forests as a root parasite of madrone (*Arbutus menziesii*) and salal (*Gaultheria shallon*) from northern British Columbia to Marin County, California.

OXALIDACEAE
Wood Sorrel (Oxalis) Family

Habit	Herbs to shrubs or trees, annual or perennial, with oxalic acid sap.
Underground Parts	Rootstocks or scaly bulbs.
Stems	Leafy or stemless or essentially so.
Leaves	Usually compound with 3 obovate or inversely heart-shaped leaflets. Leaves alternate or the basal leaves opposite. Stipules commonly present as thin, dry margins to the bases of the leafstalks.
Inflorescence	Umbellike or forking cymes or rarely solitary on mostly rather long stalks.
Flowers	Bisexual, regular. Sepals 5. Petals 5, sometimes somewhat united at base, white, purple, or yellow. Stamens 10–15, the outer 5 opposite the petals, filaments joined near base and at least some with basal, glandlike appendages. Ovary superior, 5-celled, 2 to many ovules per cell. Styles 5, separate or united. Stigmas club shaped or stigma slightly split to about the middle into 2 stigmas.
Fruit	Capsule or berrylike, spherical or columnar, splitting longitudinally through the middle of the back of the fruit wall between the partitions into the cavity.
Seeds	Embryo straight, endosperm fleshy.
Distribution	About 10 genera and over 500 species widely spread in temperate and tropical regions.

139   OXALIS OREGANA   Nutt.
Redwood Sorrel

Perennial with short, reduced stem. Rootstocks branching, scaly, slender, and creeping. Leaves long stalked, compound, stalks 5–17 cm long; leaflets 3, broadly inversely heart shaped, hairless and green above, deep purple and long haired beneath. Flower stalks shaggy haired, 5–25 mm long, flower solitary, subtended by 2 bracts. Sepals 5; petals 5, white or pink, often purple veined, 8–20 mm long. Capsule round-ovoid, 7–8 mm long. Seeds white, 1–3 mm long. *Flowering:* February–December. *Fruiting:* September–December.

Often forming solid carpets in dense redwood forests, on seepage slopes, and on alluvial terraces. Found in shady woods from western Washington to Monterey County, California, from the coast to about 1000 m elevation.

PHILADELPHIACEAE
Hydrangea (Syringa) Family

Habit   Shrubs or subshrubs, rarely small trees (.5–2 m).

Stems   Erect, woody or twining, creeping. Branches opposite.

Leaves   Opposite or whorled, rarely alternate, toothed, sometimes 3-nerved from the base, usually deciduous, short stalked. Stipules absent.

Inflorescence   Flowers in terminal racemes, cymes, or heads, rarely solitary.

Flowers   Bisexual, or some plants with both bisexual and unisexual flowers. Sepals united, forming a tube fused to the ovary, rarely free from it. Calyx lobes 4–6, overlapping or meeting without overlapping. Petals 5–7, contorted, overlapping, or meeting without overlapping, free, mostly white. Stamens 4 to twice the number of petals. Filaments sometimes lobed or toothed, free or united at base. Anthers short, 2-celled. Ovary superior to inferior, 3–5-celled. Styles 1–7, free or nearly so, rarely united. Ovules numerous, attached centrally or, rarely, along the walls, or solitary and pendulous.

Fruit   Capsule, splitting through the cells or, rarely, a berry or follicle.

Seeds   Small, with fleshy endosperm and small, straight embryo.

Distribution   From southern Europe to eastern Asia; North America; Philippines, New Guinea. About 12 genera and 75 species of the subtropics and North Temperate Zone; several genera endemic to the southwestern United States.

Uses   Some genera such as *Hydrangea* and *Philadelphus* considered choice ornamental shrubs.

---

140   **WHIPPLEA MODESTA**   Torr.
Yerba de Selva

Semiwoody plants, trailing and freely rooting with semievergreen foliage. Surface roots often forming dense mats. Branches mostly opposite. Leaves opposite, almost sessile, ovate to elliptical and coarsely hairy with remotely sawtoothed margins. Inflorescence a terminal to open panicle with 5–10 bisexual flowers. Petals 5 or 6, white. Stamens 10–12, whitish. Fruit a leathery, black capsule. *Flowering:* April–June. *Fruiting:* June–September.

Often forming dense mats on dry, rocky sites in open to light forests from the Olympic Peninsula, Washington, to Monterey County, California. Below 1500 m elevation.

PINACEAE
Pine Family

Habit Resinous, mostly evergreen, coniferous trees, sometimes shrubs, with linear, needlelike, spirally arranged, solitary or bundled leaves.

Cones Stamens and ovules in different cones on the same tree, surrounded at base by persistent bud scales. Staminate cones with many spirally arranged stamens, each having 2 pollen sacs beneath, the cones drying and falling soon after flowering. Ovulate cones with spirally arranged scales, each of which is subtended by a bract. Ovules naked, 2 at base of each scale, hanging.

Fruit A woody cone, maturing in 1–3 years.

Seeds Usually bearing a terminal wing made of tissue from the surface parts of the cone scale.

Distribution About 9 genera and 200 species, widely distributed.

Uses Of great economic importance as timber trees and source of resinous compounds.

Key to PINACEAE

1 Needles bunched into fascicles of 2 or 3.   **PINUS**   2

1 Needles borne singly.   3

2 Needles 2 per fascicle, dark yellow green, 10–15 cm long. Mature cones sessile, 5–7 cm long.   **PINUS MURICATA**

2 Needles 3 per fascicle, pale yellow green, 8–17 cm long. Mature cones short stalked, 7–15 cm long.   **PINUS ATTENUATA**

3 Cones erect. Scales falling at maturity leaving a naked axis on the branchlet. Terminal buds blunt, enveloped in resin.   **ABIES**

Bracts of the cones hidden, narrowed into a point. Cones oblong, 12–18 cm long, 3–4 cm thick, green. Needles 2-ranked, notched at the tip, forming flat sprays, glossy dark green above, with white bands of stomates beneath.   **ABIES GRANDIS**

3 Cones hanging. Scales persistent, falling with the cone. Terminal buds distinctly pointed, not enveloped in resin.   4

4 Bracts extending conspicuously beyond the cone scales, prominently 3-cleft. Needles without woody bases, leaving the branchlets smooth on falling. Needles persistent for several weeks on cut branches.   **PSEUDOTSUGA**

Cones 5–8 cm long, the scales flexible. Needles rounded at the tip, usually spreading in all directions, or turned upward.   **PSEUDOTSUGA MENZIESII**

4 Bracts concealed by the cone scales. Branchlets roughened by the persistent, woody needle bases. Needles deciduous in a few days if the branch is cut.   5

5   Needles narrowed rather gradually (but not greatly) to the woody stalklike bases, square in cross section or slightly flattened. Stomates on the upper surface, lower surface not much whiter. Needles prickly and pungent. Top of tree erect. **PICEA**

Needles flattened, stiff, and prickly pointed. Bark divided into thin, loose, red brown scales. Cones soft, papery-woody, yellow to reddish brown, aging to brown, narrowly oblong-ovoid, 5–10 cm long. Cone scales ovate, irregularly toothed. **PICEA SITCHENSIS**

5   Needles abruptly narrowed to a short, slender stalk, flattened in cross section. Stomates in white bands under the needles, underside much paler than top surface. Needles not prickly and not pungent. Top of tree often distinctly drooping. **TSUGA**

Needles flat, 2-ranked, grooved on the upper surface, rounded at the tip, with whitish bands of stomates below but not above. Cones oblong-oval, 20–25 mm long. **TSUGA HETEROPHYLLA**

141   **ABIES GRANDIS**   (Dougl.) Lindl.
Grand Fir, Lowland White Fir

Tall, evergreen tree, 50–90 m, with straight, massive bole and flat, rounded crown at maturity and with distinct whorls of horizontally spreading branches. Bark whitish to grayish brown, thin, smooth and checkered, flaking. Needles 20–50 mm, flat, spreading, glossy green, blunt or notched at tip. Male conelet crowded densely near branch tips, yellowish brown. Female cone erect, yellowish green, 50–110 mm. Seeds olive brown, triangularly pointed with large wing. *Flowering:* April–June. *Fruiting:* September–November.

Aggressive colonizer of partly shaded to small forest openings. Prefers moist hillsides and alluvial, sandy flood plains, usually in mixed second-growth hardwood, conifer forests. From Vancouver Island on both sides of the Cascades, south to Sonoma County, California, up to 1000 m elevation.

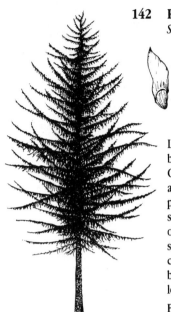

142   PICEA SITCHENSIS   (Bong.) Carr.
Sitka Spruce

Large, forest tree up to 65 m tall. Bark thin, dark red brown to gray brown to grayish purple, deciduous in small, roundish scales. Crown pointed even in old age, with drooping, large branches with ascending tips. Needles light green to bluish green, very stiff, sharp pointed, spreading from all sides of branches, 15–25 mm long, somewhat flattened in cross section with 2 white bands of stomates on upper side and 2 narrower, whitish stomate bands on lower side. Male conelets dark rose, oblong, 25–50 mm long. Female conelets reddish green, 30–45 mm long, erect. Mature cone light brown with oblong, papery scales, toothed at apex, 50–100 cm long. Bracts one-half as long as scales, completely concealed.

From southern Alaska along the Pacific coast to Mendocino County, California, below 500 m elevation, along the western slopes of the Cascades in Washington, coastal foothills of Oregon and northern California, often dormant close to ocean. Common associate of redwood forest in Del Norte and Humboldt counties, California.

143   PINUS ATTENUATA   Lemmon
Knobcone Pine

Tree 2–15 m tall with a straggling crown. Branchlets pale brown turning to brown. Bark light brown with low ridges and loose scales. Needles 3 per fascicle, stiff, pale yellow green, 8–17 cm long, with distinct rows of stomates. Male conelets yellow, 12 mm long. Female conelets short stalked, whorled. Mature cone 70–150 mm long, light brown, outer scales with knoblike tips and stout prickles. Cone persisting unopened for many years. Seeds dark brown, roundish, flattened, 5–7 mm long, wings narrow, 25–35 mm long.

Dry, barren, rocky places, below 4000 m elevation. Orange and Mariposa counties, California, to Siskiyou County, California, to southern Oregon. In cutover redwood lands, occasionally invading extremely dry sites in Santa Cruz and Monterey counties, California.

144 **PINUS MURICATA** D. Don
Bishop Pine

Small tree 15–25 m tall with heavy, spreading branches and round-ish crown. Bark thick, furrowed with dark purplish brown scales. Needles 2 per bundle in crowded clusters, dark yellow green, 10–15 cm long. Male conelets whorled, yellowed, 8 mm long. Female conelets without stalk, ovoid, nearly terminal, whorled, erect. Mature cone 50–70 mm, brown, curved, asymmetrical with enlarged outer scales that have stout, recurved prickles persisting unopened for many years. Cones lateral and often on main branches or trunk. Seeds dark brown, 6 mm long, nearly triangular, wing 3–4 times as long.

In the redwood forests near the Pacific coast occasionally as an invading species following fires. Thrives in dry, gravelly sand, in cold clay soils and in boggy places. Coastal foothills and flats, Humboldt County to Santa Barbara County, California.

145 **PSEUDOTSUGA MENZIESII** (Mirb.) Franco
Douglas Fir

Giant forest tree up to 90 m tall. Bark very thick, rough, dark brown. Crown of young tree pyramidal, roundish and flattened in old age. Branching rather irregular, alternate or opposite. Buds without resin, sharp pointed, dark red brown, glossy. Needles with round to pointed apex, yellow green to dark blue green, 20–30 mm long, spreading and ascending. Leaf scar elliptical-oval. Male conelets yellow red, 6–10 mm long, axillary. Female conelets pendant, purplish green, axillary. Mature cone reddish brown, 40–100 mm long, bract 3-toothed, distinctly protruding and exceeding the scales. Entire cone shed in fall. Seed light brown, 5–6 mm.

In the redwood forests a common associate on mesic and dry sites and invading into clear-cut areas. Moist to very dry areas from sea level to high elevations, southwestern British Columbia to Monterey County, California, inland to southwestern Alberta, Montana, Wyoming, Colorado, West Texas, and northern and central Mexico.

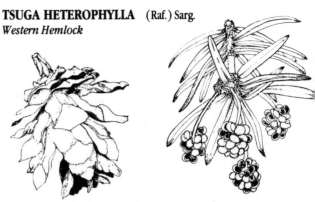

146   TSUGA HETEROPHYLLA   (Raf.) Sarg.
Western Hemlock

Trees 30–60 m tall, relatively narrow crown, typically drooping leader and down-sweeping branches, young twigs slightly hairy. Bark checkered with small scales, brown to reddish brown. Needles flat, grooved, glossy with 2 whitish stomatiferous bands beneath, 6–20 mm long, rounded at tip, markedly unequal in length, spreading at right angles to form flat sprays. Male conelets stalked, white to yellow. Female conelets sessile, greenish purple. Mature cone dark brown, small 15–25 mm, oblong-ovoid, scales papery, bract minute, winged seed, 4 mm long.

Moist woods, Alaska to Sonoma County, California, northern Idaho, northwestern Montana from sea level to 5000 m elevation. One of the most common forest trees in the Pacific Northwest. In the redwood forests common in Del Norte and Humboldt counties, California, on slopes and ridges, disappearing in Mendocino County, California, as an associate tree.

PLATANACEAE
Sycamore Family

Habit	Large trees, with scaly, thin bark and watery sap.
Stems	Bark thin, scaling, pale greenish to whitish when young, thick and deeply furrowed with age.
Leaves	Alternate, deciduous, palmately lobed. Leafstalks widened at base and largely covering the buds. Stipules thin, sheathing, entire or toothed.
Inflorescence	A raceme of unisexual, spherical heads on long, slender, drooping stalks, male and female flowers usually in different racemes on the same tree.
Flowers	Unisexual, minute, sepals 3–8, minute, scalelike. Petals 3–6, minute, in the male flowers wedge shaped, the narrow end at point of attachment, longitudinally grooved, thin, dry at points and longer than the sepals; in the female flowers sharp pointed to rounded and longer than the rounded sepals. Stamens as many as the sepals and opposite them. Style terminal with stigmatic surface on the inner side. Carpels as many as the sepals, 1-celled, surrounded by persistent hairs and a few sterile stamens. Ovule 1, rarely 2.
Fruit	An achene, aggregated into a dense, spherical head with intermingled hairs and sterile stamens.
Seeds	Elongate-oblong, hanging. Endosperm, fleshy.
Distribution	Found in North America, Europe, southwestern Asia and Central America, 1 genus.

147 PLATANUS RACEMOSA Nutt.
California Plane-Tree, Sycamore

Large tree, 10–25 m tall, widely branching. Bark dark brown and furrowed at the base, becoming thin and whitish along the branches. Leaves woolly haired when young, becoming hairless above with age, 15–25 cm × 15–25 cm, deeply 5-lobed. Raceme of unisexual, spherical heads. Male heads several, 8–10 mm wide. Female heads 3–5, 2–3 cm wide in fruit. Petals of female flower light green, enlarged at tip, styles 5–6 mm long, slightly club shaped with a dark reddish tip. Petals of male flowers slender, with a swollen base. Stamens 3–4 mm long with wedge-shaped anthers. Achene brownish white with light orange brown stiff hairs. *Flowering:* February–April. *Fruiting:* April–May.

Found along stream banks and watercourses in canyons from the northern Central Valley and interior valleys of the Coast Ranges south to northern lower California, below 1300 m elevation.

POACEAE
Grass Family

Habit
Annual or perennial herbs, rarely shrubs or trees, usually with hollow stems (culms) solid at the nodes.

Stems
Some creeping and rooting (stolons), or with rootstocks.

Leaves
Parallel veined, alternate, 2-ranked, consisting of 2 parts: the sheath and the blade. The sheath surrounds the culm with the margins overlapping or rarely grown together. The blade is usually narrow and elongate, generally flat, but often folded or rolled. At the junction of the sheath and blade, on the inside, is a membranous, transparent or hairy appendage, the ligule. Sometimes auricles arise as free, earlike projections on both sides of the lower margins of the blade.

Inflorescence
Flowers mostly perfect, sometimes unisexual, without a distinct perianth, arranged in spikelets consisting of a shortened axis (rachilla) and 2 to many bracts, the 2 lowest (glumes) being empty, rarely 1 or both absent. Spikelets arranged in spikes, racemes, or panicles with bractless branches.

Flowers
In the axil of each succeeding bract (lemma) is borne a single flower, subtended and usually enveloped by a 1- or 2-nerved bract (palea). The lemma, palea, and enclosed flower constitute the floret. At the base of the flower between it and the lemma are usually 2 very small, slightly obovate, flattened balloonlike structures (lodicules), tipped with minute, uneven hairs. Stamens usually 3, but sometimes 1, 2, or 6, with delicate filaments and 2-celled, versatile anthers. Pistil 1, with a 1-celled, 1-ovuled ovary, usually 2 styles and plumose stigmas.

Fruit
A grain seed with pericarp fused to seed, commonly referred to as a caryopsis, usually enclosed at maturity in the lemma and palea.

Seeds
Endosperm starchy.

Distribution
About 450 genera and 4500 species distributed around the world.

Uses
Most economically important family of flowering plants, providing the major staple foods of the world (wheat, rice, rye, corn, oats, millet).

Poaceae = Gramineae.

148 CORTADERIA SELLOANA (Schult.) Asch. & Graebn.
[ARUNDO S. Schult.]
Pampas Grass

Perennial reed, in large tussocks, 2–4(7) m tall, separate male and female plants. Leaves long and linear, with tufted hairs at the throat of the sheath. Leaf blade folded, 2–9 mm wide with midrib and margins bearing minute teeth. Spikelets 2- to 3-flowered, 15–18 mm long, arranged in panicles 30–100 cm tall. Female spikelets with long, silky hairs, male spikelets naked (bisexual spikelets have also been reported). Glumes white, papery, long, slender. Lemmas bearing a long, slender awn. Fruit a slender, light brown grain, with 2 persistent style beaks. *Flowering:* April–May, September–November. *Fruiting:* May, June, October–December.

Found on plains and open slopes. Native to Brazil, Argentina, and Chile; escaped from Ventura to Monterey and Del Norte counties, California.

PODOPHYLLACEAE
May Apple Family

Habit	Perennial herbs with usually fleshy rootstocks.
Roots	Tuberous or cylindric and creeping, usually fleshy rootstocks.
Leaves	Basal or on the stem, simple and palmately lobed, or compound with 2 or 3 leaflets, without stipules.
Inflorescence	Flowers solitary or in various types of inflorescence.
Flowers	Bisexual, regular. Perianth of 2 or 3 whorls variously differentiated, rarely absent (*Achlys*), each with 4 or 6 members, differentiated into outer sepals, inner sepals (when present), and petals. Petals usually with nectar-bearing glands and sometimes spurred at base or reduced to nectar-bearing scales or sacs, overlapping. Stamens usually as many as petals and opposite them or twice as many, free. Anthers opening by slits lengthwise or by valves from the base upward. Pistil of 1 carpel. Ovary superior, 1-celled.
Fruit	A berry or dry, inflated fruit splitting regularly, irregularly, or not at all.
Seeds	Endosperm copious. Embryo small, straight. Arillus sometimes present.
Distribution	In temperate parts of the Northern Hemisphere, 8 genera and 25 species.

Key to PODOPHYLLACEAE

1   Leaf blade consisting of 3 large, sessile, wedge-shaped leaflets. No petals or sepals. Stamens 6–13. Fruit a 1-seeded follicle, not opening.   **ACHLYS**

Flowers perfect in erect, terminal spike. Stamens 6–13. Stigma broad, sessile. Fruit reddish tinged, 3–4.5 mm long, with a hardened, convex outer side and a concave inner side, not opening. **ACHLYS TRIPHYLLA**

1   Leaf blade with compound divisions of 3 leaflets, long stalked. Sepals 2 rows of 6, unequal in size. Petals 6. Stamens 6. Fruit 1–10-seeded follicle, splitting open to its base.   **VANCOUVERIA**

2   Leaves deciduous, compound with division of 2 or 3 leaflets. Leaflets thin, soft. Panicles not glandularly hairy. Flowers white, 10–14 mm long. Filaments of stamens broad, white dotted with red-tipped, glandular hairs. Ovary dotted with glandular hairs.   **VANCOUVERIA HEXANDRA**

2   Leaves persistent, compound with divisions of 3–5 leaflets. Leaflets hardened with thickened margin. Panicles dotted with glandular hairs. Flowers white, often purplish tinged, 6–8 mm long. Filaments of stamens not widened nor hairy. Ovary without glandular hairs. **VANCOUVERIA PLANIPETALA**

149 **ACHLYS TRIPHYLLA** (Sm.) DC.
Deer-Foot, Vanilla Leaf

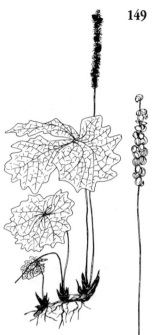

Perennial herbs 15–50 cm tall with slender, creeping, extensive rootstocks. Leaves large, long stalked, with 3 large, wedge-shaped leaflets. Spike terminal, long and dense, 2.5–10 cm long. Flowers white. No sepals, petals, or bracts. Stamens 6–13, white, filaments and anthers white. Ovary green, 1-celled, with 1 seed. Fruit a follicle, not opening, reddish purple with fine, minute hairs, broadly half-moon shaped with outer bony ridge. Reddish seed, 3–4.5 mm long. *Flowering:* April–June. *Fruiting:* June–September.

Found in moist woods with rich soils and on flood terraces along streams. Below 1700 m elevation. From British Columbia south from the eastern side of the Cascades to the coast in Washington, to the Columbia River Gorge. In Oregon and California strictly west of the Cascades and in the Coast Ranges to Mendocino County, California.

150 **VANCOUVERIA HEXANDRA** (Hook.) Morr. & Dec.
Inside-Out Flower

Perennial herb 10–50 cm tall with deciduous, long-stalked, 2 or 3 times divided basal leaves. Leaflets sparsely hairy, 2–6 cm, light green above, paler bluish green beneath, thin, with heart-shaped base and 3-lobed tip, the midlobe often largest. Panicle open, drooping, 5–30-flowered, up to 12 cm long. Flower stalk drooping, 30–40 mm long. Outer sepals 4–6 mm wide, greenish red, soon falling off. Inner sepals 6–15 mm, strongly reflexed, white. Petals 6, 10–14 mm long, strongly reflexed. Stamens pressed against style. Filaments dotted with red, glandular hairs. Follicle 10–15 mm long, 1–6 seeded. *Flowering:* May–June. *Fruiting:* June–September. (See Plate VI.)

Found in shaded, moist woods along the Pacific coast. From Puget Sound, Washington, to Mendocino County, California. Below 1500 m elevation.

151   VANCOUVERIA PLANIPETALA   Calloni
Evergreen Vancouveria

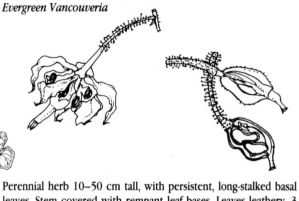

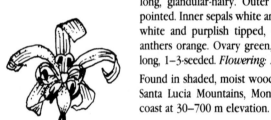

Perennial herb 10–50 cm tall, with persistent, long-stalked basal leaves. Stem covered with remnant leaf bases. Leaves leathery, 3 times divided, sometimes 5. Leafstalks 10–25 cm, densely hairy, and widened at base. Leaflets 15–40 mm long, glossy green with thickened margin, bluntly 3-lobed. Flowers in an open, drooping panicle, 25–50-flowered, up to 50 cm tall. Flower stalks 15–30 mm long, glandular-hairy. Outer sepals 6, 2–3 mm long, greenish, pointed. Inner sepals white and purplish tinged, 4–6 mm. Petals 6, white and purplish tipped, 4 mm. Stamens 6, filaments white, anthers orange. Ovary green, style cup shaped. Follicle 3–6 mm long, 1–3-seeded. *Flowering:* April–June. *Fruiting:* July–September.

Found in shaded, moist woods from southwestern Oregon to the Santa Lucia Mountains, Monterey County, California, along the coast at 30–700 m elevation.

POLYGALACEAE
Milkwort Family

Habit	Perennial herbs, shrubs, or rarely trees.
Leaves	Simple, alternate or opposite or whorled. Stalks short, without stipules.
Inflorescence	Usually a raceme or spike, occasionally solitary; subtended by 3 small bracts.
Flowers	Bisexual and irregular. Sepals 3, small and ovate. Petals 4, the 2 large outer petals broad, oval, often slightly 2-lobed at the tip, pinkish; upper, inner petal 2-forked with curling tip and dark purple base, whitish to pink; lower, inner petal pinkish, upturned with whitish, blunt, curled tip, partly constricted, thus sheathing style and stamens. Style distinctly kinked 90 degrees. Stamens 5–8, partly fused at the base.
Fruit	Capsule, drupe, or winged achene.
Distribution	In temperate and tropical regions, 10 genera and about 1000 species.
Uses	Some species of horticultural importance.

152 POLYGALA CALIFORNICA Nutt.
California Milkwort, Polygala

Perennial herb with numerous slender stems, 20–40 cm tall, from a woody base. Leaves elliptic to oval, 1–4 cm long, on short stalks. Flowers in terminal racemes; a small, self-fertilizing, unopening flower may be present at the base of the stem. Sepals 3, short and ovate, 2–4 mm long. Petals 4, the inner, upper 1 elongate, the tip forked or recurved and dark purple, the inner, lower petal inflated and keeled, pinkish to white, partly sheathing over the style; 2 large, outer petals pinkish, flaring outward from the flower. Stamens usually 8 but sometimes less, filaments united. Style with a 90 degree kink below the middle. Capsule thin walled, notched at tip. *Flowering:* March–July. *Fruiting:* July–September. (See Plate VI.)

Rocky ridges and slopes, common in redwood–tan oak forests. In the Coast Ranges from northern San Luis Obispo County, California, to southern Oregon; below 1000 m elevation.

POLYPODIACEAE
Polypody Fern Family

Habit   Ferns with creeping or ascending scaly rootstocks. Typically growing as epiphytes on trees or rock outcrops.

Fronds   Mostly simple to pinnate, firm in texture, usually net veined, on commonly jointed stalks.

Sori   Typically round, indusium lacking. Sporangia sometimes merged and spread over the leaf surface.

Indusium   Absent.

Sporangia   Surrounded by a ring (annulus) of 12–14 cells, stalked. Stalk of about equal length as the sporangium.

Spores   Have 2 sides.

Distribution   About 65 genera widely distributed.

Key to POLYPODIACEAE

Only 1 genus, *Polypodium,* is represented. Rootstocks creeping, with thin, dry scales. Frond stalks jointed, arising singly from rootstock. Sori on back of frond or sometimes terminal, round to elliptic, relatively large, without an indusium.

1   Fronds thick, leathery, evergreen. Sori 2.5–5 mm broad, orange brown, crowded close to the midribs of the upper pinnae. Pinnae mostly over 1 cm wide, rounded at the tip, the midrib scaly beneath, the top lobe or pinna the longest or largest. Rootstock 6–10 mm thick, covered with a coarse, white, waxy powder, tasteless. **POLYPODIUM SCOULERI**

1   Fronds not leathery, not evergreen. Sori 1–2.5 mm broad, between the margins and midribs of all the pinnae. Pinnae seldom over 1 cm wide, the midrib not scaly. The top lobe or pinna not distinctly the longest or largest. Rootstock 3–5 mm thick, not covered with a white powder, licorice flavored.   **2**

2   Fronds 4–15(20) cm long. Pinnae usually less than 2.5 cm long, oblong to elliptical, rounded at the tip, obscurely lobed or toothed. Sori commonly a little closer to the margins than to the midribs of the pinnae. Occurring more inland on rock outcrops. **POLYPODIUM CALIFORNICUM**

2   Fronds 15–50 cm long. Pinnae mostly over 3 cm long, linear-oblong, tapering to a distinct point, finely sawtoothed. Sori commonly a little closer to the midribs than to the margins of the pinnae. Occurring near the Pacific coast on moss-covered hardwoods and rarely on conifers or rocks. **POLYPODIUM GLYCYRRHIZA**

153   POLYPODIUM CALIFORNICUM   Kaulf.
Licorice Fern

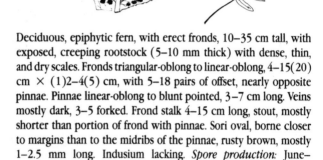

Deciduous, epiphytic fern, with erect fronds, 10–35 cm tall, with exposed, creeping rootstock (5–10 mm thick) with dense, thin, and dry scales. Fronds triangular-oblong to linear-oblong, 4–15(20) cm × (1)2–4(5) cm, with 5–18 pairs of offset, nearly opposite pinnae. Pinnae linear-oblong to blunt pointed, 3–7 cm long. Veins mostly dark, 3–5 forked. Frond stalk 4–15 cm long, stout, mostly shorter than portion of frond with pinnae. Sori oval, borne closer to margins than to the midribs of the pinnae, rusty brown, mostly 1–2.5 mm long. Indusium lacking. *Spore production:* June–September.

Common on rock ledges and crevices in more inland areas. From Coast Ranges and foothills of the Sierras to Humboldt and Butte counties, California, to the Santa Barbara Islands and Baja California. Below 1300 m elevation.

154   POLYPODIUM GLYCYRRHIZA   D. C. Eat.
Licorice Fern

Deciduous, epiphytic fern, with long, hanging fronds 15–70 cm long. Rootstock firm, 3–5 mm thick, with deciduous, pointed scales. Fronds lance shaped, 15–70 cm × 5–20 cm, with 10–30 pairs of offset pinnae. Pinnae linear-oblong, tapering to a point, with finely sawtoothed edges. Veins free and mostly 3-forked. Frond stalk 6–30 cm long, straw colored and naked. Sori borne closer to midribs of pinnae than to margins, round-oval, rusty brown, mostly 1.5–2.5 mm long. Indusium absent. Fertile fronds persisting into the following growing season, sterile fronds changing to light yellow, deciduous. Rootstocks have a licorice taste. *Spore production:* June–October.

Found on rocks, logs, mossy tree trunks (maples and alders), and rarely on moist banks. Chiefly near the coast from Alaska to Monterey County, California. Below 600 m elevation.

155   POLYPODIUM SCOULERI   Hook. & Grev.
Leather Fern

Epiphytic, perennial fern 10–40 cm long, on stumps and conifer trees in shaded, redwood forests. Rootstocks woody, 6–10 mm thick, exposed, white, waxy, with thin, dry scales. Fronds triangular-ovate, pinnately divided into 2–14 pairs of pinnae, evergreen, few and leathery. Pinnae oblong-elliptic, shallowly scalloped on margins, 2–9 cm × 7–25 mm, extending slightly down midrib. Veins form a network. Frond stalk stout, rigid, naked, orange rusty brown. Conspicuous orange brown sori crowded mostly near midribs of upper pinnae. Indusium lacking. *Spore production:* February–June. (See Plate VI.)

Found on mossy logs, cliffs, and banks along the coast. From southern British Columbia to Santa Cruz County, California, and on Guadalupe Island, Baja California.

PORTULACACEAE
Purslane Family

Habit	Annual or perennial herbs, more or less succulent, rarely somewhat woody.
Leaves	Alternate, opposite, or in basal rosettes, simple, usually entire, with or without stipules.
Inflorescence	Flowers solitary or in racemes or cymes.
Flowers	Bisexual, regular or nearly so. Sepals commonly 2 (or rarely 8), sometimes united at the base, persistent (rarely, deciduous), usually unequal in size. Petals 5(2–16), sometimes united at the base, quickly withering. Stamens usually numerous or equal in number to petals and joined to their bases. Anthers free moving. Pistil 1, of 2 or 3 or more carpels. Ovary usually superior, 1-celled, with few to many ovules on a free central or basal placenta. Styles 2–8 or 2–8-cleft.
Fruit	Capsule membranous to papery or firm, splitting from the tip by 2 or 3 valves or opening as a lid.
Seeds	Usually lens shaped, 1–many, smooth and shining, often appendaged. Endosperm abundant. Embryo curved.
Distribution	About 20 genera and 580 species, widely distributed; 9 genera native to the United States.
Uses	Several genera with showy flowers of horticultural interest; some cultivated or collected in the wild for consumption as tasty vegetables.

156 MONTIA SIBIRICA (L.) Howell
Miner's Lettuce

Succulent annual or biennial from a slender taproot, often developing short rootstocks. Stems several, 10–50 cm tall. Basal leaves broadly or narrowly ovate, the blades 1–5 cm long. Leafstalks 5–15 cm long, sometimes becoming fleshy at the base or with bulblets in the axils. Stem leaves opposite, 2 per stem, broadly ovate, 1–7 cm × 1–5 cm, sessile, subtending the branched racemes. Racemes loose, 6–30 cm long, 10–20-flowered, 1–4 flowers per stem with long bract. Sepals green, round to ovate, 2–6 mm long. Petals 5, pink or white with pink veins, notched at the tip, 6–12 mm long. Stamens 3–5. Capsule brown, shorter or as long as the calyx. Seeds 1–3, black and shining, 2 mm long. *Flowering:* March–September. *Fruiting:* May–November.

Found in moist places, especially under hardwoods during the spring; from eastern Siberia to Alaska and south to Santa Cruz County, California, east to Utah and Montana.

PRIMULACEAE
Primrose Family

Habit   Perennial or annual herbs.

Leaves   Opposite or basal, simple, without a stipule.

Inflorescence Flowers solitary in the axils or in terminal or axillary racemes, spikes, umbels, or flattopped racemes.

Flowers   Bisexual, regular, typically 5-parted, varying from 3–9-parted. Sepals united, greenish or, rarely, colored, 4–9-parted or lobed, persistent or, rarely, deciduous. Petals united, deeply parted or merely lobed, the lobes spreading or reflexed or, rarely, coherent, contorted, overlapping, or 5-clawed in bud. Stamens 5, situated on the floral tube opposite the petal lobes. Ovary superior, 1-celled, ovules on a basal or a free, central axis. Style 1, simple, stigma round to lobed, stout.

Fruit   Capsule, commonly 2–6-valved.

Seeds   Achene, few to many, with endosperm.

Distribution About 25 genera and 700 species, of wide geographic distribution but most abundant in the Northern Hemisphere.

Uses   Of minor economic importance as a source of ornamentals.

---

157   TRIENTALIS LATIFOLIA   Hook.
Pacific Starflower

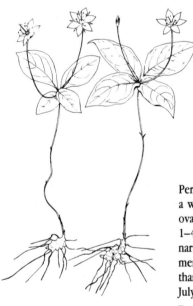

Perennial herb with an erect, unbranched stem, 5–20 cm tall, with a whorl of leaves on the stalk and a tuberous root. Leaves 4–6, ovate to obovate, pointed, 20–80 mm × 25–50 mm. Leafstalks 1–4 mm long. Flowers solitary on stalks 1–4 cm long. Sepals 5–9, narrow, 4–6 mm long. Petals pinkish, 5–9, ovate and pointed. Stamens 5–9. Fruit a capsule, whitish with glandular, black dots, less than 4–6 mm long. Seeds white. *Flowering:* April–July. *Fruiting:* July–August.

Found in woods and prairies and on shaded banks in mesic forests; from Vancouver Island and western Washington south to San Luis Obispo and Mariposa counties, California, below 1500 m.

PYROLACEAE
Wintergreen Family

Habit	Herbaceous perennials from slender rootstocks, mostly with evergreen, simple leaves.
Roots	Rootstocks slender, creeping, branched, scaly. Roots sometimes associated with mycorrhizal fungi and plants become saprophytic and leafless.
Stems	Low, more or less woody, not branched.
Leaves	Stalked, simple, alternate, often crowded into false whorls, evergreen, leathery, mostly sawtoothed, without stipules.
Inflorescence	Bisexual, solitary or in elongated or flattopped racemes or corymbs, with bracts. Flowers in almost all cases drooping when flowering.
Flowers	Bisexual, regular. Sepals 4 or 5, more or less united at the base. Corolla of 5 or, rarely, 4 not united or slightly united petals. Stamens 8 or 10, filaments more or less widened at the base, anthers inverted during flowering, opening by round or oblong pores, often pores at the ends of small tubes. Pollen in tetrads. Ovary superior, usually with a fleshy disk around its base, 5-celled or, rarely, 4-celled, sometimes incompletely 10-celled and bluntly 5-angled. Ovule inverted, numerous, on central axial placentae. Styles wholly united or sometimes free, short or slender, often curved downward but ascending at tip. Stigmas round or 5-lobed, with short, stout lobes.
Fruit	Capsule a 5-angled sphere flattened at its upper end splitting along midveins of the carpels.
Seeds	Minute, numerous, with a loose seed coat and a large arillus.
Distribution	Widely distributed in the extratropical regions of the Northern Hemisphere, 5 genera and about 25 species.

Key to PYROLACEAE

1   Leaves mostly in whorls or scattered on stems, not predominantly in basal rosettes. Flowers in small, terminal, flattopped racemes or corymbs. Filaments hairy. Styles short, usually not protruding beyond the corolla. Half-shrubby with trailing, woody stems.
CHIMAPHILA   **2**

1   Leaves mostly basal. Flowers solitary or in a terminal raceme. Filaments not hairy. Styles elongate, visible in the flowers. Nearly stemless herbs.   **3**

The family Pyrolaceae is sometimes considered as a part of the Ericaceae family (Hitchcock) or is sometimes treated to include the Monotropaceae (Munz). Here the Ericaceae and Monotropaceae are considered as separate families. Most saprophytic Pyrolaceae have forms with green leaves and forms without leaves, sometimes on the same rootstock. Originally, these leafless forms were considered a separate species. Now they are regarded as forms of the main species.

2   Stems reddish or purplish. Flowers usually 3 or less. Perianth creamy white. Leaves not distinctly whorled, elliptic to ovate, dark glossy green, often whitish mottled, with regularly sawtoothed margins. Filaments hairy over entire swollen portion of base. Floral bracts obovate, persistent.   **CHIMAPHILA MENZIESII**

2   Stems usually light greenish. Flowers usually more than 3 arranged in a long-stalked umbellike corymb. Perianth rose colored. Leaves oblanceolate, light green, in distinct whorls of 3–8 with remotely toothed margins. Swollen base of filaments fringed with hairs. Floral bracts linear, deciduous.   **CHIMAPHILA UMBELLATA var. OCCIDENTALIS**

3   Flower solitary or rarely in a 2- or 3-flowered raceme. Petals spreading and nearly flat. Anthers conspicuously 2-horned. Capsules splitting from the top downward. Valves of capsules without cobwebby margins.   **MONESES**

Stems 1–3 cm high. Leaves rather thin, round-ovate, with sawtoothed margins, 1–3 cm long. Flowering stalk, 3–15 cm high, with a single, nodding, white or pinkish flower at the stalk tip. Petals round to ovate, 10–12 mm long.   **MONESES UNIFLORA var. RETICULATA**

3   Flowers in terminal racemes, not solitary. Petals concave, more or less covering the stamens and pistil. Anthers not 2-horned. Capsule splitting from the base upward, its valves with cobwebby margins.   **PYROLA**   **4**

4   Leaves mottled with white along the principal veins on the upper surface. Style about same length as corolla. Petals yellowish to greenish white, rarely pink or purplish. Calyx lobes scarcely longer than broad. Anthers opening with pores on the sides of short tubes. Grows on dry soils with thick humus layers.   **PYROLA PICTA**

4   Leaves not mottled. Style protrudes beyond corolla. Petals usually pinkish to rose. Calyx lobes much longer than broad. Anthers opening with pores near the ends of short tubes. Grows on moist ground or in swampy sites.   **PYROLA ASARIFOLIA var. BRACTEATA**

158 CHIMAPHILA MENZIESII (R. Br. *ex* D. Don) Spreng.
Little Prince's Pine, Pipsissewa

Low, sparingly branched, erect perennial to 20 cm tall. Leaves 2–6 cm long, somewhat lance shaped, dark green and shiny above, paler beneath, sometimes white mottled. Corymb with 1–3 nodding flowers and obovate, persistent bracts. Sepals pinkish, 3 mm long, rounded, raggedly toothed. Petals white or pinkish, 6 mm long, nearly circular. Widened portion of filaments hairy. Fruit a capsule, 5–6 mm in size, becoming erect at maturity. *Flowering:* June–August. *Fruiting:* July–October.

Found in coniferous woods, mostly in dense shade at middle elevations. From British Columbia south to the Sierra Nevada and southern California, northeast to Idaho and Montana.

159 CHIMAPHILA UMBELLATA (L.) Barton
var. OCCIDENTALIS (Rydb.) Blake
Western Prince's Pine

Low, often branched, erect perennial, 10–30 cm tall. Leaves in whorls of 3–8, mostly inversely lance shaped, 2–7 cm long, dark glossy green above, yellowish green below. Corymb of 3–15 nodding flowers, flower stalk finely hairy and glandular, with linear, deciduous bracts. Petals oval, pinkish, 5–6 mm long, fringed with hairs. Fruit a capsule, 5–7 mm in size, sparsely hairy, erect at maturity. *Flowering:* May–August. *Fruiting:* July–October.

Usually found on dry, shrubby slopes and in open woods, often as a locally patchy dominant. From Alaska to southern California; to the eastern United States; and Eurasia.

160   MONESES UNIFLORA   (L.) Gray
var. RETICULATA   (Nutt.) Blake
Moneses

Low, delicate, perennial herb, 3–15 cm tall, with creeping root-stock and a single, drooping flower. Leaves light green, in 1–4 whorls of 2–4 leaves each, rather thin and obscurely veined, round to ovate, 10–30 mm long, with finely sawtoothed margins. Sepals whitish, 3 mm long, fringed with hairs. Petals white or pinkish, 10–12 mm long. Fruit a light brown capsule, 6–8 mm in size, erect at maturity. *Flowering:* May–August, *Fruiting:* June–September.

Found in cool, moist woods, usually on rotting logs in dense shade, from Alaska through the Coast Ranges to Humboldt County, California, to eastern North America; and Eurasia. Rare within the redwood forests.

161   PYROLA ASARIFOLIA   Michx.
var. BRACTEATA   (Hook.) Jeps.
Oregon Wintergreen

Low, creeping perennial with basal leaves. Sometimes the plants are saprophytic and lacking green leaves. Leaves dark green, usually purplish beneath, not mottled, round to obovate, 3–8 cm long, long stalked. Leaf margins with sharp points formed by vein tips. Elongated raceme of 5–25 flowers. Flowering stems 15–60 cm tall. Perianth reddish. Sepals triangular to lance shaped, 2.5–5 mm. Petals ovate, 5–8 mm long. Style quite long, curved downward and upward. Fruit a capsule, 7–8 mm. *Flowering:* May–September. *Fruiting:* September–November.

Found on moist ground in coniferous forests throughout the western United States to Alaska and across Canada to northeastern North America.

162   PYROLA PICTA Sm.
Shinleaf, White-Veined Wintergreen

Low, branched perennial with basal leaves (these sometimes lacking). Some plants saprophytic without green leaves. Vegetative stems mostly 2–5 cm. Flowering stems 10–20 cm. Leaves ovate to round-elliptic, 2–7 cm long, distinctly mottled with white along the main veins on the upper surface, margins thickened and entire to irregularly toothed. Elongated raceme of 10–25 flowers. Sepals ovate, barely 2 mm long. Petals distinctly yellowish to greenish white (rarely purplish), with transparent margins. Style short, curved downward. Fruit a capsule, 6–7 mm in size. *Flowering:* June–August. *Fruiting:* July–October.

Found in coniferous forests on dry soils with a thick humus layer. From British Columbia to southern California and east to the northern Rocky Mountains. Common inland in redwood forests.

RANUNCULACEAE
Buttercup Family

Habit	Annual or perennial herbs, sometimes shrubs or woody climbers with bitter and sharp, colorless juice.
Leaves	Usually alternate, or opposite or basal, blades simple to palmately compound. Stalks expanded at base, sheathing. Stipules absent.
Inflorescence	Flowers solitary or in racemes or flattopped panicles. Flower parts inserted on a convex receptacle, distinct, variable in number.
Flowers	Bisexual, rarely unisexual, superior, regular or irregular. Flower parts usually all present, free and distinct, but with many exceptions. Petals may be lacking and sepals petallike; sepals and petals may be spurred; sepals mostly 3–15. Petals usually the same, commonly yellow, white, red, or blue. Stamens usually many, attached below the ovary, maturing from the outward whorls toward the center. Pistils few or many, may be somewhat united. Ovary 1-celled, with 1–many ovules and basal or walled placentae.
Fruit	Generally a dry, single, carpellated fruit, opening only along the ventral seam, less commonly an achene, sometimes a berry or capsule.
Seeds	With hard endosperm, containing oil.
Distribution	About 35–40 genera and 1500 species, perhaps as many as 70 genera and 2000 species, of cooler regions of the Northern Hemisphere. About 21 genera native to the United States.
Uses	Many ornamentals, a few medicinal plants, and important toxic plants, such as *Delphinium.*

Key to RANUNCULACEAE

1   Sepals 5, small and green. Petals 1–16, yellow, 2–17 mm long. Leaves simple or compound, mostly basal. Usually in moist areas. **RANUNCULUS**   **2**

1   Sepals petallike, petals absent. Sepals 4–20, white, 15–25 mm long. Leaves simple or compound, basal and on the stem in a whorl just below the flower. Usually in dry forests.   **ANEMONE**

     Perennial herb with 3 sessile stem leaves and a showy, single, terminal, white flower. Fruit a thin-walled achene, purple to green with a light yellow base.   **ANEMONE DELTOIDEA**

2   Creeping stem, 10–50 cm, producing runners (20–80 cm) that root at the nodes. Petals yellow, 6–17 mm long, usually 5, often 6–9 or more. Roots threadlike.

     Perennial herb with runners. Flowers terminal, solitary. Fruit, 20–40 achenes (2–3 mm).   **RANUNCULUS REPENS**

2   Stem usually single, erect (15–90 cm). Petals yellow, 5, 2–6 mm long. Roots coarse, fibrous.

Annual or perennial herb, bearing solitary, terminal or axillary flower and 5–30 achenes. **RANUNCULUS UNCINATUS**

163 ANEMONE DELTOIDEA Hook.
Columbia Windflower

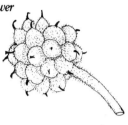

Perennial herb with slender, creeping rootstocks, and 10–30 cm high stems that wither in winter. Leaves basal and along the stem. Stem leaves 3, in a whorl, simple, ovate, sawtoothed on the margin, 4–7 cm long, with very short stalks. Basal leaves mostly solitary, with 3 ovate leaflets 3–6 cm long. Flowers large and showy, mostly solitary on a long stalk, without petals but with 5, white, petallike sepals 15–25 mm long. Achenes shaggy haired below, purple green with light yellow base. *Flowering:* April–July. *Fruiting:* June–August.

Found in dry, mixed, conifer forests in partial shade from Mendocino, Humboldt, and Siskiyou counties, California, north to British Columbia, below 1800 m elevation.

164 RANUNCULUS REPENS L.
Creeping Buttercup, Crowfoot

Perennial herb with threadlike roots and runners rooting at the nodes (20–80 cm). Stems creeping, 10–50 cm, floral stems ascending, 30–60 cm. Leaves compound with 3 lobed and toothed leaflets. Stem leaves alternate, stalked. Flowers terminal, solitary, with 5 sepals and usually 5 bright yellow petals 6–17 mm long. Fruit, 20–40 compressed achenes. *Flowering:* April–August. *Fruiting:* August–September.

Found in open, wet areas, often locally dominant, weedy. From British Columbia and western Washington south to Monterey and Fresno counties, California. Also found in the Rocky Mountains and eastern North America. Native to Europe.

165   RANUNCULUS UNCINATUS   D. Don in G. Don
Little Buttercup

Annual or perennial herb with coarse, fibrous roots and single, erect, sparingly branched, hollow stem. Basal leaves 2–9 cm broad with 3-lobed parts. Stem leaves larger than the basal. Flowers solitary, terminal or axial, with 5 sepals and 5 yellow petals (2–6 mm). Fruit, 5–30 achenes. *Flowering:* April–July. *Fruiting:* May–August.

Moist, shady soils of the Coast Ranges from Alaska south to Sonoma County, California, south to the Sierra Nevada and San Bernardino mountains, California, below 2700 m elevation.

RHAMNACEAE
Buckthorn Family

Habit	Small trees, shrubs, or a few climbers, deciduous to evergreen.
Stems	Often thorny.
Leaves	Simple, generally alternate. Stipules present, small and deciduous or sometimes corky, spiny, and persistent.
Inflorescence	Usually axillary or terminal corymbs, cymes, or panicles.
Flowers	Bisexual or with bisexual and unisexual flowers on same plant, or with male and female flowers on separate plants, regular. Sepals 4 or 5 united, toothed. Petals 4 or 5, inserted on the calyx, sometimes absent. Stamens 4 or 5, opposite the petals, anthers 2-celled, short, versatile. Ovary superior, free from or sunken in a fleshy, glandular disk. Ovary 2–5-celled, ovules 1 in each cell.
Fruit	Capsule, berry or fleshy, nonsplitting, often 3-celled, 1 or, rarely, 2 seeds per cell.
Seeds	Strong, hardened seed coat with fleshy endosperm or, rarely, no endosperm, embryo large.
Distribution	About 50 genera and 600 species, inhabiting the temperate and tropical regions.
Uses	Economically of little importance; some of limited medical value or with edible fruits, like the jujube. Several species ornamental; others important pioneer species with nitrogen-fixing root nodules.

Key to RHAMNACEAE

1 Leaves large, pinnately veined. Inflorescence inconspicuous. Flowers in umbels, few flowers per umbel. Flowers greenish, petals short clawed or lacking, 4- or 5-parted. Fruit fleshy, berrylike, nonsplitting. **RHAMNUS**

Leaves deciduous, rather thin and leathery, minutely sawtoothed, 8–20 cm long. Flowers 5-parted. Fruit a berry, purple black at maturity, 6–9 mm long. Small tree or tall shrub, 3–10 m tall. **RHAMNUS PURSHIANA**

1 Leaves smaller, 3-veined from the base or strictly pinnately veined, veins distinctly bulging on the leaf underside. Inflorescence large and showy, flowers in branched panicles with many flowers per panicle. Flowers white to blue, petals long clawed, 5-parted, calyx lobes deciduous. Fruit a 3-celled capsule. **CEANOTHUS**

Large shrub to small tree, 1–6 m high, densely branched with numerous fine branches. Leaves oblong-elliptic, pointed at tip, narrowed at base. Flowers showy, deep blue to light blue, rarely white. Fruit coat nearly smooth, somewhat veined and sticky. **CEANOTHUS THYRSIFLORUS**

166 CEANOTHUS THYRSIFLORUS Eschs.
Blue Brush, Blue-Blossom

Treelike shrub, 1–6 m tall. Leaves evergreen, oblong to elliptic, obscurely glandular, finely sawtoothed, dark green and without hairs above; pale green and sparsely hairy on prominent veins beneath, 2–6 cm long. Leafstalks 3–12 mm long. Inflorescence a dense panicle 4–8 cm long. Flowers 5-parted, petals long clawed, pale to deep blue, rarely nearly white. Fruit a capsule 3 mm broad, somewhat sticky, nearly smooth. Seed a black nutlet barely 2 mm long. *Flowering:* March–August. *Fruiting:* August–October.

Found on wooded slopes and in canyons, seeds dormant for many years, germinating only after forest fires, then a dominant pioneer species. Coast Ranges from Santa Barbara County, California, to southern Oregon, below 700 m elevation.

167 RHAMNUS PURSHIANA DC.
Cascara Sagrada

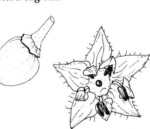

Treelike shrub or tree 3–12 m high. Leaves deciduous, elliptic to oblong, rounded at tip, rounded to nearly heart shaped at base, hairy to sparsely haired, minutely sawtoothed, 6–15 cm long. Leafstalks finely woolly haired, 5–25 mm long. Inflorescence an umbel. Flowers bisexual or entire plant unisexual, 5-parted, 3–4 mm. Petals short clawed, greenish. Fruit a purplish black berry with 3(2) nutlets, 6–9 mm long. *Flowering:* April–July. *Fruiting:* July–September.

Found on moist soils in lowlands and canyons, often dominant in partly cutover areas. From British Columbia south along the coast to Mendocino and Placer counties, California, east to northern Idaho and western Montana, below 1700 m elevation.

ROSACEAE
Rose Family

Habit   Herbs, shrubs, or trees with alternate or, rarely, opposite, simple or compound leaves.

Leaves   Usually alternate, rarely, opposite, simple or compound, deciduous or evergreen, usually with stipules.

Flowers   Usually bisexual, mostly regular. Receptacle free from the ovary. Sepals usually 5(4–10), frequently bearing bractlets between them, sometimes united at the base. Petals 5(4–10), sometimes absent, separate, attached to the rim of the floral cup and alternating with the sepals, rarely absent. Stamens usually numerous and in series of 5 per whorl. Anthers 2-celled, mostly opening by slits, rarely by pores. Carpels 1–many, united or separate, ovary superior or partially inferior.

Fruit   Follicle, achene, drupe, fleshy and applelike, or a fleshy aggregate of drupelets.

Seeds   Without endosperm usually.

Distribution   Over 100 genera and 3000 species of worldwide distribution; most common in north temperate and boreal regions.

Uses   Of great economic importance, producing most of our common fleshy fruits (pear, plum, strawberry, blackberry, apple); includes many plants of great ornamental value (rose, serviceberry, hawthorn, meadowsweet).

Key to ROSACEAE

1   Low, perennial herb. Leaves compound, the 3 leaflets with sawtoothed margin.   **FRAGARIA**

      Leaves and flowering stalks arising from a central base, plant producing runners with leaves at the nodes. Leaflets 2–5 cm long, leafstalks 3–15 cm. Flowers in long-stalked racemes or cymes, petals white. Achene fruits many, small, embedded in the surface of, or in shallow pits of, the red, fleshy, swollen receptacle; a "strawberry," 10–15 mm in size.   **FRAGARIA CALIFORNICA**

1   Erect, woody shrubs or small trees or sprawling, vinelike perennials. Leaves simple and entire, or lobed and toothed, or 3–9 times compound with sawtoothed margin.   **2**

2   Leaves simple, lobed but not compound. Plants usually without prickles at or between the nodes of the branches.   **3**

2   Leaves compound, with 3–9 leaflets. Usually with prickles at or between the nodes of the branches.   **6**

3   Flowers large, 2–4 cm across. Inflorescence a terminal, 1–4-flowered corymb.   **RUBUS**

Erect shrub, 1–3 m high. Bark shredding with age. Leaves with palmate main veins and 5 lobes, irregularly sawtoothed. Flowers white. Fruit an aggregation of red, fleshy drupelets, which separate from the receptacle as a loose thimble-shaped unit.   **RUBUS PARVIFLORUS**

3   Flowers small, at the most 1.5 cm across. Inflorescence a dense, many-flowered panicle, corymb, or nodding axillary raceme.   **4**

4   Leaves entire, not sawtoothed on the margins. Flowers white, in nodding axillary racemes.   **OSMARONIA**

Shrub or small tree with smooth, purple to brown bark. Flowers greenish white, fragrant, blossoming as the leaves develop. Leaves oblong, 5–12 cm long, on stalks .5–1 cm long. Fruit a bitter, bluish black to purple drupe, .8–1 cm long.   **OSMARONIA CERASIFORMIS**

4   Leaves with smooth or sawtoothed margins, more or less lobed. Flowers white, in dense, many-flowered panicles or corymbs.   **5**

5   Leaves shallowly lobed, mostly deeply sawtoothed, greenish and slightly hairy above, pinnately veined. Flowers very small, 5 mm across. Fruit 3–5 achenes per flower.   **HOLODISCUS**

Erect shrub with brown or purplish peeling bark. Leaves ovate to oval, 4–10 cm long, with 15–25 lobes or deep teeth. Flowers white, in dense panicles. Fruit a gray brown achene.   **HOLODISCUS DISCOLOR**

5   Leaves with 3–5 lobes, dark green and hairless above, palmately veined. Flowers larger, about 1 cm across. Fruit 3–5 follicles per flower.   **PHYSOCARPUS**

Spreading to erect shrub with shredding bark, producing runner-like new growth (suckers). Leaves ovate to heart shaped, 3–10 cm long. Follicle .5–1 cm long.   **PHYSOCARPUS CAPITATUS**

6   Leaves pinnately compound with 5–9 leaflets, the stalks of the leaflets meeting the main leafstalk at 2–4 different points. Pistils barely protruding from the mouth of the concave floral cup. Fruit an orange red to purple, leathery drupe enclosing many small achenes.   **ROSA**   **7**

6   Leaves palmately compound with 3 leaflets, sometimes 5, the stalks of the leaflets meeting the main leafstalk at a single, common point. Pistils inserted on a convex, rounded, fleshy receptacle above the point of insertion of the stamens. Fruit an aggregate of fleshy drupelets; blackberries and raspberries.   **RUBUS**   **8**

7   Petals dark rose, light rose on the back side; flowers 2–3 cm across. Mature hip orange red, 1 cm long, without sepals attached. Branches usually prickly throughout, the prickles numerous, all slender and similar to each other.   **ROSA GYMNOCARPA**

7   Petals light pink to deep rose, whiter at the base; flowers 4–6 cm across. Mature hip purplish, 1–2 cm long, with persistent sepals. Branches usually prickly throughout, a pair of larger, stout prickles usually present at the nodes.   **ROSA NUTKANA**

8   Petals red purple. Branches erect, usually without prickles, except for first-year shoots. Yellow or reddish aggregate of fleshy drupelets usually separating as a whole from the receptacle, forming a hollow cone.   **RUBUS SPECTABILIS**

8   Petals white or pink. Branches arching, often trailing and rooting, with numerous, persistent prickles throughout. Reddish purple to black, or yellowish red aggregate of fleshy drupelets remaining attached to the receptacle, forming a solid fruit (except in *Rubus leucodermis*).   9

9   Sepals exceeding the petals in length. Branches usually with a whitish bloom, especially when young. Branches erect but arching and rooting at tip. Reddish purple to black, or yellowish red, fleshy aggregate of drupelets separating as a unit from the receptacle, forming a hollow fruit.   **RUBUS LEUCODERMIS**

9   Sepals equal to or shorter than the petals. Branches lacking a whitish bloom; usually trailing and rooting. Black to deep red aggregate of fleshy drupelets solidly attached to the receptacle.   **10**

10   Inflorescence a large panicle or corymb, 5–20-flowered. Flowers always bisexual with pinkish petals. Prickles stout, broad based, often flattened; stems thick. Leaflets 3 or 5, the lateral and terminal ones equal in size, 6–12 cm long.   **RUBUS DISCOLOR**

10   Inflorescence a small corymb, 4–10-flowered. Flowers sometimes unisexual, with white petals. Prickles slender, scarcely flattened, mainly bristly; stems slender, trailing. Leaflets 3 or 5, the lateral ones 3–7 cm long, the terminal one largest, up to 12 cm long.
RUBUS URSINUS

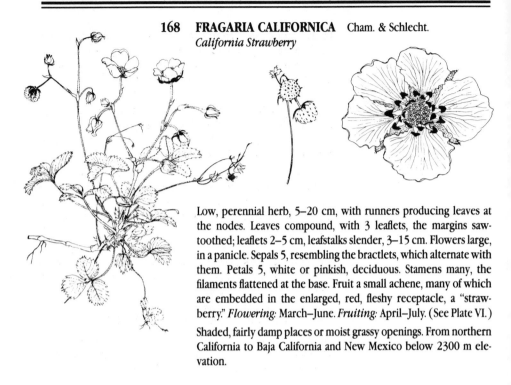

168   FRAGARIA CALIFORNICA   Cham. & Schlecht.
California Strawberry

Low, perennial herb, 5–20 cm, with runners producing leaves at the nodes. Leaves compound, with 3 leaflets, the margins saw-toothed; leaflets 2–5 cm, leafstalks slender, 3–15 cm. Flowers large, in a panicle. Sepals 5, resembling the bractlets, which alternate with them. Petals 5, white or pinkish, deciduous. Stamens many, the filaments flattened at the base. Fruit a small achene, many of which are embedded in the enlarged, red, fleshy receptacle, a "strawberry." *Flowering:* March–June. *Fruiting:* April–July. (See Plate VI.)

Shaded, fairly damp places or moist grassy openings. From northern California to Baja California and New Mexico below 2300 m elevation.

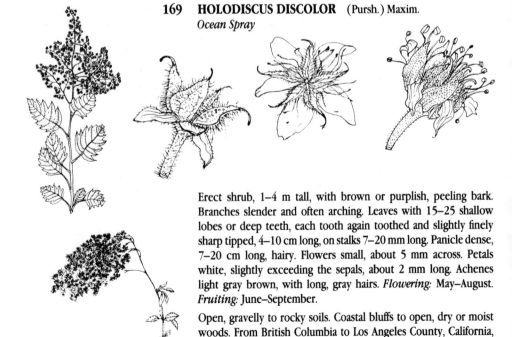

169   HOLODISCUS DISCOLOR   (Pursh.) Maxim.
Ocean Spray

Erect shrub, 1–4 m tall, with brown or purplish, peeling bark. Branches slender and often arching. Leaves with 15–25 shallow lobes or deep teeth, each tooth again toothed and slightly finely sharp tipped, 4–10 cm long, on stalks 7–20 mm long. Panicle dense, 7–20 cm long, hairy. Flowers small, about 5 mm across. Petals white, slightly exceeding the sepals, about 2 mm long. Achenes light gray brown, with long, gray hairs. *Flowering:* May–August. *Fruiting:* June–September.

Open, gravelly to rocky soils. Coastal bluffs to open, dry or moist woods. From British Columbia to Los Angeles County, California, western Montana, and northern Idaho; below 1500 m elevation.

170 OSMARONIA CERASIFORMIS (T. & G.) Greene
Oso Berry, Indian Plum

Deciduous shrub or small tree, 1–5 m high, with erect branches and smooth purplish brown or gray bark. Leaves simple, oblong to inversely lance shaped, 5–12 cm long. Racemes nodding at the end of the leafy branchlets. Flowers usually unisexual, greenish white, blossoming as the leaves develop. Female flowers with smaller and narrower petals than male flowers. Fruit a bluish black to purple drupe, 8–10 mm long, bitter, on a light yellow stalk with light red bands. *Flowering:* February–April. *Fruiting:* May–August. (See Plate VII.)

Found on stream banks, in canyons, at roadsides, and in open woods, in moist to fairly dry areas. From British Columbia south to Santa Barbara and Tulare counties, California, below 1800 m elevation.

171 PHYSOCARPUS CAPITATUS (Pursh.) Kuntze
Pacific Ninebark

Deciduous, spreading to erect shrub with shredding bark, 1–5(6) m tall, often forming dense thickets. The branches angled, sometimes producing runnerlike new growth (suckers). Leaves ovate to heart shaped, 3–10 cm long, 3–5-lobed, the lobes doubly sawtoothed and less than one-half the length of the leaf. Flowers in a dense corymb. Flower stalks and floral cup densely covered with hairs, which are branched at the tip. Petals white, nearly round, about 4 mm. Stamens about 30, equaling or exceeding the petals. Fruit a follicle, 3–5 per flower, swollen, 5–11 mm long, usually hairless. *Flowering:* May–September. *Fruiting:* June–October.

Moist banks, swamps, and north slopes. From southern Alaska to Santa Barbara County, California, west of the Cascades, also in the Sierra Nevada (California), Idaho, Montana, and Utah; below 1500 m elevation.

172 ROSA GYMNOCARPA Nutt.
Wood Rose

Slender, loose shrub, usually prickly throughout, the prickles all similar to each other. Leaflets 5–9, usually 7, elliptic to almost round, doubly sawtoothed with gland-tipped teeth. Flowers 2–3 cm across, mostly solitary, scattered at the tips of the branches. Petals 5, dark rose, light rose on the back side, sometimes 2-lobed at the tip, concave. Flowers lose petals easily. Mature hips ovoid to pear shaped, orange red, 5–10 mm × 4–6 mm. Sepals deciduous in fruit. *Flowering:* May–August. *Fruiting:* January–December.

In moist or dry shady woods, sometimes in open places. From southern British Columbia, Montana, and western Idaho in and west of the Cascades to the Sierra Nevada of California; below 2000 m elevation.

173 ROSA NUTKANA Presl.
Nootka Rose

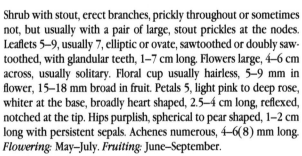

Shrub with stout, erect branches, prickly throughout or sometimes not, but usually with a pair of large, stout prickles at the nodes. Leaflets 5–9, usually 7, elliptic or ovate, sawtoothed or doubly saw-toothed, with glandular teeth, 1–7 cm long. Flowers large, 4–6 cm across, usually solitary. Floral cup usually hairless, 5–9 mm in flower, 15–18 mm broad in fruit. Petals 5, light pink to deep rose, whiter at the base, broadly heart shaped, 2.5–4 cm long, reflexed, notched at the tip. Hips purplish, spherical to pear shaped, 1–2 cm long with persistent sepals. Achenes numerous, 4–6(8) mm long. *Flowering:* May–July. *Fruiting:* June–September.

Damp flats and slopes. Mostly in wooded regions from Alaska to Mendocino County, California, northern Rocky Mountains; below 500 m elevation.

174   RUBUS DISCOLOR   Weihe & Nees.
Himalaya Berry

Robust, sprawling shrub to 3 m high. Stems stout, to 10 m long with stout, broad-based, and flattened prickles. Leaves compound, leaflets 3–5, oblong to ovate, bright green above, grayish beneath. Lateral and terminal leaflets equal in size, 6–12 cm long. Panicle or corymb large, 5–20-flowered, prickly and woolly. Sepals reflexed, woolly, 7–12 mm long. Petals red tinged, pink, or white, 10–15 mm long. Fruit an aggregate of fleshy, black, and shiny drupelets remaining firmly attached to the receptacle. Berries ripen late. *Flowering:* June–August. *Fruiting:* August–September.

Common along roadsides, railways, creeks, and in waste places. Native to Europe; naturalized widely from British Columbia to northern California.

175   RUBUS LEUCODERMIS   Dougl.
White-Stemmed Raspberry

Deciduous perennial, branches with numerous stout prickles and a whitish bloom; branches arching, sometimes rooting at the tip. Leaves compound, usually with 3 leaflets, irregularly sawtoothed, with prickly stalks and veins. Compact, few-flowered umbel or corymb. Sepals lance shaped, narrowed to a long point, exceeding the petals in length. Petals white, narrowed at the base, broadly spatula shaped. Fruit a reddish purple to black or yellowish red, fleshy aggregate of drupelets with a whitish bloom; separating as a unit from the receptacle forming a hollow cone. *Flowering:* April–July. *Fruiting:* July–September.

Open woods, fields, slopes, canyons, and in cutover areas. From Canada to Tulare County, California, east to Montana, Utah, and Nevada; below 2300 m elevation.

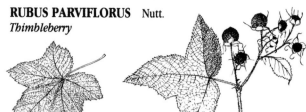

176   RUBUS PARVIFLORUS Nutt.
Thimbleberry

Erect shrub, 1–3 m tall, forming dense patches from the spreading rootstock. Bark shredding with age, branches with minute, soft, gland-tipped hairs. Leaves with palmate main veins and 5 lobes, irregularly sawtoothed, hairless to woolly haired, (5)10–15(25) cm long and broad. Leafstalks glandular-hairy. Terminal corymb with 2–9 flowers, stalks glandular-hairy. Sepals narrowed at the tip into a long tail. Petals white, obovate to elliptical, 10–25 mm long. Flowers large, 2–4 cm across. Fruit an aggregate of fleshy, red drupelets, which separate as a hollow, thimblelike unit from the receptacle when ripe. *Flowering:* March–August. *Fruiting:* May–October.

Moist to dry places, open woods and canyons, in cutover areas and along roadsides. From Alaska to throughout California, east to western Ontario and the Great Lakes region, the Dakotas, Wyoming, Colorado, New Mexico, and northern Mexico; below 2600 m elevation.

177   RUBUS SPECTABILIS Pursh.
Salmonberry

Thicket-forming shrub, 1–4 m tall, with yellowish bark that shreds with age. Stems erect or arching. First-year growth usually with small prickles. Leaves compound, usually with 3 leaflets. Terminal leaflet 4–11 cm, lateral leaflets smaller. Flowers usually solitary on short, leafy branches in leaf axils, appearing prior to foliage development. Flowers red to reddish purple, showy, 4–5 cm across. Fruit an aggregate of fleshy drupelets, easily separated from the receptacle, forming a hollow cone, yellowish or reddish. *Flowering:* March–June. *Fruiting:* May–August.

Moist woods, swamps, and stream banks, often forming dense, dominant thickets in open, alluvial flood plains. From Alaska to Mendocino County, California, east to Idaho; below 300 m elevation.

178   RUBUS URSINUS   Cham. & Schlecht.
Pacific Blackberry

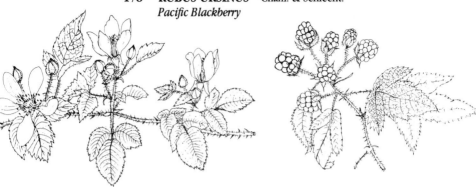

Weak and trailing woody perennial. Stems slender, 1–6 m tall, rooting at the tip, with abundant, slender, recurved prickles. Leaves compound, with 3, rarely 5, leaflets. Lateral leaflets lance-ovate, 3–7 cm long, sawtoothed on the margin; terminal leaflet larger, up to 12 cm long. Small corymb of 4–10 flowers, stalks with purplish, gland-tipped hairs. Sepals 7–11 mm long, with woolly, usually gland-tipped hairs. Petals white. Flowers usually bisexual, occasionally unisexual. Fruit a black to deep red aggregate of fleshy drupelets, which adhere to the receptacle, forming a firm, solid fruit, 25 mm × 10 mm. *Flowering:* April–August. *Fruiting:* September–June. (See Plate VII.)

Prairies, woodlands, clearings, especially on logged or burned-over forest land. From British Columbia to northern California, east to Idaho.

RUBIACEAE
Madder Family

Habit   Herbs, shrubs, or trees.
Leaves   Simple, opposite or whorled, entire, with stipules.
Inflorescence Flattopped panicle type.
Flowers   Bisexual or rarely unisexual, regular, nearly symmetrical, mostly 4-, sometimes 3- or 5-parted. Sepals sometimes obsolete. Petals regular, fused, forming a tube, lobed. Stamens as many as the lobes and inserted on the tube. Ovary inferior, 2-celled, rarely splitting when dry into 2 or 4 nonsplitting, 1-seeded carpels, styles 1 or 2, short or elongated, simple or lobed, ovules 1 to many in each cell.
Fruit   Capsule, berry, drupe or nutlet, nonsplitting.
Seeds   Various, embryo in fleshy or hardened endosperm.
Distribution   About 400 genera and 7000 species, of worldwide distribution but most abundant in tropical regions.
Uses   Many species of great economic importance, including Coffea and Cinchona (for coffee and quinine); some ornamentals (Gardenia, Bouvardia).

Key to RUBIACEAE

Only 1 genus, *Galium,* is represented.

1   Leaves in whorls of 4–8.   2

1   Leaves in whorls of 4.

    Stem erect, grayish shaggy haired. Flowers yellowish, 2–2.5 mm wide. Fruit fleshy, whitish, 3–4 mm wide, with or without hairs. **GALIUM CALIFORNICUM**

2   Leaves in whorls of 6–8, linear to linear-oblong or inversely lance shaped, with stiff hairs. Stems readily clinging to other vegetation by means of hooked bristles. Plants annual. Flowers greenish white, 2 mm in diameter. Fruit bristly-hairy, 1.5–5 mm, very rarely without hairs.   **GALIUM APARINE**

2   Leaves mostly in whorls of 6, oblong to obovate, mostly without hairs. Stems not readily clinging to other vegetation. Plants perennial. Flowers greenish white, 2–3 mm wide. Fruit 1.5–2 mm, densely covered with hooked hairs.   **GALIUM TRIFLORUM**

179   GALIUM APARINE L.
Cleavers Grass, Goose Grass

Annual herb, bristly stems and foliage, slender, weak, usually scrambling over bushes. Roots slender. Leaves per whorl 6–8, linear to inversely lance shaped, bristle tipped, spreading marginal bristles and stiff hairs on surface. Flowers, flattened panicles (1–5) on axillary stalks, surpassing the whorl of leaves at top. Sepals absent. Petals 4, fused and lobed, greenish white. Fruit, covered with many stiff, hooked bristles, rarely without hair. Stone oval, grayish. *Flowering:* March–August. *Fruiting:* August–September.

Common on shaded banks, especially in moist sites, alluvial flats, and at edges of thickets to open woodland. West of the Sierra crest, California; Channel Islands; occasional on deserts; to Alaska and the east coast; said to be introduced from Europe. Below 2500 m elevation.

180   GALIUM CALIFORNICUM   Hook. & Arn.
California Bedstraw

Perennial, tufted herb. Roots slender, branching, woody rootstock. Stem erect, forming tufts or more diffuse, slender, grayish shaggy haired throughout. Leaves in whorls of 4, elliptic, oblong-lance shaped to ovate, abruptly terminates in little point, thin, shaggy with spreading hairs on both surfaces rarely on margins. Male and female flowers on separate plants, male flowers 2 or 3 per axillary stalk in flattopped panicles, petals yellowish with or without hairs externally. Fruit small, fleshy, whitish translucent when ripe, dark when dry. Stone oval, with fleshy whitish coating. *Flowering:* March–July. *Fruiting:* July–August.

Open hills and woods, shades, rocky slopes, more common in drier sites. Coast Ranges from Humboldt to Los Angeles counties, Santa Cruz Island, locally in central Sierra and Amador counties; below 1200 m elevation.

181   GALIUM TRIFLORUM   Michx.
Sweet-Scented Bedstraw

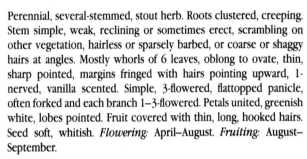

Perennial, several-stemmed, stout herb. Roots clustered, creeping. Stem simple, weak, reclining or sometimes erect, scrambling on other vegetation, hairless or sparsely barbed, or coarse or shaggy hairs at angles. Mostly whorls of 6 leaves, oblong to ovate, thin, sharp pointed, margins fringed with hairs pointing upward, 1-nerved, vanilla scented. Simple, 3-flowered, flattopped panicle, often forked and each branch 1–3-flowered. Petals united, greenish white, lobes pointed. Fruit covered with thin, long, hooked hairs. Seed soft, whitish. *Flowering:* April–August. *Fruiting:* August–September.

Moist, shaded canyons and wooded places. Fruits distributed by deer, frequently found along deer trails. Alaska to southern California and across the continent; also Japan; the Himalaya Mountains; and Europe; from sea level to below 2600 m elevation.

SALICACEAE
Willow Family

Habit Deciduous trees or shrubs with simple, alternate leaves with stipules. Male and female flowers borne on separate plants.

Stems Shoots often producing new roots. Wood soft, light, mostly pale. Winter buds scaly.

Inflorescence Catkins appearing at the same time or before the leaves, maturing in a few weeks, entire catkin falling off. Each flower subtended by by a scalelike bract.

Flowers Perianth represented by a cup-shaped, glandular disk (*Populus*) or 1 or 2 enlarged, basal glands (*Salix*). Male flowers with 2–many (rarely 1) stamens. Female flowers with a single pistil of 2–4 carpels and as many stigmas with or without a common style. Ovary 1-celled, ovoid or spherical.

Fruit Capsule, 2–4-valved.

Seeds Numerous, minute, without endosperm, covered with long, white hairs, adapted for aerial dispersal.

Distribution *Populus* and *Salix* (2 genera only) widely distributed but most abundant in the north temperate and subarctic regions.

Key to SALICACEAE

1   Trees with hanging catkins. Buds with numerous overlapping scales, resinous. Floral bracts fringed or torn at the margins. Calyx represented by a cuplike, often asymmetrical disk. Stamens 6–many. Capsules 2–4-valved.   **POPULUS**

Large, rough-barked tree, 40–60 m tall, with a broad, roundish crown. Buds large, pointed, the terminal bud about 2 cm long. Leaves ovate, narrowed to a point, 3–7 cm long, 2–5 cm long, on stalks 2–4 cm long. Stamens 20–60. Styles 3. Fruit 3-valved. **POPULUS TRICHOCARPA**

1   Trees or, more often, shrubs, usually with erect or ascending catkins. Buds with a single, nonresinous scale. Floral bracts entire or merely toothed. Calyx represented by a minute, glandlike structure. Stamens 1–10, usually 2 or 5. Capsules 2-valved.   **SALIX**

2   Stamens 3–8, typically 5. Filaments conspicuously hairy toward the base. Ovary not hairy. Style .5–1 mm long. Floral bracts yellowish. Capsule lance shaped, not hairy, on a 1.5–2 mm long stalk. Leaf veins not sunken.   **SALIX LASIANDRA**

2   Stamen 1. Filament not hairy. Ovary woolly-hairy. Style .3–.8(1.2) mm long. Floral bracts brown, often darker toward the end. Capsule ovoid-conical, silky haired, on a .3–.6 mm long stalk. Leaf veins sunken.   **SALIX SITCHENSIS**

182   POPULUS TRICHOCARPA   T. & G.
Black Cottonwood

Tree up to 70 m tall and 3 m thick, usually smaller. Bark ashy gray, buds dark red brown, the terminal bud about 2 cm long, bud scales resinous. Leaves ovate to oblong-lance shaped, with wavy, saw-toothed margins. Leaves dark green above, pale whitish beneath, 3–7(20) cm × 2–5(12) cm, strongly resinous. Upper surface of leaf sticky when rolling out of bud. Male flowers in 2–3(5) cm long, red purple catkins. Floral bract gray green, triangular, withering early. Female flowers in 8–20 cm long green red catkins. Floral bract frizzled at the margins, light reddish brown. Styles 3, stigma yellow, spreading. Fruit a capsule. *Flowering:* February–April. *Fruiting:* March–May.

Found in well-drained but moist river flood plains. From Alaska south to Baja California and southwestern Alberta, western Montana, Idaho, Wyoming, and Utah. Below 3000 m elevation.

183   SALIX LASIANDRA   Benth.
Red Willow

A shrub or small tree, 3–15 m high, up to 60 cm wide, the smooth bark becoming dark and fissured with age. Twigs deep red, lustrous, and finely hairy when young. Leaves lance shaped, narrowed to an elongated tip, finely sawtoothed, green above, white beneath, 6–15 cm × 1–4 cm or up to 30 cm × 5 cm. Leafstalks stout, 3–15(25) mm. Stipules leafy in texture, rounded, deciduous, 2–10 mm. Male flowers in 2–7 cm long catkins. Floral bract yellow, toothed, deciduous. Stamens 3–8, mostly 5. Female flowers in 3–12 cm long catkins. Floral bracts same as in male flower. Style 1 mm long, stigma broad. Fruit a capsule, straw color or brown, not hairy, 4–8 mm long on 1–2 mm long stalk. *Flowering:* March–May. *Fruiting:* March–June.

Found in wet places from Alaska to southern California; central North America. Below 2700 m elevation.

184   SALIX SITCHENSIS   Sanson
Sitka Willow

Shrub or small tree 1–7 m tall with smooth, gray bark. Young twigs velvety-hairy, light gray green becoming dark and hairless with age. Leaves obovate, pointed to the tip, tapered to the base, with sunken veins above, densely whitish hairy beneath, greener above, 4–9(18) cm × 1–3(6) cm. Leafstalks 5–10(20) mm. Stipules small and withering to leafy and persistent. Male catkins 2–5 cm long, the female 2–11 cm long. Catkins on 1–2 cm long stalks, subtended by bracts or nearly sessile and bracts inconspicuous. Floral bract inversely lance shaped, brown, 1–2 mm long. Male flower, stamen 1 by fusion of 2. Female flower style about 1 mm long, stigma less than .5 mm long. Fruit a capsule, 4–6 mm long on a .3–.6 mm long stalk. *Flowering:* March–April. *Fruiting:* March–June.

Found in moist places from southern Alaska south to San Luis Obispo County, California, east to northern Idaho.

SAXIFRAGACEAE
Saxifrage Family

Habit	Annual or in North America perennial herbs with simple leaves or, less often, compound, mostly alternate, commonly all basal.
Inflorescence	Racemes or panicles. Flowers rarely solitary.
Flowers	Mostly bisexual, regular. All the flower parts are frequently joined near the base in a cuplike enlargement of the receptacle. Calyx well-developed, greenish or white to strongly bluish and sometimes petallike, the lobes usually 5(4–6). Petals usually equal in number to and alternate with the calyx lobes, frequently smaller and less showy than the sepals. Stamens usually 5, 10, or, occasionally, only 3. Filaments not joined together, often flattened. Anthers 2-celled, splitting lengthwise. Pistil of 2 (rarely 3–6) carpels, separate to wholly united. Ovary 1–2(5)-celled, from superior to inferior.
Fruit	Capsule or sometimes consisting of separate follicles.
Seeds	Endosperm abundant, fleshy.
Distribution	About 50 genera and nearly 800 species, mostly in the temperate zones.

Key to SAXIFRAGACEAE

1   Stamens 10.   **2**

1   Stamens 5 or 3, rarely 2.   **3**

2   Stamens well exerted beyond the corolla. Petals entire, linear to awl shaped. Capsules unequally 2-valved. Floral tube nearly free from ovary. Ovary superior. Seeds few.   **TIARELLA**

       Flowering stems 10–50 cm high, glandular-hairy or sticky above. Basal leaves broadly heart shaped, 3–5-lobed, the lobes spine tipped, on 5–20 cm long stalks. Capsule papery, light brown, the seeds borne basally at the edges of the splitting valves.   **TIARELLA TRIFOLIATA var. UNIFOLIATA**

2   Stamens not exerting beyond the corolla. Petals pinnately divided into narrow divisions. Capsules splitting by 2 equal valves. Floral tube joined to ovary for one-third to one-half its length. Ovary partly inferior. Seeds many.   **TELLIMA**

       Flowers drooping on 1–3 mm long stalks, subtended by minute bracts. Flowering stems 30–80 cm high. Basal leaves heart to kidney shaped, shallowly 3–7-lobed, irregularly toothed or scalloped, 3–10 cm broad, on very hairy, 5–20 cm long stalks. Capsule about equal in length to the persistent calyx, the persistent styles divergent and hardened, on a thickened, erect stalk.   **TELLIMA GRANDIFLORA**

3   Stamens 3, rarely 2. Floral tube free from ovary. Ovary superior, on a short stalk. Petals generally 4, threadlike, entire. Calyx unequally

5-lobed, split much more deeply on 1 side than between the rest of the lobes. **TOLMIEA**

Stems and leaves hairy. Flowering stems 30–80 cm tall. Basal leaves heart shaped, palmately veined, shallowly 5–7-lobed, irregularly once or twice toothed, 2–12 cm wide, on stalks 5–20 cm long, with well-developed membranous stipules. Capsule slender, projecting from the slit on the lower side of the floral tube. Plant reproduces vegetatively by developing spontaneous buds at the base of leaf blades. **TOLMIEA MENZIESII**

3 Stamens 5. Floral tube fused to the base of the ovary. Ovary partly to completely inferior. Petals 5.   4

4 Petals pinnately cleft into featherlike, linear divisions. Flowers in a spikelike raceme. Runners often produced. **MITELLA**   5

4 Petals entire to clawed. Flowers in a panicle. No runners.   6

5 Flowering stems with 1–3 stem leaves. Raceme blossoming from the top downward, with up to 25 flowers on 2–8 mm long stalks. Ovary about half inferior. Petals greenish, often purplish at the base. Filaments purple. Calyx 5–7 mm broad. Styles about 1 mm long. Stigmas clublike. **MITELLA CAULESCENS**

5 Flowering stems leafless. Raceme blossoming from the bottom upward, with 8–60 flowers on stalks less than 2 mm long. Ovary nearly completely inferior. Petals whitish with 3–5 divisions. Filaments white. Calyx 2.5–3.5 mm broad. Styles about .3 mm long. Stigmas 2-lobed. **MITELLA OVALIS**

6 Ovary 2-celled, with the placentae on its axis. Flowering stems leafy. Calyx nearly or almost regular. **BOYKINIA**

Plant glandular-hairy, 15–60 cm high. Leaves 5–7-lobed, kidney to heart shaped, toothed, ultimately bristle pointed, 2–8 cm wide, on 5–15 cm long stalks, with bristly stipules. Panicle many-flowered, consisting of 1-sided cymes, with leafy bracts. Capsule light yellow brown with blackish brown veins. Petals white, often pinkish in age, obovate to spatula shaped, usually narrowed to a short claw. **BOYKINIA ELATA**

6 Ovary 1-celled, with the placentae along its walls. Flowering stems 0–4-leaved, with membranous bracts. Calyx often irregular. **HEUCHERA**

Flowering stems 30–70 cm high, with white or brown hairs, at least below, woody at base. Basal leaves round to ovate or heart shaped with 5–7 rounded, sharp-tipped lobes, 3–10 cm long, on densely hairy 5–18 cm long stalks. Capsule light brown, yellowish and hairy at the base, 4–5 mm long. Petals whitish, narrow, often rolled backward, clawed, 2–6 mm long. Styles well protruded. Floral tube tapered at the base. **HEUCHERA MICRANTHA**

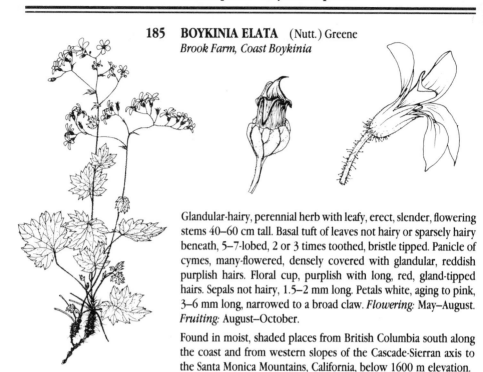

185   BOYKINIA ELATA   (Nutt.) Greene
Brook Farm, Coast Boykinia

Glandular-hairy, perennial herb with leafy, erect, slender, flowering stems 40–60 cm tall. Basal tuft of leaves not hairy or sparsely hairy beneath, 5–7-lobed, 2 or 3 times toothed, bristle tipped. Panicle of cymes, many-flowered, densely covered with glandular, reddish purplish hairs. Floral cup, purplish with long, red, gland-tipped hairs. Sepals not hairy, 1.5–2 mm long. Petals white, aging to pink, 3–6 mm long, narrowed to a broad claw. *Flowering:* May–August. *Fruiting:* August–October.

Found in moist, shaded places from British Columbia south along the coast and from western slopes of the Cascade-Sierran axis to the Santa Monica Mountains, California, below 1600 m elevation.

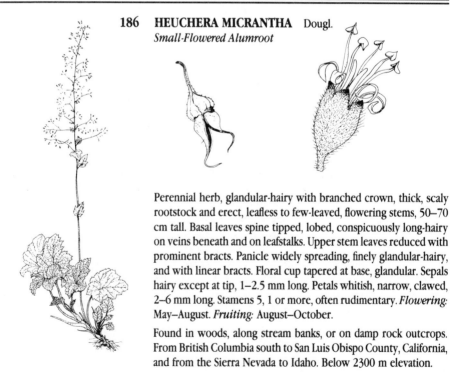

186   HEUCHERA MICRANTHA   Dougl.
Small-Flowered Alumroot

Perennial herb, glandular-hairy with branched crown, thick, scaly rootstock and erect, leafless to few-leaved, flowering stems, 50–70 cm tall. Basal leaves spine tipped, lobed, conspicuously long-hairy on veins beneath and on leafstalks. Upper stem leaves reduced with prominent bracts. Panicle widely spreading, finely glandular-hairy, and with linear bracts. Floral cup tapered at base, glandular. Sepals hairy except at tip, 1–2.5 mm long. Petals whitish, narrow, clawed, 2–6 mm long. Stamens 5, 1 or more, often rudimentary. *Flowering:* May–August. *Fruiting:* August–October.

Found in woods, along stream banks, or on damp rock outcrops. From British Columbia south to San Luis Obispo County, California, and from the Sierra Nevada to Idaho. Below 2300 m elevation.

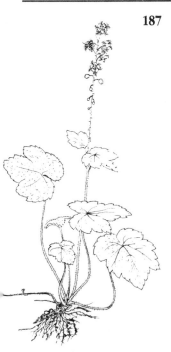

187 MITELLA CAULESCENS Nutt. in T. & G.
Star-Shaped Miterwort

Low, perennial, glandular-hairy, 10–40 cm tall. Flowering stems with 1–3 leaves, with green bracts. Leaves heart shaped, shallowly (3)5(7)-lobed, glandular-short-hairy. Raceme up to 25 flowers on 2–8 mm long stalks, flowering from tip downward. Calyx broadly bell shaped, yellowish green. Petals greenish, often purplish at base, dissected into (4)8(9) threadlike segments. Stamens 5. Ovary about one-half inferior. *Flowering:* April–June. *Fruiting:* May–August. (See Plate VII.)

Found in more or less shaded, rich forests, between 600 and 1700 m elevation. From Humboldt County, California, to British Columbia, Idaho, and northwestern Montana.

188 MITELLA OVALIS Greene
Common Miterwort

Low, perennial, glandular-hairy, flowering stems, leafless but with papery bracts, 10–35 cm tall. Leaves heart shaped to oval, shallowly 5–9-lobed with coarse white to brown hairs. Raceme (8)20–60-flowered, spikelike, flowering from base upward. Calyx shallowly saucer shaped, joined to the ovary for about one-third its length. Petals whitish, about 1.5 mm long, pinnately divided into 3–7 linear segments. Stamens 5. Ovary nearly completely inferior. *Flowering:* March–May. *Fruiting:* May–July.

Found in deep, moist woods, on creek bottoms, and on wet banks. From British Columbia south to Marin County, California.

189   TELLIMA GRANDIFLORA   (Pursh.) Dougl.
Fringe Cups

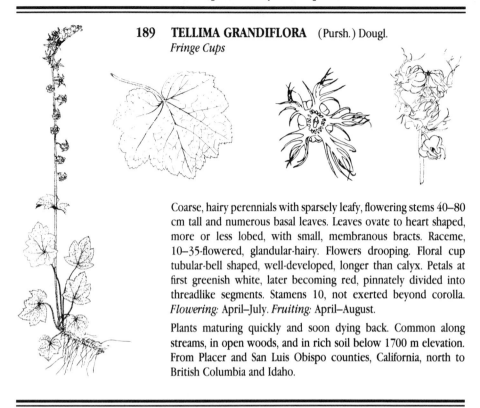

Coarse, hairy perennials with sparsely leafy, flowering stems 40–80 cm tall and numerous basal leaves. Leaves ovate to heart shaped, more or less lobed, with small, membranous bracts. Raceme, 10–35-flowered, glandular-hairy. Flowers drooping. Floral cup tubular-bell shaped, well-developed, longer than calyx. Petals at first greenish white, later becoming red, pinnately divided into threadlike segments. Stamens 10, not exerted beyond corolla. *Flowering:* April–July. *Fruiting:* April–August.

Plants maturing quickly and soon dying back. Common along streams, in open woods, and in rich soil below 1700 m elevation. From Placer and San Luis Obispo counties, California, north to British Columbia and Idaho.

190   TIARELLA TRIFOLIATA   L.   var. UNIFOLIATA
(Hook.) Kurtz
Sugar-Scoop

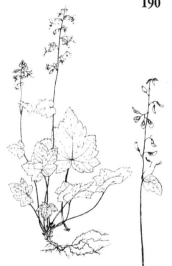

Perennial, glabrous to white hairy below, glandular above, to 50 cm tall. Leaves distinctly 3–5-lobed, double scalloped to coarsely toothed, the teeth spine tipped. Flowering stem with 1–4 reduced leaves. Inflorescence a narrow panicle of drooping flowers. Floral cup small, bell shaped, nearly free from ovary. Sepals 5, unequal, white to pinkish. Petals 5, white, linear to awl shaped. Stamens 10, well exerted. *Flowering:* May–August. *Fruiting:* August–October.

Found in shaded, moist woods and along stream banks mostly below 700 m elevation. From Santa Cruz County, California, north to southern Alaska and east to southwestern Alberta, western Montana, and northeastern Oregon.

191 TOLMIEA MENZIESII (Pursh.) T. & G.
Thousand Mothers, Youth-on-Age, Pig-a-Back Plant

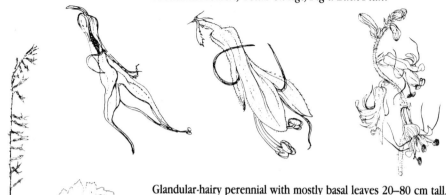

Glandular-hairy perennial with mostly basal leaves 20–80 cm tall. Leaves heart shaped, palmately veined, hairy throughout, clustered. Old leaves often sprouting a new, young plant with roots at intersection of leafstalk and leaf blade. Raceme elongate, 20–60-flowered. Floral cup cylindric-funnel form, free from ovary. Sepals in 2 forms, the 3 upper larger than the 2 lower, white. Petals 4, rarely 5, brown and threadlike. Stamens 3, rarely 2, unequal. Ovary superior. *Flowering:* May–August. *Fruiting:* August–October. (See Plate VII.)

In moist, cool woods, especially along streams. From southern Alaska to Santa Cruz County, California, below 2000 m elevation.

SCROPHULARIACEAE
Figwort (Snapdragon) Family

Habit	Herbs, shrubs, or, rarely, vines with usually irregular flowers.
Leaves	Simple, opposite or alternate, without stipules.
Inflorescence	Racemes or panicles.
Flowers	Bisexual, usually irregular or 2-lipped. Sepals 4 or 5, separate or united. Petals 4 or 5 united into a corolla, usually 2-lipped and cylindric. Stamens usually 4, in 2 pairs unequal in their filament length, sometimes only 2 stamens, or 5 with the fifth one sterile or, rarely, fertile (*Verbascum*). Ovary superior, 2-celled, of 2 carpels, with placentae on the axis. Style usually also united, with separate or united stigmas.
Fruit	Capsule, 2-celled opening with 2 valves from the top downward.
Seeds	Many to few, with fleshy endosperm.
Distribution	About 200 genera and 3000 species, especially numerous in western North America.

Key to SCROPHULARIACEAE

1   Stigmas 2, flattened or platelike.   2

1   Stigma 1, pointed.   7

2   Corolla cylindrical to bell shaped with a widened, obscurely 2-lipped corolla opening. Sepals deeply parted to nearly separate. Stem leaves alternate. Flowers in long, terminal, erect, leafy raceme. **DIGITALIS**

Tall biennial herb, 50–180 cm high, with toothed or lobed leaves. Raceme often branched at base, flowers drooping or hanging, capsules erect.   **DIGITALIS PURPUREA**

2   Corolla 2-lipped. Sepals united, the calyx tube usually inflated and creased like a fan. Leaves opposite. Flowers solitary in the upper leaf axils (5 species).   3

3   Flower stalk shorter than calyx. Plants woody at base to stubby. Dry, rocky places. Capsule splitting into 4 valves to base.   **MIMULUS**

Leaves glandular, hairy at least beneath, toothed somewhat entirely, 2.5–7 cm long, with sunken veins. Corolla semipersistent, deep to yellow orange, funnel shaped, 35–50 mm long, the upper lip strongly reflexed. Seed spindle shaped, 1 mm long, dark red brown. **MIMULUS AURANTIACUS**

3   Flower stalk longer than calyx. Plants not at all woody. Wet or marshy places. Capsule not or only partly splitting.   4

4   Flowers strongly flattened sideways, scarlet, sometimes orange red, 40–50 mm long. Leaves finely toothed, with 2–5 lengthwise veins.

Capsules 16–18 mm long, splitting through the top of cell partition. Seed pointed at base, wrinkled lengthwise. Plant coarse or shaggy haired, sticky. Corolla strongly 2-lipped, the lobes curled backward. **MIMULUS CARDINALIS**

4 Flowers not strongly flattened sideways, yellow, mostly 10–14 mm long. Leaves toothed, pinnately veined. Capsules 6–12 mm long, not splitting. Seeds rounded at both ends, smooth or finely lined. **5**

5 Mature calyx strongly inflated, lower calyx lobes curved upward. Corolla throat almost closed by large red-spotted, hairy ridges. Annual or biennial herb, not hairy. Seed oblong, marked lengthwise with fine furrows. **MIMULUS GUTTATUS**

5 Mature calyx not inflated, the lobes straight or nearly so. Corolla throat open. Perennial herb, soft-hairy or sticky-hairy, becoming smooth. **6**

6 Corolla 30–40 mm long, yellow, externally often brownish, purple dotted on the lower side.

Throat widely bell shaped. Stem unbranched, erect or ascending. Herbage soft-hairy, becoming smooth. Anthers hairy. Seeds dark olive brown, oblong, pointed, honeycomb pitted, 6 mm long. **MIMULUS DENTATUS**

6 Corolla 18–25 mm long, yellow, with fine, brown spots and blackish lines in narrowly bell-shaped throat. Stems diffusely branched, creeping.

Herbage with shining white hairs, sticky to slimy, musk scented. Anthers obscurely hairy. Seeds brown to light yellow brown, somewhat spherical warty, 3 mm long. **MIMULUS MOSCHATUS**

7 Stamens 2. Flowers blue to white, corolla wheel shaped without or almost without a corolla tube, unequally 4-lobed, the upper lobe the largest. **8**

7 Stamens 4, fifth stamen sterile, scalelike. Flowers greenish yellow or greenish purple to dark maroon, with distinct small 2-lipped tube. Corolla never wheel shaped. Upper and lateral lobes more or less vertical, the lower lip shorter, turned downward. **SCROPHULARIA**

Stem coarse, finely hairy, purple brown, 100–180 cm tall. Leaves 3–11 cm long × 2–8 cm wide, on stalks 1.5–5 cm long. Corolla 8–15 mm long. Fruit dark brown, 6–8 mm long, beaked by the persistent style. **SCROPHULARIA CALIFORNICA**

8 Flowering stems leafless except for reduced bracts. Leaves all basal, long and slender stalked. **SYNTHYRIS**

Corolla bell shaped, 5–9 mm long. Leaves ovate to heart shaped, with shallow, toothed lobes, 2–8 cm long. Plant hairy throughout. Capsule with wide, spreading lobes, notched, hairy, 2–4 mm long × 6–8 mm wide. **SYNTHYRIS RENIFORMIS**

8 Stems leafy, leaves short stalked. **VERONICA**

Leaves lance shaped to lance-ovate, finely toothed, 10–90 mm long × 5–35 mm wide, opposite throughout. Hairless, perennial herb with shallow, creeping rootstocks. Flowers in several axillary racemes. Racemes small bracted, strongly recurved in fruit. Corolla violet blue with dark blue veins, the throat white. Capsule oval, swollen, notched at top, 3–4 mm long, 2–4 seeds per cell. **VERONICA AMERICANA**

192   DIGITALIS PURPUREA L.
Purple Foxglove

Biennial herb 50–180 cm tall with strong taproot and long, erect racemes, slightly hairy, becoming sticky on upper portion; stem leaves oblong to lance shaped, lobed or toothed, narrowed at the base to short stalks, 15–20 mm × 2–12 mm. Basal leaves rosette-like, large; flowers on 6–25 mm long stalks, in a 1-sided, long raceme, often with 2–4 side racemes; sepals green with purple tips, ovate 10–18 mm; corolla pink purple, lower side with blackish purple spots, each with white border. Filaments white, 2 pairs at unequal length, anthers yellow with red spots. Capsules brown, erect, 4-valved, hairy at tip, 12 mm. Nutlet gray brown, oblong, .5 mm. Pollinated by bumblebees. *Flowering:* May–August. *Fruiting:* June–October.

From Santa Barbara, California, to Vancouver Island, British Columbia, in western Cascades; garden escapee.

193 MIMULUS AURANTIACUS Curt.
Orange Bush Monkey Flower

Woody, perennial herb, 40–120(200) cm tall with erect, profusely branching stems; plant finely glandular-hairy throughout. Leaves 2.5–7 cm, green above, paler below, lance shaped to linear-oblong, narrowing to sessile bases, margins toothed. Calyx tube persistently ridged, inflated, 20–25 mm, lobes lance shaped. Corolla 35–50 mm, yellow orange with narrow tube enlarging to funnel-shaped throat, 2 upper lobes perpendicular to throat, notched, toothed; lower lip enlarged, hairy, with 2 orange ridges. Style white, platelike stigmas fringed with hair, white. Capsule brown, long and cylindrical, 4-valved, splitting to base, 20 mm. Seed red brown, 1 mm. *Flowering:* March–August. *Fruiting:* June–September.

Dry, open, rocky places. Coast ranges from Del Norte County to Santa Barbara County, California, Sierra foothills from Placer County to Tuolumne County, California, western Oregon. Below 600(1000) m.

194 MIMULUS CARDINALIS Dougl. *ex* Benth.
Scarlet Monkey Flower

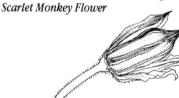

Perennial herb 20–120 cm tall, erect or lying down with tips ascending. Leaves glandular-hairy, oval to oblong-elliptical, sessile, finely toothed with 3–5 prominent veins 2–11 cm long. Calyx green, hairy, cylindrical, angular winged, 20–30 mm, lobes nearly even, 3–5 mm. Corolla 2-lipped, compressed to a vertical plane, scarlet, sometimes yellow, 40–50 mm, narrow throat yellowish with 2 hairy ridges, red striped inside, upper lip arched curving upward, lower lip bent downward. Filaments yellow, anthers brown orange, fringed with hair. Style white; stigma yellow with 2 spreading lips fringed with hairs. Capsules oblong, tapering abruptly to a point, 16–18 mm. Pollinated by hummingbirds. *Flowering:* April–September. *Fruiting:* June–October.

Frequent on stream banks and seeps. Southern Oregon through California; sparingly east of the Sierras to Inyo County, California, Nevada, and Arizona.

195 MIMULUS DENTATUS Nutt.
Tooth-Leaved Monkey Flower

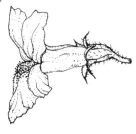

Perennial herb 20–40 cm tall, unbranched, from slender running rootstock. Leaves ovate, rounded to tapering at the base, coarsely and evenly toothed, pinnately veined, 2–7.5 cm, short stalked or clasping. Flowers solitary. Calyx 10–15 cm, bell shaped, sparsely hairy along sharp, angled ribs, lobes triangular, fringed with hair, 4–6 mm. Corolla yellow, 30–40 mm, throat flattened, with 2 ribs, bearded yellow, purple dotted on the lower side, lobes rounded 6–10 mm. Capsule elliptic-oblong, light brown, 8 mm. Seed olive brown. *Flowering:* April–July. *Fruiting:* June–August.

Ranges near the coast from Humboldt County, California, to Washington, below 400 m. Prefers alluvial flats and wet places in shaded or seepage areas.

196 MIMULUS GUTTATUS Fisch.
Large Monkey Flower, Seep-Spring Monkey Flower

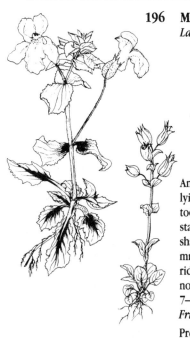

Annual or biennial herb 4–100 cm tall, with 1 to several erect or lying stems. Leaves hairless to slightly hairy, oval, rounded at base, toothed. Upper leaves sessile and joined, lower ones on long, wide stalks, 1–9 cm. Terminal racemelike inflorescence. Calyx bell shaped, strongly inflated and angled, hairless, tinged red, 15–25 mm. Corolla yellow, 15–45 mm, 2 hairy red- or brown-spotted ridges in throat that join somewhat, closing the opening. Anthers not hairy. Stigmas fringed with hair. Capsule stalked, green brown, 7–12 mm. Seed brown, oblong, plump. *Flowering:* March–August. *Fruiting:* May–October.

Prefers wet, open places along streams and springs from California to Alaska and east to the Rocky Mountains.

197   **MIMULUS MOSCHATUS** Dougl.
Musk Flower

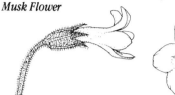

Perennial herb 5–70 cm tall with weak, creeping, branched stems; green parts of the plant with slender, flat, shining, white hairs, sticky, musk scented. Leaves oblong to ovate, toothed, pinnately veined, 1–8 cm long × 7–35 mm wide, on short stalks, upper leaves sessile. Calyx sticky haired, bell shaped, 7–13 mm long, teeth lance shaped. Corolla yellow, 15–26 mm long, throat narrowly bell shaped, 2-ridged, soft haired, with brown spots and blackish lines. Filaments yellow, anthers brownish yellow. Stigma white, 2-lobed. Capsule 6–8 mm long, brown, with persistent calyx. Seed spherical, brown to yellow. *Flowering:* May–August. *Fruiting:* July–September.

Prefers wet soil, bogs, and stream banks, not dominant. From mountains in San Diego County to Modoc County, California, Coast Ranges from Santa Cruz, California, to British Columbia, east to Rocky Mountains and, perhaps introduced, to eastern states.

198   **SCROPHULARIA CALIFORNICA** Cham. & Schlecht.
Coast Figwort

Perennial herb 100–180 cm tall, with purple brown stems and terminal flower stalks of maroon flowers. Leaves ovate to triangular, doubly sawtoothed, cut off squarely at base, .3–10 cm × 2–8 cm. Panicle narrow, with spreading, upward-curving branches, 20–40 cm × 5–10 cm. Sepals oblong to ovate, 3–4 cm long. Corolla red brown to maroon, yellowish in front, 8–15 mm long, lower lobe recurving. Sterile filament uppermost, brown, fertile stamens white, hairy, anthers maroon, blunt. Stigma knob shaped, whitish, hairy. Capsule brown, ovoid, 6–8 mm long, beaked with style, opening with 2 valves. Seeds many, minute. Pollinated by hummingbirds and bumblebees. *Flowering:* February–August. *Fruiting:* May–September.

Prefers open, moist, sandy, low ground in bushy thickets and banks, important pioneer in disturbed moist areas. From Santa Monica Mountains, California, north to British Columbia.

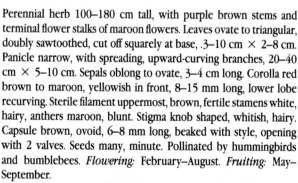

199   SYNTHYRIS RENIFORMIS   (Dougl.) Benth.
Round-Leaved Synthyris, Snow-Queen

Perennial herb 6–14 cm with hairy stems, long-stalked leaves, and a short, erect woody rootstock. Leaves ovate to heart shaped with shallow, toothed lobes, sparsely short haired above, pale beneath, 2–8 cm. Raceme sparsely flowered, 1–3 cm. Flowering stems leafless, weak. Flower stalks 7–10 mm in the axils of ovate, 3–4 mm long bracts. Sepals oval, 4 mm. Corolla bluish lavender, bell shaped, 5–9 mm, lobes shorter than tube. Filaments white, hairless, 3–4 mm. Anthers purplish black. Style red brown, 5–8 mm; stigma glandular, brown, club shaped. Capsule with spreading lobes, margins fringed with hairs, notched with persistent style, 2–4 mm × 6–8 mm wide. Seeds 2 per cell. *Flowering:* February–May. *Fruiting:* April–June. (See Plate VIII.)

Prefers moist, shaded, coniferous forests. From southwestern Washington to Marin County, California, west of the Cascades, excepting the Columbia gorge, below 900 m.

200   VERONICA AMERICANA   (Raf.) Schw.
American Brooklime

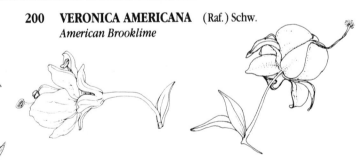

Perennial herb 10–100 cm, creeping at the base, with succulent, erect, hairless stems. Leaves on short, rounded stalks, opposite, lance to ovate, finely toothed, 10–40 mm × 5–35 mm. Axillary racemes loose, elongated, with small bracts. Corolla violet blue with darker veins, 7–10 mm, throat, pollen, and filaments white. Filaments pinkish tipped, 2.5–3 mm, anthers whitish. Stigmas light yellowish brown. Capsule light brown, oval, 3–4 mm long. *Flowering:* May–August. *Fruiting:* July–September.

Prefers stream sides and swamps in flowing or stagnant water. Temperate North America, common on the Pacific coast.

SELAGINELLACEAE
Spike Moss Family

Habit   Low, depressed or creeping, freely branched, leafy, terrestrial plants.

Leaves   Very numerous, usually overlapping, either all nearly alike, awl shaped to lance shaped, and arranged radially in many vertical rows, or of 2 kinds, in 4 vertical rows, broader and with distinctly different dorsal and ventral sides of the individual leaf, the leaves of 2 shapes corresponding to the rows.

Cones   Sporangia axillary in terminal, quadrangular, sessile spikes of modified leaves (sporophylls), each spike containing both the larger or so-called macrosporophylls (female) and the smaller microsporophylls (male). The female sporangia with 1–4 rather large spores, the male sporangia with many minute reddish or orange spores.

Distribution   A single genus.

201   **SELAGINELLA OREGANA**   D. C. Eat.
Festoon

Slender, trailing, or hanging perennial herb, much branched and epiphytic on trees, 15–90 cm long. Upper and lower leaves nearly equal, bright green, loosely overlapping, narrowly lance shaped to slenderly tapering, 2.4–3.4 mm long, with a short yellowish green bristle, 5–9 hairs on each side of leaf, .2–.6 mm. Cones 1–several at ends of many branches. The modified leaves bearing the sporangia much like vegetative leaves but evidently in 4 rows, cone therefore somewhat quadrangular.

Found hanging from hardwood trees (maple), on fallen trunks, and on damp, shaded rocks or stream banks. From Humboldt and Del Norte counties, California, to western Washington, below 330 m elevation.

TAXACEAE
Yew Family

Habit   Evergreen trees or shrubs, slightly resinous and aromatic, with fissured or scaly bark and close-grained and durable wood. Trees unisexual.

Stems   Often irregularly grooved or fluted with scaly bark.

Leaves   Needlelike, flattened, spirally arranged, twisted at the base and usually becoming 2-ranked horizontally, stiff, entire.

Flowers   Male and female flowers on separate plants. Flowers all axillary, surrounded by whorls of bud scales.

Male Flowers   Stamens 3–12, in tiny, spherical clusters in the leaf axils, subtended at the base by several bracts. Each stamen more or less shield shaped and bearing 2–9 hanging pollen sacs.

Female Flowers   Typical ovulate cones lacking. Ovules solitary (or paired), terminal on a short, scaly stalk, fruit a fleshy berry or drupe, not a woody cone, ripening in one season.

Seeds   Hard, bony, surrounded by and almost immersed in a fleshy disk that often becomes juicy and highly colored. Cotyledons 2.

Distribution   Mostly in the Southern Hemisphere, 3 genera and about 15 species.

---

202   **TAXUS BREVIFOLIA**   Nutt.
Western Yew

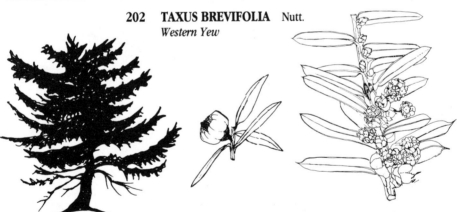

Small shrub or tree up to 5–15 m tall, evergreen, with a contorted, fluted trunk. Bark thin, consisting of outer purplish scales, newly formed inner bark reddish to reddish purple. Branches spreading, drooping. Foliage dark green to yellow green needles, flat, 2-ranked, pointed, 12–18 mm long, 1–2 mm wide. Male conelets yellowish, globose, about 3 mm long, stamens 6–14 in small, stalked cluster, axillary to needles. Female conelet solitary, axillary, light green. Ovule borne in ovoid, reddish arillus, open at apex. Seeds 5–6 mm long, yellow white. (See Plate VIII.)

Scattered in damp and shaded places and canyons below 2300 m elevation; from southern Alaska to northwestern California, northern Idaho, and northwestern Montana.

TAXODIACEAE
Bald Cypress (Redwood) Family

Habit	Evergreen or deciduous trees, the leaves needlelike or scalelike, spirally arranged, extending down the stem below the point of insertion, persistent on the deciduous branchlets.
Cones	Terminal, woody, with many thickened, wide-spreading, spirally arranged scales.
Male Conelet	Catkins terminal or axillary, of spirally arranged bracts with stamens attached. Male and female flowers both on the same trees. Stamens each bearing 2–9 pollen sacs on the underside of the flattened, scalelike connective.
Female Conelet	Solitary in axils of scalelike needles or terminal, light green, ovate consisting of fleshy, spirally arranged, green scales, each bearing 2–9 ovules, and without distinct bracts.
Seeds	Erect, small, irregularly angled, with small winglike borders. Cotyledons 2 or more.
Distribution	About 10 genera and 16 species. Many of the species are limited and isolated, resembling relic distributions of formerly more widespread ranges.

203   SEQUOIA SEMPERVIRENS   (D. Don) Endl.
Coastal Redwood

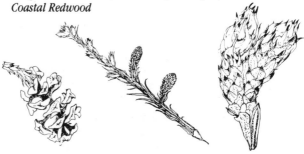

Very tall, evergreen tree growing to more than 100 m tall, trunk strongly buttressed with burls capable of resprouting. Bark very thick, 15–30 cm; spongy fibrous, reddish brown, often ridged. Needles of 2 kinds. Flat, soft needles, 12–25 mm long, pointed, 2-ranked, forming flat sprays. Exposed scalelike needles on top branchlets, 8–12 mm long, adpressed, thick, sharp pointed. Male conelets minute, greenish, erect, axillary, 4–5 mm long. Cone maturing in one season turning red brown, oblong, 20–35 mm long with 18–35 scales, deciduous as an intact cone. Seed oblong, yellowish brown, 5–6 mm long, narrowly winged on the sides.

Along the Pacific coast in alluvial flats, lower slopes up to 2500 m elevation from Monterey County, California, to southwestern Oregon, but not in the immediate ocean spray; the dominant forest cover in the coastal fog belt to about 50 miles inland locally.

TRILLIACEAE
Trillium Family

Habit	Perennial herbs with erect stem, a few short leaf sheaths at the base, and a short, thick rootstock or creeping rhizome.
Life Form	Geophyte.
Roots	Short, thick rootstalk or creeping rhizome.
Stems	Simple, erect, with a few basal leaf sheaths.
Leaves	Paired and opposite or 3 or 4 (rarely, more) in a whorl at top of stem, sessile or stalked, lance shaped to ovate or elliptic, veins distinct.
Inflorescence	Terminal flowers 1 or more, sessile or stalked.
Flowers	Bisexual, regular, variously colored or sometimes greenish. Perianth segments free, similar or if different, the outer series often broader and calyxlike, the inner series petallike or linear-threadlike. Stamens, as many as perianth segments. Filaments threadlike or slightly flattened, anthers 2-celled. Ovary superior, sessile, 1-celled, with ovules attached to wall, or 3 to more celled, with ovule-bearing surface at center of the ovary. Styles or style branches 3–5.
Fruit	Berry or fleshy capsule.
Seeds	Hard, with fleshy endosperm.
Distribution	Temperate and montane regions of the Northern Hemisphere.

Key to TRILLIACEAE

1 Stem short, underground. Flowers in an umbel, directly arising from the underground stem, appearing to be on single flower stalks. Stamens 3. Large, basal leaves 2, with brownish mottling.   **SCOLIOPUS**

   Perianth whitish green with dark purple lines, strongly recurved, segments ovate, lance shaped. Stamens 3, erect, anthers deep purple. Capsule strongly 3-angled, dark green, beaked by persistent style and stigmas.   **SCOLIOPUS BIGELOVII**

1 Stem 10–50 cm tall with stem leaves in a single whorl of 3 (rarely, 4 or 5) and a single flower per leafy stalk. Stamens 6.
TRILLIUM   2

2 Flowers distinctly stalked. Leaves green. Petals recurring, white, changing color with age to pinkish or rose purple. Filaments of stamens 3–6 mm, anthers 6–15 mm. Berry ovoid, yellowish green, 10–25 mm long.   **TRILLIUM OVATUM**

2 Flowers distinctly sessile. Leaves green and usually mottled with conspicuous darker splotches. Petals greenish yellow to white, changing color to purple with a white base. Filaments of stamens 10–20 mm, anthers 10–25 mm. Berry white to light green to pale reddish, 20–30 mm long.   **TRILLIUM CHLOROPETALUM**

204 SCOLIOPUS BIGELOVII Torr.
Slink Pod

Perennial herb with short, underground stem. Leaves 2, sheathing at base, often splotched dark brown, with 3 distinctly sunken parallel veins, 10–20 cm × 5–10 cm. Leaves spreading over ground, only erect when very young, withering in May–June. Inflorescence a sessile umbel with 1-flowered stalks 3–12. Flower stalks 3-angled, erect in flower, strongly recurved and lengthening in fruiting, 10–20 cm long. Flowers ill scented. Sepals and petals grayish green with purple lines and mottled, 14–17 mm long. Fruit a sharp, 3-angled capsule, 15–18 mm long. Seed 3 mm long. *Flowering:* February–March. *Fruiting:* April–May.

Found on concave slopes, especially with ground-water seepage in the spring season. California Coast Ranges, Humboldt County to Santa Cruz Mountains, below 500 m elevation.

205 TRILLIUM CHLOROPETALUM (Torr.) Howell
Giant Wake-Robin

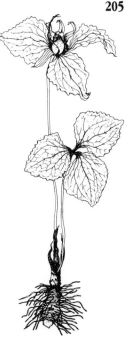

Perennial herb with 1 or more annual, unbranched, hairless stems, 10–50 cm tall. Stems greenish above, purplish at base. Leaves mostly 3 per stem, green, usually mottled with conspicuous dark splotches, broadly ovate, whorled at the top of an otherwise leafless stem, 6–18 cm long. Flower solitary, distinctly sessile, subtended by a whorl of usually 3 large leaves. Perianth segments oblong to lance shaped, pinnately veined. Petals greenish yellow aging to purple with a white base, longer than the sepals. Berry usually strongly winged. *Flowering:* March–June. *Fruiting:* June–August.

Found in moist woods and on slopes mostly close to creeks and wet places. From western Washington south to the Coastal Ranges of central California. Usually below 300 m elevation but up to 1500 m elevation in the southern Coast Ranges.

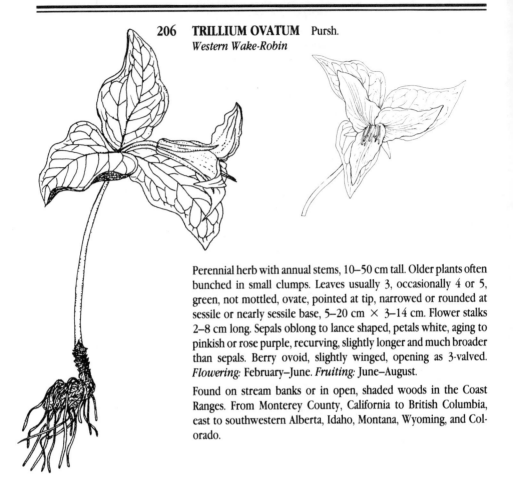

206   TRILLIUM OVATUM Pursh.
Western Wake-Robin

Perennial herb with annual stems, 10–50 cm tall. Older plants often bunched in small clumps. Leaves usually 3, occasionally 4 or 5, green, not mottled, ovate, pointed at tip, narrowed or rounded at sessile or nearly sessile base, 5–20 cm × 3–14 cm. Flower stalks 2–8 cm long. Sepals oblong to lance shaped, petals white, aging to pinkish or rose purple, recurving, slightly longer and much broader than sepals. Berry ovoid, slightly winged, opening as 3-valved. *Flowering:* February–June. *Fruiting:* June–August.

Found on stream banks or in open, shaded woods in the Coast Ranges. From Monterey County, California to British Columbia, east to southwestern Alberta, Idaho, Montana, Wyoming, and Colorado.

TYPHACEAE
Cattail Family

Habit	Aquatic herb, perennial, from creeping rootstocks with large, erect, emergent leaves and inflorescence.
Roots	Fibrous, white. Rootstock thick, fleshy, creeping.
Stems	Erect, cylindrical, without hairs and jointless.
Leaves	Alternate, elongate-linear, flattened, sword shaped, stripe ridged, sheathing at the base, and spongy.
Inflorescence	Terminal, elongated spike with male flowers in upper section and female flowers in lower section. Spike subtended by broad, sheathing bracts usually withering very early.
Flowers	Unisexual, sessile, perianth always basal consisting of many slender, jointed threads. Stamens 2–7, filaments free or united at base, anthers linear, attached at its base. Fertile female flower, ovary having a slender stalk, 1- or 2-celled, elevated, swollen, bubblelike, narrowed into a slender, long style, styles as many as the cells of the ovary, stigmas 2, narrow. Many female flowers sterile with abortive terminal ovaries and perianth hairs beneath.
Fruit	Small, dry, splitting open late.
Seeds	Striped. Endosperm abundant, mealy.
Distribution	Only 1 genus. Temperate and tropical regions.
Ecology	Wet places, marshes, ditches in stagnant to slow-flowing water. In shallow water, 1–2 m deep.

207 TYPHA LATIFOLIA L.
Cattail, Soft-Flag

Perennial emerging from shallow water, drying back to water level in winter. Stem stout, fleshy and unbranched. Leaves light green, erect. Top section of spike male, in flower dark green brown to reddish brown, becoming yellowish when pollen is released. Bottom section of spike female, dark green brown to red brown, becoming whitish as stigmas wear off. Both female and male flowers have white, silvery, hairlike perianth. Light brown fruit. *Flowering:* June–July. *Fruiting:* July–August.

Found throughout California to Alaska; on the Atlantic coast; in Europe; below 1700 m elevation. Fresh-water marshes and shallow ponds, drainage ditches, slow-moving water, and stagnant pools.

URTICACEAE
Nettle Family

Habit   Herbs, annual or perennial. Some tropical species are trees or shrubs.
Leaves   Alternate or opposite, mostly with stipules, simple.
Inflorescence Male and female flowers borne either on different branches of the same plant or on different plants, or flowers having both male and female parts. Flowers borne in small, clustered, flattopped panicles, or singly, but sometimes on a spike.
Flowers   Bisexual or unisexual, perfect, small greenish. Petals none. Sepals united and 2–5-cleft or separate. Male flower with stamens as many as the sepals or sepal divisions and opposite them. Female flower, ovary superior, 1-celled, with a solitary erect or straight ovule. Style 1, stigma 1.
Fruit   Nutlet, 1-seeded, small, dry, hard, nonsplitting.
Seeds   With oily endosperm.
Distribution   About 40 genera and 550 species of wide geographic range, but mainly tropical or subtropical.
Uses   Of little importance economically; however, ramie one of the world's most beautiful and strongest fibers (though not widely known). Several species ornamental.

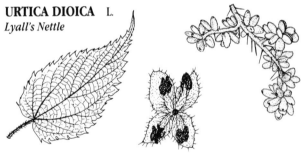

208   URTICA DIOICA   L.
Lyall's Nettle

Perennial herbs with an underground stem or rootstock, branching from the base 1–3 m tall, with hairs. Leaves 3–15 cm long, ovate to heart shaped, thin, coarsely toothed, with minute hairs. Leafstalks 3–8 cm long. Stipules rounded at tip, about 1 cm long. Male and female inflorescences on different plants or on the same plant with male flowers borne in the lower axils. Flowers borne on hanging stalks in the leaf axils. Sepals 4, united at base. Petals 0. Male flowers with 4 stamens. Female flowers, stigmas, sessile, many white, hairlike. Fruit an achene, broadly ovate, 1–2 mm long. *Flowering:* April–September. *Fruiting:* July–October.

Found in moist places near the coast and along river flats from Mendocino County to Del Norte County, California, north to Alaska, Idaho.

VACCINIACEAE
Huckleberry (Blueberry, Cranberry, Bilberry) Family

Habit Shrubs, with simple, alternate leaves, mostly 5-parted flowers, and a berry or drupe fruit.

Stems Woody; erect, or slender and trailing, or treelike.

Leaves Simple and alternate, without stipules, deciduous or evergreen, entire or finely toothed.

Inflorescence Flowers solitary or clustered, commonly subtended by bracts.

Flowers Bisexual; sepals fused, mostly 4 or 5, deciduous or persistent, adhering to the ovary for all or the greater part of its length. Petals fused, corolla mostly 4- or 5-lobed, deciduous, mainly urn shaped. Stamens twice as many as the corolla lobes; anthers prolonged at the apex into a slender tube with a terminal pore, sometimes with slender appendages. Ovary inferior, 4–10-celled, ovules many, attached centrally. Style 1, thin; stigma undivided.

Fruit Berry or drupe, many-seeded.

Seeds Compressed, the seed coat often bony. Endosperm fleshy, embryo straight.

Distribution About 20 genera and over 300 species, widely distributed throughout the Northern and Southern Hemispheres.

Key to VACCINIACEAE

Only 1 genus, *Vaccinium*, is represented.

1 Leaves thick, evergreen, the margins finely sawtoothed; glossy green above, paler beneath. Twigs smooth and rounded. Filaments brownish yellow, densely hairy. Corolla bright pinkish to white, narrowly urn shaped. Berry deep purplish black, 4–7 mm in diameter. Dry slopes and canyons.   **VACCINIUM OVATUM**

1 Leaves thin, deciduous (sometimes tardily so), mature leaves with entire margins; dull green above, paler beneath. Leafy twigs angled and slightly winged. Filaments purple, not hairy. Corolla waxy, pale yellowish pink, spherical. Berry bright red, 6–10 mm in diameter. Deep woods and mesic to moist slopes.   **VACCINIUM PARVI-FOLIUM**

209   VACCINIUM OVATUM   Pursh.
Huckleberry

Erect, evergreen shrub .5–4 m high. Leaves spirally arranged, leathery and persistent, glossy green above, paler below, finely and sharply toothed, pointed at the tip, 1–5 cm long. Flowers 3–10 in racemes or corymbs with red, deciduous bracts. Corolla bell shaped, 5–7 mm long, with short, spreading lobes, bright pinkish to white. Stamens hairy, not protruding, yellowish. Purplish black berries, 4–7 mm broad. Seed dark orange brown, 1 mm long. *Flowering:* March–August. *Fruiting:* July–October. (See Plate VIII.)

Found below 800 m elevation in dry areas, often forming dense entanglements in open, coniferous forests. From British Columbia to Santa Barbara County, California, on the west side of the Cascades and Sierra Nevada to the coast.

210   VACCINIUM PARVIFOLIUM   Sm.
Red Huckleberry

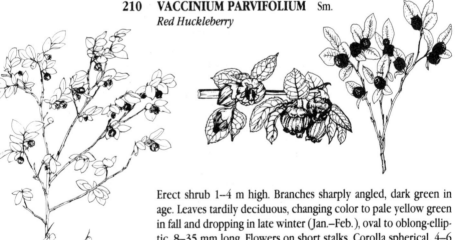

Erect shrub 1–4 m high. Branches sharply angled, dark green in age. Leaves tardily deciduous, changing color to pale yellow green in fall and dropping in late winter (Jan.–Feb.), oval to oblong-elliptic, 8–35 mm long. Flowers on short stalks. Corolla spherical, 4–6 mm long, yellow pink to yellow green with 5 small, reddish lobes. Filaments purple, anthers orange with spreading, erect awns. Berries bright red, spherical, 6–10 mm. Seeds smooth, yellow. *Flowering:* May–June. *Fruiting:* July–October.

Found in deep woods and moist places in coniferous forests, often rooting on top of stumps and rotting logs. From southeastern Alaska to Santa Cruz and Fresno counties, California.

VIOLACEAE
Violet Family

Habit	Herbs, shrubs, or, rarely, trees.
Life Form	Phanerophyte, hemicryptophyte.
Leaves	Simple, alternate or basal, entire or cut into narrow lobes or segments, with stipules.
Flower	Flowers solitary or clustered, stalks usually 2-bracted. Irregular, bisexual. Sepals 5, equal or unequal, free or slightly united, usually persistent. Petals 5, the lower petal often larger or with a saclike nectar-producing pouch or short spur. Stamens 5, alternate with petals, the filaments short, broad, continued beyond the anther cells, often united into a ring around the ovary. Ovary superior, free, sessile, 1-celled, with 2–5 but usually 3 placentae on the ovary walls bearing 1–many ovules, style usually club shaped, with the simple stigma turned to 1 side.
Fruit	Capsule, splitting by 3 valves.
Seed	Large, with hard seed coat and straight embryo, endosperm abundant.
Distribution	Wide distribution, 15 genera and 400 species; 2 genera native to the United States.
Phenology	Most violet species are self-pollinating. Pollination occurs with the closed flower in the bud. No insect pollinators have been observed on violet flowers.
Uses	Crushed leaves of certain species reported in the seventeenth century to be used for boils and swellings. Violets also ground to be used in treating many types of skin diseases. Wild violets used in the South where they are called wild okra to thicken soups. Old-fashioned candied violets a colonial favorite as was violet-flavored vinegar. The leaves a tender, fresh green tasty either raw or cooked—an excellent source of vitamins A and C; violet leaf tea a common drink. The seeds eaten by several different birds, such as the mourning dove, California quail, and junco, and rabbits and rodents. Food for caterpillars or fritillaries. Many species cultivated as ornamentals.

Key to VIOLACEAE

Only 1 genus, *Viola*, is represented.

1   Stem slender, creeping or running and rooting at the nodes. Flowers are all basal, arising directly from the rosette of leaves, flower stalks 5–10 cm long. Petals lemon yellow. Capsule round-ovoid, mottled with purple, about 5 mm long, not beaked but style persistent. **VIOLA SEMPERVIRENS**

1   Stem ascending or erect, weak and not rooting at nodes. Flowers mainly terminal on the leafy stalks, flower stalks shorter, 2–8

cm long. Petals deep yellow. Capsule oblong, 7–10 mm long,
abruptly beaked, style persistent.   **VIOLA GLABELLA**

211   VIOLA GLABELLA   Nutt.
Stream Violet, Smooth Yellow Violet

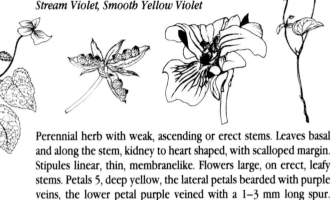

Perennial herb with weak, ascending or erect stems. Leaves basal
and along the stem, kidney to heart shaped, with scalloped margin.
Stipules linear, thin, membranelike. Flowers large, on erect, leafy
stems. Petals 5, deep yellow, the lateral petals bearded with purple
veins, the lower petal purple veined with a 1–3 mm long spur.
Fruit an oblong capsule, abruptly beaked. Seed shiny, pale brown.
Flowers self-fertilizing. *Flowering:* February–July. *Fruiting:* May–
August.

Common along streams and in shaded seepage areas. Sierra Nevada
from Tulare County, California, north, also in the Coast Ranges and
Rocky Mountains to Alaska; below 1200 m elevation.

212   VIOLA SEMPERVIRENS   Greene
Redwood Violet

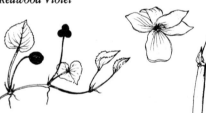

Perennial herb with slender, creeping stems rooting at nodes.
Leaves all basal, round-ovate to heart shaped, scalloped leaf margin.
Stipules ovate to awl shaped, brown, thin. Flowers all basal. Petals
5, light yellow, the 3 lower petals with faint purple veins, the lateral
ones bearded at base. Petal spur 1–2 mm long, pouchlike. Fruit a
round-ovoid capsule with purple mottling, opening with 3 valves.
Seed brown with purple. Self-fertilizing flowers in axils of stolons.
Flowering: February–June. *Fruiting:* March–July.

Coast Ranges from Monterey County, California, to British Columbia, in moist, shaded sites. Below 1200 m elevation.

Species List

ACERACEAE	001	Acer circinatum
	002	Acer macrophyllum
ADIANTACEAE	003	Adiantum pedatum
	004	Pityrogramma triangularis
ANACARDIACEAE	005	Rhus diversiloba
APIACEAE	006	Angelica hendersonii
	007	Caucalis microcarpa
	008	Heracleum lanatum
	009	Oenanthe sarmentosa
	010	Osmorhiza chilensis
	011	Sanicula crassicaulis
ARACEAE	012	Lysichitum americanum
ARALIACEAE	013	Aralia californica
ARISTOLOCHIACEAE	014	Asarum caudatum
ASPIDIACEAE	015	Athyrium filix-femina
	016	Cystopteris fragilis
	017	Dryopteris arguta
	018	Dryopteris expansa
	019	Polystichum dudleyi
	020	Polystichum imbricans
	021	Polystichum munitum
ASTERACEAE	022	Achillea borealis var. californica
	023	Adenocaulon bicolor
	024	Anaphalis margaritacea
	025	Baccharis pilularis var. consanguinea
	026	Cirsium arvense
	027	Cirsium vulgare
	028	Conyza canadensis
	029	Erechtites arguta
	030	Erechtites prenanthoides
	031	Erigeron philadelphicus
	032	Gnaphalium chilense
	033	Gnaphalium japonicum
	034	Gnaphalium purpureum
	035	Hieracium albiflorum
	036	Hypochoeris radicata
	037	Lagophylla ramosissima
	038	Leontodon leysseri
	039	Petasites palmatus
	040	Senecio vulgaris
	041	Sonchus arvensis
	042	Sonchus oleraceus
	043	Taraxacum officinale

BERBERIDACEAE	044	Berberis aquifolium
	045	Berberis nervosa
BETULACEAE	046	Alnus oregona
	047	Alnus rhombifolia
BLECHNACEAE	048	Blechnum spicant
	049	Woodwardia fimbriata
BRASSICACEAE	050	Cardamine californica
CAMPANULACEAE	051	Campanula prenanthoides
CAPRIFOLIACEAE	052	Lonicera hispidula
	053	Lonicera involucrata
	054	Sambucus callicarpa
	055	Symphoricarpos albus
CORNACEAE	056	Cornus nutallii
CORYLACEAE	057	Corylus cornuta var. californica
CRASSULACEAE	058	Sedum spathulifolium
CUCURBITACEAE	059	Marah oreganus
CUPRESSACEAE	060	Calocedrus decurrens
	061	Chamaecyparis lawsoniana
	062	Thuja plicata
DENNSTAEDTIACEAE	063	Pteridium aquilinum
EQUISETACEAE	064	Equisetum hyemale
	065	Equisetum telmateia
ERICACEAE	066	Arbutus menziesii
	067	Arcostaphylos columbiana
	068	Gaultheria shallon
	069	Menziesia ferruginea
	070	Rhododendron macrophyllum
	071	Rhododendron occidentale
FABACEAE	072	Lathyrus vestitus
	073	Lotus purshianus
	074	Lotus stipularis
	075	Melilotus alba
	076	Melilotus officinalis
	077	Trifolium pratense
	078	Trifolium repens
	079	Vicia angustifolia
	080	Vicia gigantea
	081	Vicia tetrasperma
FAGACEAE	082	Lithocarpus densiflora
	083	Quercus chrysolepis
	084	Quercus garryana
	085	Quercus kelloggii
FUMARIACEAE	086	Dicentra formosa

GROSSULARIACEAE	087	Ribes bracteosum
	088	Ribes divaricatum
	089	Ribes menziesii
	090	Ribes sanguineum
HELLEBORACEAE	091	Actaea rubra ssp. arguta
	092	Aquilegia formosa
HIPPOCASTANACEAE	093	Aesculus californica
HYDROPHYLLACEAE	094	Hydrophyllum tenuipes
	095	Nemophila parviflora
IRIDACEAE	096	Iris chrysophylla
	097	Iris douglasiana
LAMIACEAE	098	Mentha piperita
	099	Prunella vulgaris
	100	Satureja douglasii
	101	Stachys bullata
	102	Stachys chamissonis
	103	Stachys mexicana
	104	Stachys rigida
LAURACEAE	105	Umbellularia californica
LILIACEAE	106	Chlorogalum pomeridianum
	107	Clintonia andrewsiana
	108	Disporum hookeri
	109	Disporum smithii
	110	Lilium columbianum
	111	Lilium kelloggii
	112	Lilium pardalinum
	113	Lilium rubescens
	114	Maianthemum dilatatum
	115	Smilacina racemosa
	116	Smilacina stellata
	117	Streptopus amplexifolius
	118	Xerophyllum tenax
LYCOPODIACEAE	119	Lycopodium clavatum
MONOTROPACEAE	120	Hemitomes congestum
	121	Hypopitys monotropa
	122	Monotropa uniflora
	123	Pleuricospora fimbriolata
MYRICACEAE	124	Myrica californica
ONAGRACEAE	125	Circaea alpina var. pacifica
	126	Epilobium adenocaulon
	127	Epilobium angustifolium
	128	Oenothera hookeri ssp. wolfii
ORCHIDACEAE	129	Calypso bulbosa
	130	Corallorhiza maculata
	131	Corallorhiza striata
	132	Eburophyton austinae
	133	Epipactis gigantea

	134 Goodyera oblongifolia
	135 Listera cordata
	136 Piperia elegans
	137 Piperia transversa
OROBANCHACEAE	138 Boschniakia hookeri
OXALIDACEAE	139 Oxalis oregana
PHILADELPHIACEAE	140 Whipplea modesta
PINACEAE	141 Abies grandis
	142 Picea sitchensis
	143 Pinus attenuata
	144 Pinus muricata
	145 Pseudotsuga menziesii
	146 Tsuga heterophylla
PLATANACEAE	147 Platanus racemosa
POACEAE	148 Cortaderia selloana
PODOPHYLLACEAE	149 Achlys triphylla
	150 Vancouveria hexandra
	151 Vancouveria planipetala
POLYGALACEAE	152 Polygala californica
POLYPODIACEAE	153 Polypodium californicum
	154 Polypodium glycyrrhiza
	155 Polypodium scouleri
PORTULACACEAE	156 Montia sibirica
PRIMULACEAE	157 Trientalis latifolia
PYROLACEAE	158 Chimaphila menziesii
	159 Chimaphila umbellata var. occidentalis
	160 Moneses uniflora var. reticulata
	161 Pyrola asarifolia var. bracteata
	162 Pyrola picta
RANUNCULACEAE	163 Anemone deltoidea
	164 Ranunculus repens
	165 Ranunculus uncinatus
RHAMNACEAE	166 Ceanothus thyrsiflorus
	167 Rhamnus purshiana
ROSACEAE	168 Fragaria californica
	169 Holodiscus discolor
	170 Osmaronia cerasiformis
	171 Physocarpus capitatus
	172 Rosa gymnocarpa
	173 Rosa nutkana
	174 Rubus discolor
	175 Rubus leucodermis
	176 Rubus parviflorus
	177 Rubus spectabilis
	178 Rubus ursinus

RUBIACEAE	179	Galium aparine
	180	Galium californicum
	181	Galium triflorum
SALICACEAE	182	Populus trichocarpa
	183	Salix lasiandra
	184	Salix sitchensis
SAXIFRAGACEAE	185	Boykinia elata
	186	Heuchera micrantha
	187	Mitella caulescens
	188	Mitella ovalis
	189	Tellima grandiflora
	190	Tiarella trifoliata var. unifoliata
	191	Tolmiea menziesii
SCROPHULARIACEAE	192	Digitalis purpurea
	193	Mimulus aurantiacus
	194	Mimulus cardinalis
	195	Mimulus dentatus
	196	Mimulus guttatus
	197	Mimulus moschatus
	198	Scrophularia californica
	199	Synthyris reniformis
	200	Veronica americana
SELAGINELLACEAE	201	Selaginella oregana
TAXACEAE	202	Taxus brevifolia
TAXODIACEAE	203	Sequoia sempervirens
TRILLIACEAE	204	Scoliopus bigelovii
	205	Trillium chloropetalum
	206	Trillium ovatum
TYPHACEAE	207	Typha latifolia
URTICACEAE	208	Urtica dioica
VACCINIACEAE	209	Vaccinium ovatum
	210	Vaccinium parvifolium
VIOLACEAE	211	Viola glabella
	212	Viola sempervirens

Glossary

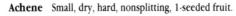

Achene

Achene   Small, dry, hard, nonsplitting, 1-seeded fruit.

Adpressed   Pressed flat against another organ.

Aerial   Growing in the air rather than in the soil.

Alternate   Any arrangement of parts along an axis other than an opposite or whorled arrangement; interspersed regularly among other organs, for example, as stamens alternate with petals.

Annual   Of one year's or growing season's duration from seed to maturity and death. A *winter annual* is a plant that germinates from seed in the fall and that fruits in the following spring. *See also* **Therophyte.**

Anther   Pollen-bearing part of the stamen. *See also* **Stamen.**

Arillus   Outgrowth of the placenta adhering about the navel (hilum) of a seed.

Ascending   Rising obliquely or curving upward.

Awl Shaped   Leaf shape in which the base gradually tapers to a sharp, curved point and in which the length of the blade is about 10 + times the width of the base of the blade. Blade is often straight but may be curved.

Awn   Terminal, slender bristle of an organ.

Axil   Upper and inside angle formed by the juxtaposition of a leaf or a branch with a stem.

Axillary   In an axil.

Alternate

Annual

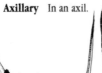
Arillus

Awl Shaped

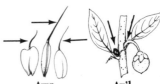
Awn   **Axil**

Banner   **Barbed**

Banner   Upper petal of the butterflylike corolla of a pea. Synonymous with *standard.*

Barbed   Bearing sharp, rigid, reflexed points similar to the barb of a fish hook.

Basal   Relating to or situated at a base.

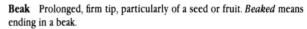

Beak

Beak   Prolonged, firm tip, particularly of a seed or fruit. *Beaked* means ending in a beak.

Berry   Pulpy, nonsplitting fruit with no true stone-enclosing seed, as the tomato. (*a*) Lengthwise section with soft-shelled seeds, (*b*) entire view, and (*c*) cross section showing soft-shelled seeds.

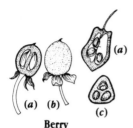

(*a*) (*b*)   (*c*)

Berry

Biennial   Plant of two years' duration from seed to maturity and death.

Bisexual   Flower possessing both fertile anther(s) and pistil(s).

Blade   Expanded part of a leaf or petal.

Bract   Reduced leaf subtending a flower, usually associated with an inflorescence.

Bractlet   Secondary bract borne on a pedicel instead of subtending it; sepallike organs subtending the sepals in many members of the Rosaceae family.

Blade

Bud   Undeveloped stem, leaf, or flower. Buds are often enclosed by reduced or specialized leaves termed bud scales.

Bulb   Leaf bud, usually underground (rarely above ground in leaf axils), with thickened scales or coats like an onion: (*a*) solid and (*b*) scales.

Bulblet   Small bulb, especially one borne aerially, as in a leaf axil or in an inflorescence.

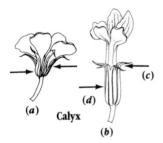

Bract   **Bractlet**   **Bud**   (*a*)   (*b*)
                                                      Bulb

Calyx   External, usually green, whorl of segments or parts of a flower, contrasted with the inner, showier, corolla segments. Calyx segments are called sepals; they can be (*a*) separate or (*b*) fused. The free, projecting parts of a fused or united calyx are (*c*) the calyx lobe; and the fused or united part of a calyx is (*d*) a calyx tube.

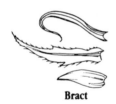

(*a*)   **Calyx**
            (*b*)

Capsule   Dry, splitting fruit composed of more than a single carpel.

Carpel   Ovule-bearing structure or component of the ovary of a flower.

Catkin   Scaly, deciduous spike of reduced flowers, either erect or drooping: (*a*) erect female catkin and (*b*) drooping male catkin.

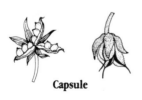

Capsule

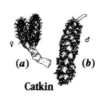

(*a*)   (*b*)

Catkin

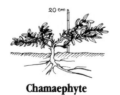

Chamaephyte

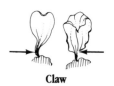

Claw

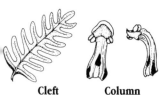

Cleft   **Column**

Compound Leaf

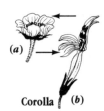

(*a*)

Corolla   (*b*)

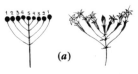

(*a*)

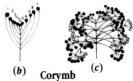

(*b*)   **Corymb**   (*c*)

Cell   Cavity of an anther containing pollen or a compartment of an ovary containing ovule(s). Also, the microscopic units of which a plant is composed. *Cellular* means made up of cells or marked so as to resemble cells.

Chamaephyte   Life form among plants that endures the unfavorable or nongrowing season in the form of perennial buds close to the ground surface but not at the ground surface. Buds are within 20–30 cm above the ground and are generally protected by the snow cover.

Claw   Narrow, petiolelike base of some petals and sepals.

Cleft   Cut more deeply than halfway and almost to the midrib.

Coherent   Congenitally united with another organ of the same kind (coalescent, or connate) or of another kind (adnate). Often used to describe parts more superficially stuck together.

Column   Body formed by union of stamens and pistil in orchids or by union of stamens in mallows and milkweeds.

Compound Leaf   Leaf with 2 or more separate leaflets, joined to the common or main stalk.

Conical   Cone shaped, with the point of attachment at a broad base.

Corolla   Inner perianth segments of a flower, composed of colored petals, which may be almost wholly united. Petals can be (*a*) separate or (*b*) fused; can be (*a*) equal in size, shape, and color or (*b*) differently shaped or colored.

Corolla Lobe   Free portion of a fused corolla tube.

Corolla Tube   Fused or united part of a corolla.

Corymb   Inflorescence flowering first from the lower or outer portion of the inflorescence and proceeding upward or inward; (*a*) flattopped inflorescence. Often the inflorescence plane is (*b*) concave or (*c*) rounded (convex), in which the inflorescence itself is compounded like a corymb of umbels.

Cotyledon   Primary leaf or leaves of an embryo, appearing immediately at germination.

Creeping   Spreading over or beneath the ground surface and usually rooting at the nodes.

Cyme   Inflorescence flowering first from the center or top and progressing outward or downward: (*a*) rounded, (*b*) flattopped, and (*c*) 1-sided inflorescence, formed by repeated branching from the bases of the flower stalks.

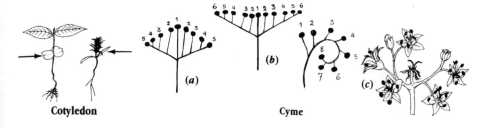

Cotyledon   (*a*)   (*b*)   (*c*)   **Cyme**

Disk

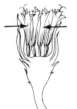

Disk Flower

Deciduous Falling off, as petals fall after flowering, or leaves of non-evergreen trees fall in autumn.

Disk Fleshy development of the receptacle about the base of an ovary.

Disk Flower Called a tube flower; with a tubelike 4- or 5-lobed corolla in the Asteraceae family. Disk flowers are usually bisexual and normally located in the center of the flower head.

Dissected Deeply divided into numerous fine segments.

Dorsal Pertaining to the back or outer surface; the surface turned away from the main axis.

Drupe Fleshy fruit in which are embedded 1–5 seeds. Seeds are seldom hard-shelled or stony. Fruit nonsplitting, fleshy enclosure gradually drying and shriveling. (*a*) Side view of fruit, (*b*) 1-seeded, and (*c*) 3-seeded, lengthwise section. *See* **Stone.**

Dissected

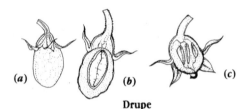

(*a*)   (*b*)   (*c*)

Drupe

Epiphyte

Elliptic In the form of a flattened circle more than twice as long as broad.

Endosperm Nutrient-enriched tissue surrounding the embryo of a seed.

Entire Undivided; the margin continuous, not incised or toothed.

Epiphyte Life form among plants that persists during the unfavorable or nongrowing season attached to another plant above the soil surface. The plant remains fully exposed to climatic impacts. Epiphytic plant roots are not in contact with the soil; they do not enter live tissue of the host plant, and they do not become dependent on moisture or nutrients received from the host plant.

Erect Upright in relation to the ground or, sometimes, perpendicular to the surface of attachment. A lip of a corolla is erect when in line with the tube.

Even-Pinnate Condition in a pinnately compound leaf when an even number of leaflets is present and a terminal leaflet is lacking. *See* **Pinnate.**

Evergreen Remaining green throughout the winter or the nongrowing season.

Floral Cup

Floral Tube

Floret

Follicle

Fertile   Describing pollen-bearing stamens and seed-bearing fruits.

Filament   Thread, especially the stalk of an anther (but not always threadlike).

Fleshy   Thick and juicy; succulent.

Floral Cup   Concave expansion of the base of a flower on which floral components such as the calyx, corolla, stamen(s), and pistil(s) are implanted.

Floral Tube   More or less elongated tube consisting of united or fused perianth or other floral parts.

Floret   Individual flower of the Poaceae family; a small flower consisting of opposite, overlapping, and paired bracts tightly enclosing the stamens and the ovary. Also used to describe individual flowers in the Asteraceae family.

Follicle   Dry fruit derived from 1 carpel, 2- to many-seeded, opening along 1 suture at maturity.

Free   Not joined to other organs; distinct and separate from other organs; the reverse of *adnate*.

Frond   Leaf of a fern.

Fruit   Ripened ovary with all its accessory parts. Fruits are of a wide variety: opening or nonopening, fleshy or dry, very large or very small, such as (*a*) a pome and (*b*) a berry, or capsule.

Funnel Shaped   Gradually widening upward and open, like a funnel.

Frond

(*a*)

(*b*)

Fruit

Funnel Shaped

Gametophyte

Geophyte

(*a*) (*b*)

Gland

Gametophyte   Sexual form of a spore-producing plant (as a fern), contrasted with the sporophyte, or asexual, form. The sexual organs are usually placed on the underside of a small, leaflike organ called a thallus.

Geophyte   Life form among plants that endures the unfavorable or non-growing season in the form of buds such as rootstocks and bulbs hidden beneath the soil surface.

Gland   Depression, protuberance, or appendage on the surface of an organ or in the leaves that secretes a usually sticky, sugary fluid or essential oil, resin, or other substance. Glands can occur (*a*) at the base of ovaries, (*b*) on leafstalks, or almost anywhere on the plant. *Glandular* means bearing glands or glandlike.

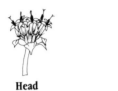

Head

Hemicryptophyte

Habit   General appearance of a plant.

Head   Dense, globular cluster of sessile or nearly sessile flowers arising essentially from the same point on a flower stalk.

Hemicryptophyte   Life form among plants that endures the unfavorable or nongrowing season in the form of dormant buds at ground level, protected by the plant's dead foliage or by the litter or duff layer, or as buds on rootstocks at the ground surface.

Herb   Plant without persistent, woody stem, at least above ground.

Herbaceous   Pertaining to an herb; opposed to woody; having the texture or color of a foliage leaf; dying to the ground each year.

Host   Plant that nourishes a parasite or that forms the substrate for an epiphyte.

Incised

Indusium

Inferior (Ovary)

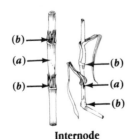

Internode

Incised   Cut rather deeply and sharply; cut slightly deeper than halfway to the midrib.

Included   Not protruding beyond a surrounding organ or envelope.

Indusium   In ferns, the epidermal outgrowth that covers or envelops and protects the sorus or the cluster of sporangia. The plural form of *indusium* is *indusia.*

Inferior   Lower or beneath. *Inferior ovary* refers to an ovary that is adnate to the floral cup and situated below the implantation of the calyx and corolla.

Inflorescence   Flower cluster of a plant.

Internode   (*a*) Portion of stem between (*b*) 2 nodes. The nodes usually bear 1 or more leaves or reduced leaves.

Interval   Space between ridges.

Involucre   Whorl or set (series) of bracts (phyllaries) or modified bracts (spines, bristles) subtending a flower cluster, as in the heads of members of the Asteraceae family, or subtending the umbels, as in members of the Apiaceae family.

Irregular   Showing a lack of uniformity of component parts of a flower; asymmetric.

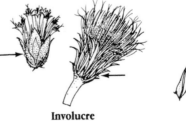

Involucre

Irregular

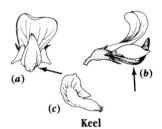

(a) **(b)** **(c)**

Keel

Jointed Having points of separation or what appear as such points.

Keel Prominent dorsal ridge (analogous to the keel of a boat) or the 2 lower petals of the butterflylike flower of a pea. (*a*) Frontal view, (*b*) side view, and (*c*) isolated keel, side view.

Lance Shaped

Lance Shaped Much longer than broad, tapering from below the middle to the apex and (more abruptly) to the base.

Lateral At or on the side.

Leaflet Single segment of a compound leaf, often sessile or stalked.

Ligule In grasses, a thin, collarlike appendage on the inside of a blade at the junction of the blade with the sheath and clasping the main stem.

Linear Resembling a line; long and narrow, of uniform width, as the leaf blade of grasses.

Lip Either the upper or lower portions of a divided corolla or calyx, usually enlarged, differently colored, or with a conspicuous shape when compared to the other segments of the corolla or calyx, as in the orchid flower.

Lobe Division or segment of an organ, usually rounded or pointed; cut less than halfway to the midrib (of a leaf).

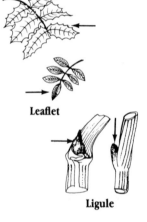

Leaflet

Ligule

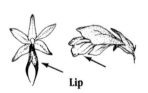

Lip

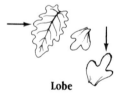

Lobe

Midrib

Membranous Of the nature of a membrane; thin, soft, and pliable.

Mesic Medium wet; medium moisture conditions.

Mesophyte Plant that grows in medium moisture conditions.

Midrib Central rib or vein of a leaf or other organ.

Net Veined

Nut

Nectary   Organ or gland that secretes nectar or a sugarlike fluid.

Nerve   Simple vein or slender rib of a leaf or bract.

Net Veined   Venation pattern characterized by connecting and forking major and minor veins forming a complex network of veins.

Node   Joint of a stem; the point of insertion of a leaf or leaves. *See* **Internode.**

Nut   Hard-shelled, 1-seeded, nonsplitting fruit derived from a simple or a compound ovary.

Nutlet   Diminutive of *nut;* applied to any small and dry, nutlike fruit. Thicker walled than an achene.

Oblong   Much longer than broad, with nearly parallel sides.

Obovate   Inversely ovate.

Obsolete   Rudimentary or not evident; applied to an organ that is almost entirely suppressed; vestigial.

Odd-Pinnate   Pinnately compound leaf with a terminal leaflet, the number of leaflets being odd. *See* **Pinnate.**

Opposite   Set against, as leaves when there are 2 at a node; or one part in front of another, as a stamen in front of a petal.

Oval   Broadly elliptic.

Ovary   Part of pistil that contains ovules.

Ovate   Having the outline of a hen's egg in longitudinal section, the broader end downward.

Ovule   Cell structure within ovary that after fertilization becomes the seed.

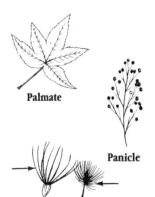

Palmate

Panicle

Pappus

Palmate   In the shape of a hand when the fingers are spread; in a leaf, having the lobes or divisions and main veins radiating from a common point.

Panicle   Inflorescence type in which the main axis is compoundly branched.

Pappus   Modified calyx in members of the Asteraceae family, consisting of a crown of bristles, scales, or spines implanted on the summit of an achene.

Parallel Veined   Having the veins extending in the same direction and equidistant; the vein pattern of most monocot leaves.

Parallel Veined

Parasite

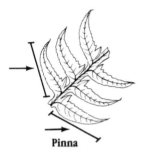

Pinna

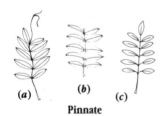

(a)   (b)   (c)

Pinnate

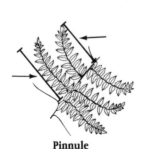

Pinnule

Parasite Life form among plants in which the parasitic plant is dependent for its moisture and nutrients on a host plant. The parasite plant dies at the same time the host plant does, being incapable of sustaining itself without the host plant.

Perennial Lasting from year to year.

Perianth Floral envelopes collectively; usually used when the calyx and the corolla are not clearly differentiated from each other.

Persistent Remaining attached, as a calyx on the fruit or leaves on a plant.

Petal Part or segment of a corolla, usually conspicuously colored.

Phanerophyte Life form among plants that endures the unfavorable or nongrowing season in the form of buds above the ground, fully exposed to climatic changes, as shrubs and trees.

Pinna Leaflet or primary division of a pinnately parted leaf or frond of a fern. The plural form of *pinna* is *pinnae*.

Pinnate Compound leaf having the leaflets arranged on each side of a common petiole; featherlike; also used with reference to a pattern of leaf venation. (*a*) Even-pinnate leaf with tendril, (*b*) even-pinnate leaf, and (*c*) odd-pinnate leaf.

Pinnule Secondary division of a pinnately parted or compound leaf or frond of a fern.

Pistil Ovule-bearing organ of a flower, consisting of a stigma and (*a*) an ovary, usually with (*b*) a style between the ovary and (*c*) the stigma.

Placenta Ovule-bearing surface in the ovary.

Pod Any dry, splitting fruit consisting of a single, folded carpel, especially a legume. The fruit splits from the top end toward its base, usually into 2 parts along both the ventral suture and midnerve; opposed to a follicle, which splits along the suture only.

Pollen Male reproductive spores found in the anther.

Prostrate Lying flat on the ground surface.

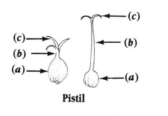

Pistil

Pod

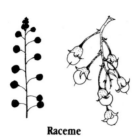

Raceme

Raceme Inflorescence type in which each flower is nearly equally stalked on an unbranched main axis.

Rachilla Minute axis of a grass spikelet.

Rachis Axis of a spike or raceme or of a compound leaf.

Ray Petallike extension of the corolla of a ray flower in members of the Asteraceae family; the primary branchlets of a flattopped panicle.

Ray Flower Flower in members of the Asteraceae family with a strap-shaped or bladelike extension of the corolla. Often ray flowers are different from disk flowers; generally, they are the showy, outer or marginal flowers of the head, usually unisexual (female) or neuter (infertile). *See* **Disk Flower.**

Rachilla

Receptacle That portion of the floral axis on which the flower parts are implanted or, in members of the Asteraceae family, that which bears in the head the involucre and the ray flowers or disk flowers or both.

Recurved Bent backward or downward.

Reflexed Abruptly bent downward.

Regular Said of a flower having radial symmetry, with all the parts in each series alike.

Rib Primary vein of a leaf or a ridge on a fruit. *See* **Midrib.**

Ribbed With prominent ribs.

Ray Flower

Riparian Adjacent to a stream or creek; may be occasionally or regularly flooded by a stream.

Rootstock Underground stem, usually with modified leaves or scales and nodes that bear roots; also called rhizome.

Rosette Crowded cluster of radiating leaves appearing to rise from or lie flat on the ground.

Runner Slender, trailing stem rooting at the nodes or end.

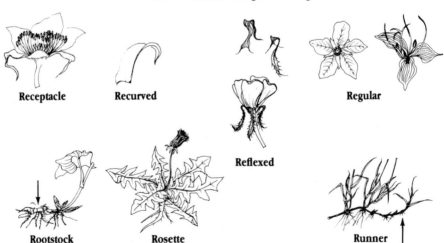

Receptacle   **Recurved**   **Regular**

Reflexed

Rootstock   **Rosette**   **Runner**

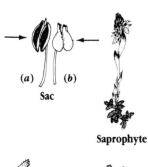

(a)   **(b)**

Sac

Saprophyte

Scale   Sheath

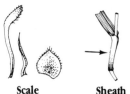

Silicle

Silique

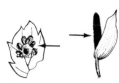

Sorus   Spadix

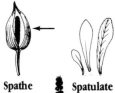

Spathe   Spatulate

Spike

Sac Cavity of an anther cell that contains pollen, often (*a*) splitting open lengthwise or (*b*) opening by a pore or tube. *See also* **Anther.**

Saprophyte Life form among plants that depends on the presence of decomposing organic matter to provide moisture and nutrients. The saprophytic plant usually combines with a soil fungus and forms a mycorrhizal association, with the fungus extracting the required moisture and nutrients from the dead organic matter. It cannot sustain itself without the presence of dead organic material and generally lacks chlorophyll in its tissues and is incapable of direct photosynthesis.

Scale Any thin, dry bract; usually a rudimentary leaf; a flat-thin hair or epidermal appendage.

Seed Ripened ovule.

Segment Division or part of a leaf or other organ that is lobed, cleft, or divided but not truly compound or dissected into separate parts. In Equisetum, *segment* is used to describe the parts of the stem that can be easily separated or pulled apart.

Sepal Part or segment of the calyx.

Sessile Attached directly by the base; not stalked.

Sheath Tubular, basal part of a leaf that encloses the stem, as in grasses and sedges. *Sheathing* means enclosed as by a sheath.

Shrub Woody plant of smaller proportions than a tree, which usually produces several branches from its base.

Silicle Short silique, not much longer than wide, often only 2-seeded.

Silique Narrow, many-seeded (or 2-seeded) capsule in members of the Brassicaceae family, with 2 valves splitting from the base toward the tip of the capsule and leaving the 2 placentae with the false partition (replum) between them. A silique is generally at least 3 times as long as wide.

Simple Unbranched, as a stem or hair; not compounded, as a leaf; single, as a pistil of 1 carpel.

Solitary Borne singly.

Sorus Cluster of sporangia on the back of the fronds of ferns, with or without an indusium. The plural form of *sorus* is *sori.*

Spadix Spike or succulent, swollen axis bearing flowers or fruits enveloped in a spathe.

Spathe Broad, sheathing bract enclosing a spadix, as in members of the Araceae family.

Spatulate Like a *spatula,* a knife rounded at its tip and gradually narrowed toward its base.

Spike Inflorescence consisting of an elongated axis with sessile flowers or spikelets.

Spikelet Secondary spike; the ultimate cluster of florets in grasses (Poaceae), consisting of 2 glumes and 1 or more florets, and of florets in sedges (Cyperaceae).

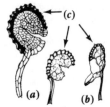

Sporangium

Spore

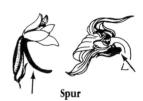

Sporophyte

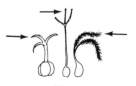

Spur

Stamen

Spine   Hard, sharp, needlelike modification of a leaf or stipule or other plant part.

Sporangium   Spore case or sac, often stalked and rupturing by means of contraction of a ring or band of thick-walled cells called an annulus. (*a*) Sporangium, side view, (*b*) frontal view, and (*c*) annulus. The plural form of *sporangium* is *sporangia.*

Spore   Reproductive body of pteridophytes and lower plants; analogous to the seed of angiosperms but consisting of a single cell only.

Sporophyte   (*a*) Asexual or diploid generation of ferns and their allies, the fern plant itself, emerging on fertilization from the (*b*) gametophyte.

Spreading   Diverging almost to the horizontal; nearly prostrate.

Spur   Slender, saclike or subulate, nectar-bearing extension from a petal or sepal.

Stamen   Male organ of a flower, which bears the pollen, consisting of a stalk (filament) and anthers (pollen sacs).

Sterile   Infertile or barren, as a stamen lacking an anther, a flower lacking a pistil, and a seed without an embryo.

Stigma   Receptive part of the pistil on which pollen germinates.

Stipule   Small, leaflike organ or appendage associated with the base of a leafstalk.

Stomate   Epidermal aperture for gas exchange, usually in leaves.

Stone   Bony or hardened inner layer of the ripened walls of an ovary within the drupe of plums and peaches, for example, enclosing the seed; the pit of such fruits. *See also* **Drupe.**

Style   Contracted portion of a pistil between an ovary and a stigma. Style branches may be only stigmatic in part, the remainder then being appendage. *See also* **Stigma.**

Subtend   To be below and close to, as a leaf subtends a shoot borne in its axis.

Succulent   Juicy; fleshy and soft.

Superior   Ovary that is placed above the implantation of the calyx and corolla but free from them.

Suture   Line of splitting of fruits and anthers; the line of a natural union or division between coherent parts, equivalent to a seam.

Stigma

Stone   **Style**   **Superior (Ovary)**   **Suture**

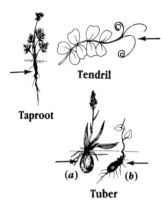

Tendril

Taproot

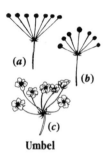

(a)   (b)

Tuber

Taproot Primary, stout, vertical root giving off small laterals but not or seldom dividing.

Tendril Slender, coiling, or twining organ by which a climbing plant grasps its support.

Therophyte Life form among plants in which the plant is perpetuated only by means of seeds on completion of a season's growth, when the plant dies; or an annual plant that endures the unfavorable or nongrowing season in the form of a seed. The same as annual.

Throat Somewhat constricted or expanded opening into a corolla tube.

Tuber Thickened, solid, and short, usually underground stem, with many buds, often (a) a separate organ or (b) a thickened, swollen root-stock.

(a)

(b)

(c)

Umbel

Umbel (a) Flat or (b) convex flower cluster in which (c) flower stalks arise from a common point, like rays of an umbrella. *Umbellate* means borne in an umbel.

Unisexual Flowers having only stamens or pistils; of one sex.

Venation Arrangement of the veins of a leaf; nervation; veining.

Ventral Relating to the inward face or surface of an organ, in relation to the axis; anterior; front; opposed to dorsal.

Whorl Circular arrangement involving 3 or more leaves or flowers at a node or at about the same point on an axis.

Wing Thin, usually dry extension bordering an organ or the 2 lateral petals of the legumelike flower of members of the pea family. (a) Frontal view illustrating 2 wings, (b) isolated wing, side view, (c) wing side view within a legume flower, and (d) wings of seeds.

Whorl

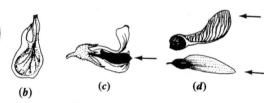

(a)   (b)   (c)   (d)

Wing

Index

Design: Marilyn Langfeld
Cover Design: Georgia Oliva
Copy Editing: Judith Chaffin
Production Coordination: Judith Chaffin
Color Separations: Balzer Shopes, San Francisco
Composition: Graphic Typesetting Service, Los Angeles
Printing and Binding: Publishers Press, Salt Lake City
Type: ITC Garamond

centimeters

5   10   15   20